MASTER EMOTIONAL INTELLIGENCE

7 Books 1: Emotional Intelligence, How to Analyze People, Cognitive Behavioral Therapy, Self-Discipline, Manipulation, Anger Management, Empath

EDWARD BENEDICT JANE ORLOFF

RAY VADEN

EMOTIONAL INTELLIGENCE

Raise Your EQ (Mastering Self Awareness & Controlling Your Emotions)

Edward Benedict

The following eBook is reproduced below with the goal of providing information that is as accurate and reliable as possible. Regardless, purchasing this eBook can be seen as consent to the fact that both the publisher and the author of this book are in no way experts on the topics discussed within and that any recommendations or suggestions that are made herein are for entertainment purposes only. Professionals should be consulted as needed prior to undertaking any of the action endorsed herein.

This declaration is deemed fair and valid by both the American Bar Association and the Committee of Publishers Association and is legally binding throughout the United States.

Furthermore, the transmission, duplication, or reproduction of any of the following work including specific information will be considered an illegal act irrespective of if it is done electronically or in print. This extends to creating a secondary or tertiary copy of the work or a recorded copy and is only allowed with the express written consent from the Publisher. All additional right reserved.

The information in the following pages is broadly considered a truthful and accurate account of facts and as such, any inattention, use, or misuse of the information in question by the reader will render any resulting actions solely under their purview. There are no scenarios in which the publisher or the original author of this work can be in any fashion deemed liable for any hardship or damages that may befall them after undertaking information described herein.

Additionally, the information in the following pages is intended only for informational purposes and should thus be thought of as universal. As befitting its nature, it is presented without assurance regarding its prolonged validity or interim quality. Trademarks that are mentioned are done without written consent and can in no way be considered an endorsement from the trademark holder.

INTRODUCTION

Congratulations on downloading this book and thank you for doing so.

We all know that letting our emotions run high is never a good thing. The last time you saw someone have an emotional outburst in public, how did that make you feel? Did you perceive them positively or negatively?

Whether you're extremely happy, you feel like you could jump through the roof right now, or feeling so angry that you could punch a hole through a wall, there's one thing that is a common factor in both scenarios. Being overly emotional is never good. Ever.

Emotions have a way of taking control over you to a point where you lose all sense of rationality. You can't think straight, you react impulsively, and worst of all, you could find yourself saying things you don't mean which end up hurting people around you. Reacting and speaking emotionally is perhaps the most dangerous thing of all. Once something has been said and done, it can never be undone. That is perhaps the most damaging thing to a relationship you could do.

Feeling extremely happy or angry is never a good idea. Even being extremely happy, for example. When you're running on an emotional high, it's easy to let your perception and judgment be clouded. How many times have you made an impulsive decision on a happy high, only to regret that decision later once the euphoria has gone? Likewise, it is also an equally bad idea to react when you're in an emotionally angry state. How many times have you found yourself saying things you immediately regret once the anger has dissipated?

Emotional Intelligence, also known as EQ, is not like the intelligence you're normally accustomed to when you hear the word *intelligent*. It isn't about being academically brilliant. It is about intelligent, yes, but *emotionally* instead of academically. Being book smart is great, but they can only get you so far in life. To achieve true success in every aspect, you're going to need to master this very crucial skill which often doesn't get enough credit as it should.

EQ is a form of intelligence which can guide all of us to make better decisions. Emotions can be more powerful than you can imagine. Without the proper tools and management techniques, you can easily find yourself overwhelmed and at a loss for what to do. Uncontrolled emotions can leave a tremendously powerful impact on your life. A classic example would be how uncontrolled emotions lead to feelings of depression and anxiety; two very real conditions which exist because of a person's inability to manage their emotions properly.

While EQ may not entirely be the cause of depression and anxiety, it certainly is a contributing factor. People who suffer from those two conditions often find themselves feeling so overwhelmed by their emotions that they completely shut down and retreat into themselves. They feel crippled, they feel despair, and everything in life seems much harder or nearly impossible because they feel hopeless.

This is a precise example of why it is so important to learn how to manage your emotions. To control your EQ matters more when it comes to achieving success than IQ does, believe it or not. No matter how brilliant you may be academically, nobody is going to follow a leader who lets their emotions run amok. To be considered a true success, you need to master EQ. It is a skill which is going to transform your life.

Which brings us to why you're reading this book right now; because you're realizing how crucial it is to learn how to manage and understand your emotions. *Emotional Intelligence* is a guidebook which is going to help you master self-awareness by learning how to control your emotions. This is going to be a very crucial step as you now move forward to take control of both your emotional and mental wellbeing.

Emotional Intelligence is going to explore what it means to possess high EQ, how to master and control your emotions, turn your attention within and start to live a life where your emotions don't run your day.

There are plenty of books on this subject on the market, so thanks again for choosing this one! Every effort was made to ensure it is full of as much useful information as possible. Please enjoy!

I

WHAT IS EMOTIONAL INTELLIGENCE

EMOTIONS. THEY CAN BE A VERY POWERFUL FORCE IN our lives.

BECAUSE IT IS SO POWERFUL THAT IT MAKES *EMOTIONAL intelligence* one of the most valuable assets we could cultivate for ourselves. Emotional intelligence is simply the ability to identify, manage and regulate your own emotions. It is also about being able to identify the emotions of others around you, and what you do with that information you receive. Emotional intelligence is about your ability to capitalize on these emotions and use them to your best advantage.

EMOTIONAL INTELLIGENCE IS OFTEN ALSO REFERRED TO as EQ or EI. It was a term which was first introduced by John Mayer and Peter Salavoy, who were two researchers at the time. This term was later brought to popularity by Dan Goleman, who wrote a book in 1996 with the same name.

THE 5 CORE PRINCIPLES OF EMOTIONAL INTELLIGENCE

Emotional intelligence can essentially be summed up in two ways - the ability to recognize, understand and manage your emotions, and the ability to influence the emotions of others. In Goleman's book, he divided emotional intelligence into five core principles:

- Self-awareness
- Self-regulation
- Motivation
- Empathy
- Social skills

THESE FIVE CORE PRINCIPLES ARE THE QUALITIES THAT everyone with high EQ should possess. This is going to be the framework that you are going to work towards as you work on mastering self-awareness and controlling your emotions.

SELF-AWARENESS

How aware are you about the state of your emotions? Do you recognize them as they happen? Or do you only notice how emotional you were after you've had some time to look back and reflect on your actions? As you learn to master self-awareness, EQ is going to teach you how to recognize your emotions as they happen, how to tune in and be mindful towards what you're experiencing. EQ will teach you how to recognize the effects that your emotions have, and what to do about them.

Self-Regulation

Having an awareness of your emotions alone is not going to be enough. It is *what you do with them* that matters just as much. Are you going to let your emotions control you? Or are you going to be the one who is in control? It is easy to lose control when you don't know how to regulate your emotions, especially when they first happen. This is why self-regulation is an important step in the EQ process because it teaches you to be adaptable and flexible in handling changes. It teaches you to take responsibility for your actions, and it helps keep you in check, so you don't give in to your disruptive impulses.

Motivation

Motivation is what gives you a sense of achievement to keep on pushing forward. To constantly push yourself to be even better. To strive for high levels of excellence and to have the initiative needed to act on opportunities that present themselves. These are qualities which are displayed by a lot of successful and influential leaders. Do you notice how they always have the optimism needed to keep pursuing their goals despite the curveballs and challenges that life throws at them? That's because they've got high levels of emotional intelligence. It keeps them going to accomplish the task and the goals that they have committed themselves to while remaining optimistic in the process. They never think about quitting because they have trained their minds always to see things from a positive perspective. They've trained themselves to see the silver lining in every situation, and they have reprogrammed their minds to focus on solving the problem at hand.

Empathy

Empathy helps emotionally intelligent individuals recognize and anticipate the needs of another individual. They then use this ability to work on fostering and building powerful relationships with a diverse group of people. Because they have the capacity to identify the needs and wants of another person, they can decipher the feelings of others, sometimes even preventing conflict before it happens because they can sense what's brewing underneath the surface. The more you can decipher the feelings of people, the better you can manage the thoughts and approaches you send them.

Social Skills

Emotionally intelligent people make such successful leaders because they are able to inspire and guide groups of individuals. They have the ability to develop good interpersonal skills, and it is these people skills which allow them to negotiate, understand and empathize with others. Their social skills help them to form meaningful bonds with a diverse group of people, especially in a work environment. They can easily influence others with their effective, persuasive techniques. They are seen as a catalyst for change because they have developed their social skills to a point where they are seen as influential and likable individuals.

THESE FIVE CORE PRINCIPLES ARE THE REASON WHY emotionally intelligent people are so successful at what they do. This is how they rise to the top, to become the affluent leaders that others look up to. It isn't a skill that they were born with. It is a skill that they cultivate for themselves over time and practice. EQ is a skill that you too, are going to learn to master by the time you reach the end of this guidebook.

The Qualities of People with High Emotional Intelligence

It isn't just academic intelligence that runs the world we live in. In fact, it takes a combination of several factors and intelligence types to accomplish true success — one of them is emotional intelligence. The term that is used to measure a person's intelligence is called the *quotient.*

Some examples of quotients include IQ (*intelligence quotient)*, which is focused on one's ability to memorize and retrieve information from memory and logical reasoning which is also known as being academically brilliant. The emotional quotient (*EQ or emotional intelligence*) on the other hand, is focused on one's ability to manage, understand and recognize not just their own emotions, but the emotions of the people around them too.

Our emotions make up a large part of who we are. We are emotional, and sometimes we respond according to those emotions. We even make decisions based on those emotions. Having emotional intelligence is just as important - if not more- to a person's success. Not only will you be able to manage and regulate your own emotions, but you can learn to influence the minds of the people around you too, as you learn to master and become better at EQ.

It is easy to spot someone with high EQ, and if there are people around you that you can use as examples of what to strive for, that's going to be a big help. Essentially, when someone displays any of the following qualities below, it is a safe bet to say that they've got high levels of emotional intelligence:

- **They Have a High Sense of Self-Awareness -** A person with high EQ has a very clear idea of how they perceive themselves, and how others around them perceive them. Someone with high EQ has mastered the art of self-awareness to the point that they completely understand themselves and how they work. They understand what factors trigger their emotions and they have learned how to manage themselves in the most proactive manner possible. They are also not afraid to seek out honest feedback from others, and they welcome constructive criticism because it helps them develop a better understanding of themselves.

- **They've Emphatic Towards Others -** A person with high EQ has the ability to relate to the people around them in a way that many others do not. They have a strong sense of empathy, and they use that quality to see things from another person's perspective. To truly understand how someone feels, you need to be able to *walk a mile in their shoes,* as the saying goes. This quality is exactly what helps them mirror someone else's emotions and feelings, to feel what they feel. It enables them to understand what the person is going through emotionally. This is a skill which they have cultivated through practice and experience.

- **They Are Curious Creatures -** They are always on the lookout for ways they can improve, and they're ever ready to learn something new. Curiosity is one of the key traits that you need to achieve success because successful people never stop learning and growing. They are passionate about life and knowledge, and they are driven every day to look for ways to become a better version of themselves. People with high EQ are always curious, and this leads to them never wanting to stop learning.

- **Their Mind Works in Analytical Ways** - People with high EQ don't just receive information and leave it at that. On the contrary, what they do instead is process and analyze the information that they receive on a deeper level. Emotionally intelligent individuals are deep thinkers, and they are always analyzing how information can be improved on and what could be done better. This is part of what makes them such great leaders, to begin with. They are problem solvers, and they always think about the *why* behind a certain action. They think about *what* benefit that course of action brings, and if this is the best scenario for everyone involved.

- **They Think Positive** - This isn't just another cliche saying for emotionally intelligent individuals. In fact, they are the living embodiment of this aspect. Despite the obstacles and challenges that come their way, those who possess high EQ maintain an optimistic attitude because they know how important it is for the mind to maintain this level of positivity. If they allow themselves to wallow in self-pity and let themselves be consumed by negative emotions and desires, they know it is only a matter of time before things quickly spiral out of control, as it often does when negativity takes over. Being optimistic and positive is the only way to keep increasing the opportunities and improve the relationships that come their way constructively and productively.

2

HOW TO MASTER SELF-AWARENESS

EXPERIENCING AN EMOTION IN EXCESS IS NEVER A GOOD thing. When something is experienced in excess, it makes it that much easier for you to feel overwhelmed and on the brink of losing control. Even excessive amounts of happiness is not a good thing, because that euphoria and happiness can result in you making decisions you normally would not.

WHICH BRINGS US TO WHY IT IS IMPORTANT TO MASTER self-awareness, becoming more self-aware of your emotional reactions is part and parcel of becoming more emotionally conscious. When you're actively mindful and aware, you become more attuned to your needs. Eventually, you'll start to develop the ability to tune into someone else's emotions too, because you're able to recognize these emotions as they are happening.

SELF-AWARENESS IS THE FIRST AND MOST IMPORTANT CORE PRINCIPLE

Because managing your emotions starts with you. Nobody can help you learn how to manage and regulate your own emotions; it has to come from within which is why the path towards developing a greater level of emotional intelligence begins with self-awareness, the first and perhaps most important core principle of EQ as a whole. Before you can move onto the next four principles, you *must* master self-awareness. Think of it in this context, if you're not *aware* that there is a problem, how would you begin fixing it? When you're not aware of what's going on with you, how would you know what the best way to regulate your actions are?

SELF-AWARENESS IS GOING TO REQUIRE THAT YOU MAKE the connection between the part of your brain that *thinks* and the part of your brain that *feels* so that you're not driven by one extreme or the other. It prevents you from acting out impulsively, and more importantly, it saves you from doing something that you may regret several hours later.

THERE'S A REASON WHY LEADERS SOMEHOW APPEAR TO have the ability to remain as cool as a cucumber, even in the most stressful of times. That's not to say they aren't experiencing any emotional turmoil within; it just means they are *aware* of the way that they feel, and they are regulating their responses to manage the situation better. Anyone who aspires to become a leader must learn to possess self-awareness, or it is never going to work.

LIKE EVERYTHING ELSE ABOUT EMOTIONAL

intelligence, self-awareness is a skill which you can learn, develop and exercise on until you get better at it. Imagine self-awareness is a brand-new muscle which you have discovered within your body, and to work on making that muscle stronger, you need to constantly exercise it until it gets better over time.

HOW TO START MASTERING SELF-AWARENESS

This is going to happen in stages. As you work towards mastering your self-awareness, remember to be patient with yourself every step of the way, and don't rush through the process.

Phase One

The first stage of the process is going to require that you start monitoring yourself daily. From the moment you wake up, until the time you go to bed, keep checking in with yourself. Observe the things, people or situations that tend to trigger your emotions, and ask yourself *why* this is the case.

As you feel each emotion, write it down and then assess what triggered this emotion. Write down how this particular emotion made you feel, and what you were tempted to do when it occurred. Get a little notebook that you can carry around with you and write down each emotion as you feel it pop up. Next, ask yourself if this emotion was worth the time, effort and energy you spent on it. Doing this regularly helps you get to know yourself and your triggers much better.

Phase Two

The second phase of the process towards mastering self-awareness is an exercise that is going to require you to *step outside yourself*. Imagine you're viewing yourself from an outsider's perspective. What important roles do you play in your life on a daily basis? How many people rely on you? How do you think others perceive you? In this second phase, meditation is a tool that is often helpful. Meditation requires you to reconnect with yourself, mind, body, and soul. It helps you find your focus, feel centered and feel more connected to your surroundings in a way you've never had before. Finding a quiet spot for you to meditate daily. If you can't manage this daily, contemplating several times a week would be good enough to start. Meditation is a great tool to help you feel centered emotionally again, teaching you to practice feelings of calm and learning to let go of all the stress you may have encountered during the day.

LEARN TO OBSERVE YOUR EMOTIONS WITHOUT judgment, assess them for what they are. Analyze them and what triggered them without being too harsh on yourself. This is an exercise for you to become aware of your current emotional state, and what triggered it. That is all.

Phase Three

Next, you'll move onto the third phase of the process, where you begin to evaluate your values. For example, as you spent time analyzing your emotions and triggers from phase one, are you spending your time wisely in the way that you react to those emotions? If you let those emotions consume you, why? Was it worth exerting that much energy and effort over it? Is the way that you're reacting based on those emotions in line with your current beliefs and values? If they aren't then why do you keep doing it?

By this stage, hopefully, you are more attuned to your emotions and able to write them down as they are happening. If you have no time to reflect on them there and then, that's okay, write down the emotions and come back later and analyze it.

Assessing your emotions and defining its causes and triggers are going to require that you spend several minutes daily just by yourself and your thoughts. Find a quiet space in your home that is free from distractions, and take a few moments to sit down and begin reflecting on everything that went on today and how it made you feel. Spending some quiet reflection time alone is important towards developing your self-awareness because it forces you to go into your mind and face your emotions instead of ignoring them or blocking them out; especially, if they happen to be unpleasant emotions. Part of becoming more self-aware is being able to confront exactly why you find yourself in such an emotional state. What is causing your distress and why do you have difficulty managing it sometimes?

Phase Four

Our lives are so busy, constantly on the go that there barely seems enough time to get in touch with ourselves. Or to even make time for ourselves for that matter. But if you are to become more self-aware, you *must make the time* to get in touch with your feelings. Not just get in touch with them, but truly understand where they are coming from. Life can sometimes seem so busy and overwhelming that it can be tempting to sweep things under the rug and not have to deal with them at all.

REMEMBER THAT LITTLE NOTEBOOK YOU WERE CARRYING around you from Phase One? That's why you need to carry it around with you. So that when you need it, whip it out and immediately write down your emotions are you identify them. If you feel joy, write it down. If you feel sadness, write it down. If you feel stress, write it down. If you feel agitation, write it down. Absolutely anything that you're feeling, write it down. Keep an emotional journal of your daily life, which you can later reflect on at the end of the day. This is the best tool to develop self-awareness because when you're writing something down, it forces you to think about and reflect on it, to consciously think about it and acknowledge its presence.

DOCUMENT YOUR EMOTIONS AND FEELINGS throughout the week. At the end of each week, start on a fresh page of your notebook or journal, and separate that page into two columns. One column is for your emotions listed throughout the week, and the other column is for the context that resulted in this emotion. Dividing them into two columns like this makes it easier for you to analyze what's going on. How many emotions did you feel this week that were positive? How many were negative? Which emotions do you think dominated the way that you felt? What caused such a reaction with you? Remember not to repress or try to ignore any emotion, especially the unpleasant ones; it is important that you be as brutally honest with yourself as possible if you want to master self-awareness and develop a deeper level of emotional intelligence.

3

THE ART OF CONTROLLING YOUR EMOTIONS

One of the first few things you must do for yourself in your efforts to become more emotionally intelligent is to make a personal commitment. Commit to yourself that from now on, you're no longer going to dwell on past emotional mistakes or failures. Commit to yourself that from now on, you're only going to look forward and towards improvement. Commit to doing the things you know you must do to become better.

As part of this commitment, you will not allow yourself to make excuses to justify your behavior when you do have an emotional outburst. Yes, this is going to be challenging. And yes, it is going to require some self-discipline to stick to the commitments you've made. But becoming more emotionally intelligent is just as much about the process and the journey to get there, not just about the result alone.

It is about the small changes you make daily that

progress you forward, which will help you become more emotionally intelligent. Fix a routine for yourself that works and stick to it every day as best you can. Make it a habit of writing in your emotional journal at least once or several times a day.

Robert Collier couldn't have said it better himself when he uttered the phrase *success is the sum of small efforts which are repeated day in and day out*. This is what you're going to do for yourself now, slowly cultivate habits which are going to help increase your EQ levels as you move forward. Learning to control your emotions is going to be one of the hardest things to do. You're trying to learn how to control a powerful force within you, and it is going to take immense self-awareness, self-regulation, and willpower to be able to pull it off successfully.

THE ART OF CONTROLLING YOUR EMOTIONS STARTS WITH YOU

The art of controlling your emotions first starts with your commitment to change. You have to *want* to see change, *desire* to make that change happen. That's the only way you're going to give this your 100% effort. You need to want to become a person with higher EQ because you know it is the only way you're going to achieve the success you envision for yourself. When you commit to change who you are, you're mentally preparing yourself to take the necessary action needed. You're dedicating f yourself to making this change for the better. For a successful and sustainable change, you need this level of commitment.

This is going to be what fuels your desire to master all the five core principle levels required for high EQ. This is what fuels your desire to take the next step, to keep things ongoing and to always look for solutions whenever there's a problem.

HOW TO START MAKING THAT PERSONAL COMMITMENT TO CHANGE

Begin by asking yourself why is it important to you to make this change? To develop a higher EQ? Why am I committing myself to this journey? You must be able to answer the fundamental question of *why you're doing this,* or you may find yourself lost along the way then things get challenging. Knowing your *why* is how you remind yourself to keep moving forward. Especially during the most difficult moments. When you have a clear reason for doing what you're doing, you're never in any doubt, and you always know why you must persevere.

CONTROLLING YOUR EMOTIONS IS SOMETHING THAT requires a deep commitment from you. This is going to be what engages you to change and to be able to maintain this change for the rest of your life.

COMMIT TO LEARNING HOW TO CONTROL YOUR emotions by following these guidelines below:

- **Have a Clear Purpose -** Make a focus list of the aspects you would like to change. For example, if anger is something you want to work on controlling first, make that your first point of focus or if it is anxiety, or nervousness, or excessive happiness for example. Any emotion that you think you would like to choose on focus controlling first. When your purpose is clear, you're less likely to lose sight of your goals.

- **Start Small** - Trying to do too much too soon is often how we find ourselves stumbling and falling along the way. While there's a wide range of emotions that you would like to control, start with one at a time and work your way up from there. Once you've mastered one, then move onto the next one. Take it one step at a time; this isn't a race to the finish line. Take as much time as you need, as long as you successfully learn how to control your emotions at the end of the day, that's all that matters.

- **Reflect On Your Progress** - Make time for reflecting and to assess just how far you've progressed. Have your efforts been working well so far? If not, what needs to be changed? Reflection gives you a chance to pinpoint the success of your efforts thus far, and it gives you a chance to look back and see how far you've come from where you were.

- **Take a Moment to Express Yourself Freely** - The art of controlling your emotions is not just about suppressing everything that you're feeling, keeping it locked inside. Suppressing one's emotions is just as bad as being overly expressive with them. Take a moment whenever you need to find a quiet space away from everyone else where you can freely express all the emotions you feel you need to let out. Let it out, take a deep breath, get it off your chest and feel better. Once you feel much better, you can rejoin the rest of the world again.

- **Stick To It** - Follow through, no matter how difficult or challenging it may be. Change is never the easiest process in the world, but as long as you keep moving forward, the hardest part of the process will soon be behind you. Never stop trying to learn how to control your emotions, because it won't be long before you've mastered the art of doing so, as long as you keep trying. No matter how hard it gets, remember why you're doing this and the commitment that you made to yourself. Stick to it and follow through.

SURROUND YOURSELF WITH EMOTIONALLY INTELLIGENT PEOPLE

Success is contagious. If you want to become an emotionally intelligent person you desire, you need to start surrounding yourself with those who have already succeeded in mastering the qualities of EQ. The company that you keep has a way of influencing and rubbing off on you which is why successful individuals always preach about being careful who you let into your life, to get rid of those who hold you back and to only surround yourself with positive, like-minded individuals.

It might be time to take a good, hard look at the current company that fills your life right now. Family, friends, and colleagues. Are these people who inspire you? Are they successful role models that you could emulate? More importantly, are they emotionally intelligent individuals that you could learn from? When you spend time with the right kind of people, you will subconsciously start to mimic the things that they do. You'll find yourself observing their every action, every movement, and slowly, you'll start to include these traits and habits into your own life. Do you know any emotionally intelligent people that you could start spending your time with? Time to start spending more time with them.

GET YOURSELF A MENTOR WITH HIGH EQ EVEN, someone who will be more than happy to guide you through the process of becoming a more emotionally intelligent person yourself. Getting a mentor is one of the best things you can do for yourself because these will be individuals who have already been through the journey and have reached the point that you want to be. Learning directly from them is one of the best better mindset habits you can adopt. Who better to spend your time around than with someone you look up to who can teach you what else you need to do to improve. Find someone whom you admire, preferably one that you regularly see to make it easier to stay in contact. Make it a habit of meeting regularly and plucking their pearls of wisdom.

SURROUNDING YOURSELF WITH PEOPLE WHO WANT TO achieve the same goal as you can make you do things you otherwise will not do. Successful people recognize that change is inevitable and that it must take place. Unsuccessful people will begrudge the changes in you whereas successful people will be glad that it happened and welcome it. Remember how emotionally intelligent people are always curious? Because they constantly seek out new ways of improving and reinventing themselves? They never settle, and they never get complacent, they're always motivated to be better. They welcome to chance to improve, and they never shy away from a challenge.

WITH WILLPOWER, DETERMINATION, CONSISTENCY, AND perseverance, becoming a master controlling your emotions is yours for the taking. Developing the art of controlling your emotions needs to become a part of your life, not just something you do as a once off. Whether you're looking to improve your personal or professional life or both, the way that you handle yourself and control your emotions makes a huge difference in the way that people view and perceive you. Do you want them to view you as an emotional liability? Or someone with leadership qualities because of how well you manage to stay calm under pressure?

4
TURNING YOUR ATTENTION WITHIN

Do you notice how your mood elevates when your favorite some comes on the radio? Or that feeling of excitement when you smell something delicious cooking. What about the way your heart races in nervous anticipation as you're about to take the stage and make a big speech in front of a large audience? It requires your attention to tune into the way that your body responds and reacts to different scenarios and situations. When the attention is focused on what's happening internally, that is known is turning your attention inwards.

Scientists believe that your attention involves the prefrontal cortex of the brain. It is this part of the brain which is unique and what makes us human because it is the prefrontal cortex that is responsible for a lot of the complex and unique thoughts which occur in your brains.

When we think of having to focus our attention

on something, a lot of the times, we often look outside ourselves for this to happen. We look for something external which we can focus our attention on. Whether it is a family member, friend, a show on TV you're watching, the long task list as work you need to attend to, these are all examples of external factors which we focus our attention on. Very rarely do we consider turning our attention inwards, tapping into our emotions and the way that we feel. Turning our attention inwards is something we should probably work on doing more often because it is our internal workings that determine the way that we feel, our happiness or sadness, the amount of stress that we feel and more.

EMOTIONALLY INTELLIGENT PEOPLE ARE ABLE TO TURN their attention inward through self-awareness, which is why they often respond differently to certain situations. For example, where one person could feel annoyed and angrier by the minute being stuck in traffic, an emotionally intelligent person is still able to remain calm, cool and collected, perfectly happy and content with being in the present moment.

THE DEMANDING LIVES THAT WE LEAD REQUIRE A LOT OF our attention to be focused outwards that we forget turning our attention inwards is just as much of a priority. It is because we don't pay enough attention to what's happening within us that we find ourselves being overwhelmed by emotions, sometimes experiencing outbursts and losing control. Our emotions have a way of creeping up on us and taking us by surprise. We may think we have everything under control, but all it takes is one trigger for the emotional floodgates to be unleashed.

WHERE TO BEGIN - HOW TO WORK ON TURNING YOUR ATTENTION WITHIN

Our emotions can be our own worst enemy. If we let it get out of control, they can pull us down in unimaginable ways and threaten every chance we have of wanting to achieve success. The reason that you may not yet have the level of emotional intelligence you desire is that learning to listen to your emotions is something that is entirely new to you. Nobody taught you that this was a crucial life skill that you need to master. In fact, most of the time people are dismissive of their emotions, either choosing to suppress them entirely or deny them altogether. Some may even have convinced themselves that emotions are nothing but a liability, designed to slow you down and prevent you from making the cold, hard decisions that you sometimes need to.

How often have you found yourself apologizing for your reactions and outbursts because your "emotions got the best of you." Living with the guilt of those actions is not a burden you want to be carrying around for the rest of your life. Once something has been said and done, that's all there is to it. It can never be undone, and the words that have been spoken can never be forgotten. This is why you constantly need to work hard at maintaining control over one of the most powerful forces going on within you.

Learning to turn your attention inwards is a skill that needs to be learned through practice. Use the following strategies to help you practice learning how to listen to your emotions and improve your self-awareness:

- **Put a Name to Your Feelings** - Noticing your feelings alone is just one part of the process. Don't notice the way that they make you feel physically, but give them a name so you can identify with them even better. Friendly, happy, proud, nervous, angry, upset, disappointed, and thrilled are just some of the names you could give the emotions that you're feeling. Put them in a sentence and say *This makes me feel proud* or *This makes me thrilled.* Clearly defining your emotions is how you train yourself to focus on pulling your attention inwards, to where it matters the most.

- **Keeping Tabs on One Emotion a Day** - Pick an emotion a day and make it a point to keep tabs on it throughout the day. Whenever you notice the emotion happening, make a note of it or write it down in your emotional journal about the level of intensity you experience that emotion today. For example, if the emotion of your choice for today is happiness, keep tabs on it for the whole day. How often did it happen? Was the feeling strong and intense? Or just a mild passing sensation. The more detailed you are, the more attention it is going to require from you to properly focus on describing your emotions as accurately as possible.

- **Reframing the Way You Think** - Your emotions have a lot to do with the way that you perceive certain situations and events. For example, if you're already feeling nervous and worried, getting an email from your boss saying that they want to see you might aggravate your emotions even further. You may perceive it as bad news, that you're about to be told off for a mistake that you made. Perhaps even fired. You'd probably be envisioning all the worst possible scenarios. Now, if you were to receive that same email from your boss, but you were feeling happy or jubilant that day, you'd perceive the situation in a whole different life. You might think that your boss wants to discuss a new opportunity, or give you some great feedback. Maybe even promote you. This is the perfect example to illustrate just how big of an influence our emotions can have on the way that we perceive things, and why it is important to start focusing on what's going on internally within you. Being able to identify your emotions makes it easier to reframe your thoughts by viewing situations from a realistic perspective. Does the situation warrant such an emotional reaction? Or are you letting your emotions get the best of you again?

- **Create Different Responses to Different Scenarios -** This is a little practice in self-regulation too. Think about all the times in the past where you may not have had the best reaction to certain situations because your judgment was impaired by your emotions. If faced with a similar situation again in the future, how would you handle things differently and why? Practice listing out all the different responses and reactions you would have, and ask yourself if this is what an emotionally intelligent person would do? How well are you regulating your reactions to these challenging emotional situations? You're not dwelling on the past, but rather using these past experiences as lessons which you can learn from. Observing what didn't work in the past, so you don't repeat those same mistakes in the future.

THE MORE YOU NOTICE AND BECOME AWARE OF YOUR emotions, the better your self-awareness skills will become. Noticing them, and accepting them for what they are is how you successfully self-regulate and determine the best course of action for yourself — one where your emotions no longer get the best of you.

5

LIVING A MORE POSITIVE LIFE

IT'S PRETTY OBVIOUS THAT THOSE WITH HIGH EQ AND A positive mindset live on a whole other level from everyone else. Their habits, behavior, the way they talk, the way they express themselves, there's something distinctively different that they do which set them apart from the crowd. Rising each morning and choosing to live life positively is how they remain motivated to keep doing what they do, to keep on succeeding and keep their success flowing.

IF YOU WANT TO START LIVING A MORE POSITIVE LIFE, take a look at the 15 qualities below that are often displayed by individuals with high emotional intelligence and a positive mindset. If you aspire to live a more positive life just like they do, then it's time to start doing what they do:

15 TRAITS OF PEOPLE WHO LIVE A POSITIVE LIFE

Individuals who live a positive life each day are always optimistic. They're hopeful, passionate, creative and in everything that they do, they give it their full effort without any complaints or cynicism in the mix. They always see the glass as half full, despite what everyone else thinks, and it is precisely this optimistic, happy, positive outlook of life that has driven them to achieve success where so many have failed to do so.

LET'S TAKE A LOOK AT SOME OF THE TOP 15 TRAITS OF people who make it a habit to live a positive life:

- They are focused on achieving their goals, and they never let any challenge defeat them or bring them down. They've always got a smile on their face, no matter how many setbacks they face, and they always stand up, brush themselves off and keep moving forward one step at a time.

- They live a happier, more satisfied life. They are grateful for everything that they have, and they make it a point to stop and appreciate life and everything that they've been given, which is why they're always happier than everyone else.

- They have more self-discipline than others because they view discipline in an optimistic way. Where others might see self-discipline as a burden having to sacrifice a lot of things that they're not happy about doing, a person with a positive outlook never sees it as a burden. They see it instead as a step that must be taken to bring them one step closer to where they want to be.

- They enjoy overcoming challenges because it is like a personal accomplishment to them. To overcome something difficult, something which pushed them out of their comfort zone and tested their boundaries, and still emerging victorious on the other side with a smile on their face is what keeps a positive thinking person going.

- They live in the present moment. They never look back and dwell on past mistakes, because they know it isn't going to bring them any benefit. Instead, they live in the now and enjoy the present opportunities that they have because they know it is preparing them for a better future at hand.

- They're not afraid to push their boundaries because they are confident in themselves and their abilities. They are optimistic, and constantly tell themselves they are capable of doing anything that they set their mind to.

- They live a life that is free from the constraints of worrying about what other people think. They never let themselves be worked up or bothered by what other people think about them, and that's how they manage to live their life with such positive energy. They don't let the negative perceptions of others cloud their judgment.

- They are more successful in achieving their goals because you'll never find the words *I can't...* in the vocabulary of someone who has a positive mindset about them. They always believe they are capable of absolutely anything, and it is that belief and that confidence in themselves that fuels them towards success.

- The respect and accept themselves for who they are. They don't need anyone else's opinions to feel validated. They don't focus on whether people like them or not, because they're more focused on building themselves up and creating a version of themselves that they like and respect. When they can look in the mirror and feel happy with the person they see looking back at them, that's all they need to go through the day with a smile on their face and a happy, positive outlook of life.

- They focus more on just getting things done, instead of focusing on how talented they are, or how good they may be at something. Even if they may not be the best, what matters to them is that they at least try to get things done. They are realistic, and they know that nobody can be the best at everything all the time, which is why they never use it as an excuse to hold themselves back.

- They read a lot. There's a lot to be learned between the pages of the book, which is why the successful individuals make it a habit of reading on a regular basis. The read books which inspire, motivate, empower and re-energize them, or give them ideas about what their next move towards success should be. The books that they read help them put things into perspective, which is why they manage to maintain the constant optimistic outlook towards life, even when they struggle.

- They make it a point to focus on the opportunities. Positive and high EQ people are always on the lookout for what their next move could be. The next step that is going to elevate their status just one step higher. They view everything which happens to them as an opportunity to either learn from or take advantage of.

- They actively avoid negativity like a plague. If there ever was an emotion that is so toxic it could completely unravel your life if you let it take control, it's negativity which is why positive minded and high EQ individuals avoid it like a plague and slam the door shut on that emotion. The minute they allow negativity into their lives, they know, it's only a matter of time before things could start to spiral, which is why they actively work at avoiding it and staying far away from it.

- They don't let the fear emotion overcome them and give into it. If you let your life be run by fear, you're always going to be held back and miss the opportunities that come your way. High EQ and positive minded people know this, which is why even though they may be afraid, they never let it stop them from making a big move and taking risks. They know that it is important to try at least, or you'll never know what could have been.

- They live a nutritious life. High EQ and positive minded individuals keep their mind sharp, and their body fit by eating a well-balanced diet which meets all their nutritional needs. They steer clear of anything which is going to impact their body negatively or prevent them from thinking clearly or impact their judgment. They keep themselves well-fed because they know how easy it is to become emotional when your body is running low on nutrition, especially when you're hungry. A well-balanced diet is a key to a happy, healthy mind.

CREATING YOUR PERFECT ENVIRONMENT FOR SUCCESS

Success is attributed to several variables, some which you can control, and some which you can't. Having determination, willpower and emotional intelligence on your side are some examples the variables which are within your control. Having a little bit of luck on your side and the right opportunity at the right time are examples of variables which you cannot control.

THERE IS ONE THING THAT YOU CAN DO, HOWEVER, which ensures that your environment is always one that is conducive to success. An environment which always fosters positivity, making you want to live your best life every day. Having the mental attitude to want to live a life full of positivity alone is not enough, you need to build and create an environment which also stimulates you to do so. Our external environments have some degree of influence over the state of our minds. If we are in a surrounding which is dank, dark and downright depressing, it makes it very hard to have a positive outlook. Compare that to an environment which is bright, open, warm, inviting and cozy. Obviously, the latter scenario is the one where we'll find it much easier to live a more positive life because the environment has been designed to foster that success.

YOUR THOUGHTS AND BEHAVIOR WILL BE INFLUENCED to some degree by the environment which you surround yourself with daily because this is where you spend most of your time. An environment that increases productivity and allows freedom of expression is a great place to spend your time in as it will motivate and inspire you. A conducive environment keeps your positivity going, making it easier to live life with a happy, healthy, positive outlook every day. With the right kind of environment, you're less likely to be influenced by negative elements because you'll be so happy with what you have going on right now that you're not willing to let anything disrupt that happiness.

. . .

HERE'S HOW YOU CAN CREATE AN ENVIRONMENT THAT encourages you to live a more positive life every day:

- **Stick Motivational Quotes Around Your Home -** Quotes, sayings, and mantras which encourage your development of a higher EQ are an excellent addition to your home or work space. Find a quote you like, get it printed out in whatever color you want and stick it right next to your goals that you have written down. With these bright, colorful quotes all around your home and office cubicle, they'll be hard to miss, and they'll serve as constant positivity reminders.

- **Have a Vision Board -** Another great element which encourages and fosters a positive mindset is to have a vision board with appealing imagery that is related to all the goals and desires you want to achieve. Use bold designs and vibrant colors, images which are your mind is attracted to. The minute you look at these pictures, you should feel a burst of happiness, have a smile on your face and feel infused with the right kind of positive energy. A vision board is especially great to have in the workspace because this is where you spend most of your time in each day. It can be easy to lose your motivation when your workspace is just a dull, uninspiring cubicle which seems to do nothing for you. But you can create a little positivity paradise of your own.

- **Have a Daily To-Do List** – Where important tasks always come first. That's how you ensure you remain productive throughout the day. Establishing a routine for yourself will make you much more productive. A routine allows you to get right down to the tasks that need to be done for the day, makes you more efficient because you know what needs to be done for the day without having to think too much about it, minimizes the time you need to spend on planning and helps to create structure in your life as well as instil good, productive habits when you do something in repetition.

NOW IS THE TIME TO START THINKING POSITIVE AND start building your confidence one step at a time. Remember that nobody else can do this for you, so it is up to you to start.

6

UNDERSTANDING THE IMPORTANCE OF SELF

THE IMPORTANCE OF SELF CAN ENCOMPASS SEVERAL different aspects. Self-worth, self-esteem, self- awareness, and self-regulation, all of which are equally important in your quest for better emotional intelligence. Having a strong sense of self is a pivotal tool which you need to become someone who has high EQ successfully. Especially in today's world where it is so easy to let the hecticness and the constant stress make us lose touch with who we are.

DEFINING A STRONG SENSE OF SELF

A strong sense of self here is defined as the way that you perceive yourself. How big your belief in yourself is? When you have a strong sense of self, you're more confident, ambitious, determined and focused on what you want to get out of your life. Your belief in yourself is so strong that nothing can waver your confidence, and you don't need validation from anyone else to assure you of what you're capable of. That is what it means to have a strong sense of self.

. . .

LET'S DO A QUICK EXERCISE HERE FOR A MINUTE TO determine where your current sense of self is:

- Do you love the person that you are right now?
- How much do you value yourself right now?
- Can you name 5 of your best qualities which you see as strengths?
- If you had to lead a group of people right now, would you be able to do it?

TO INCREASE YOUR CONFIDENCE, THAT SENSE OF BELIEF in yourself has to come from within you. That is where it all begins. No amount of external sources will be able to give you the level of confidence you desire if you don't believe in yourself, to begin with. The support and encouragement that you receive from others are just a bonus, to give you that extra bit of reassurance that you did do a good job. However, it is what you think that matters more, not what they say. If you constantly rely on others for validation, you're never going to be fully satisfied, and you'll constantly be searching for something more because it never seems to be enough.

A STRONG SENSE OF SELF IS GOING TO BE A CRUCIAL tool that you need as you work on improving your EQ levels. Self-awareness and self-regulation are the first two out of the five major principles which make up what emotional intelligence is. Self-awareness is going to require that you be connected with and attuned to who you are. What are your strengths, weaknesses, what emotional triggers set you off, how well you're able to cope with them, and how confident you are in handling the different situations that come your way? Self-regulation is then going to focus on how well you manage and control these emotional episodes when they occur. How well you're able to cope under pressure. How well you manage, yourself is going to be one of the most important things you do as you work on developing your emotional intelligence. EQ is going to require a high sense of self, and the belief in yourself to pull it off.

WHY HAVING A STRONG SENSE OF SELF MATTERS

Although emotional intelligence isn't a subject you're going to find being taught in schools, it is one of the most important things that a person can learn, and it has a strong connection with your sense of self. When you've got high EQ, your relationships are healthier, you control your emotions instead of it controlling you, and it infuses you with a strong, healthy sense of self-esteem.

LIFE CAN BE A REAL CHALLENGE, ONE THAT IS FULL OF surprises, some of which can take you on an emotional roller coaster. In the moments where you experience emotional turmoil or discomfort, having a strong sense of self is the inner strength that is going to help you see it through. Having a strong sense of self does not necessarily mean you're immune to experiencing emotional upheaval, it just means that you react differently than you normally would, especially when high EQ is involved in the mix. With a strong sense of self, your inner strength is the one that is going to help you self-regulate, soothe and calm yourself in the emotional moments when you need it the most.

. . .

HAVING A STRONG SENSE OF SELF MATTERS BECAUSE:

- It enhances your level of self-awareness (high EQ) and knowledge about yourself. You know what your values, your beliefs, your strengths, and your weakness are and how to use them to your advantage.

- It makes self-acceptance easier. You stop trying to be someone that you're not, and you accept yourself wholeheartedly, including both the good and the bad. You acknowledge what your talents are, and you're perfectly fine admitting which areas might need some improvement. You accept that you're not 100% perfect, and that's okay.

- You're more confident affirming your boundaries. You no longer succumb to the pressure always to please others, because you realize that is something which can be detrimental and damaging to your sense of self. You are willing to compromise for the relationships that matter, but not to the extent where it violates your boundaries and affects your sense of self. This is how you maintain control of your emotions and avoid feeling overwhelmed or pressured into doing things you don't want to do.
- You take responsibility for your actions, which is what a good leader does. Wherever you go, people will look to you for guidance and leadership, because of the strong sense of self that you've got. Your strong sense of self guides your

every decision and choice that you'll be displaying leadership qualities without even realizing it.

- You no longer have such strong emotional reactions to the things which are being said to you. That's because you know what you are worth, and when you know someone is saying something about you that isn't true, why let yourself get emotional about it? A strong sense of self makes you more accepting and attuned to the kind of person that you are, and that what others say about you does not define who you are in any way.
- It makes you comfortable with knowing when to say no. Sometimes, as much as you would like to help, it simply isn't worth it if it is going to affect your mental and physical health by doing so. Knowing when to say no comes from having a strong sense of self, because you know your limits and what you're capable of, and you don't feel pressured into agreeing just because you're worried about offending the person who asked for a favor.

INCREASE YOUR SENSE OF SELF BY SETTING YOURSELF FREE

If your sense of self is not where you want it to be right now, ask yourself why that is? What is holding you back? Do you constantly worry about the opinions of others? Are you worried if your actions are being judged? If you are, then it is time to set yourself free and reclaim your sense of self once more.

People with high emotional intelligence live a happier, more fulfilled life, one where they are always in control because they do not themselves be bothered by the judgments and opinions of others. They know that if they were to get all worked up and let it bother them, their emotions could quickly spiral out of control, their self-esteem gets affected and they find themselves taking several steps back instead of progressing forward the way that they should. Think about the last time that you were so worked up and bothered about what someone said about you. You spent weeks dwelling on it, and because it festered in your mind for so long, you sense of self was affected before you even realized what was happening.

HAVING HIGH EQ MEANS YOU NEED TO BELIEVE IN yourself enough and be confident in your own decisions and choices not to care what others may think. As long as you know, the course of action you chose is the right one for you at that time, believe that you made the decision that was best. Allowing yourself to constantly care about whether others are going to approve of your decision or not is just trapping yourself in an emotional prison. It is a restrictive and unhealthy thought pattern that has been holding you back all this time and messing with your emotions, causing you to obsess and worry over unnecessary things.

RECLAIM YOUR SENSE OF SELF ONCE MORE BY reminding yourself that the only opinion that matters here is yours. This is your life, and you're the one who's living it, making choices and decisions which you have to live with. Your opinions, and the opinions of the people who matter (like family and friends who genuinely care about you), are the only thoughts that should matter. The people who care about you will always want only what's best for you. They will lift you, be supportive and build up your confidence because they care about seeing you succeed.

. . .

DON'T LET THE OPINIONS OF OTHERS AFFECT THE WAY that you see yourself. When someone thinks or has anything negative to say about you, it is a reflection on them, not you. If you allow yourself to give in to your emotions because of what they say, it is going to eat away at your sense of self and diminish your confidence over time. Someone else's opinion can only matter if you allow it to matter.

7
BECOMING AN EFFECTIVE AND AWARE LEADER

Being a leader is a position which commands huge responsibility. All eyes are constantly on you. When a challenge or conflict arises, you're the one people turn to for solutions and answers. It is a big responsibility to oversee and manage a team of people, and the pressure to perform, to ensure that things are always running smoothly, rests on your shoulders.

No team, project or organization can succeed without good leadership leading the way which is why emotional intelligence is so important. When you've got so much on your plate to deal with, you're bound to go through all sorts of emotions. If you don't learn to manage and control those emotions, they're going to overwhelm you easily. Being a leader, and being an *effective* leader, are two very different things. The latter is the one that is destined for success.

Managing a company alone is overwhelming, but

being an effective leader to a team of people who are the backbone of your company is an even more overwhelming task. You must be an effective leader if you're going to bring out the best in the people that you work with. A leader needs to constantly evaluate their leadership method to see if their approaches are working as well as they should.

PART OF BEING AN EFFECTIVE MANAGER IS KNOWING the strengths and weaknesses of your team members, and what each person brings to the table. This part can be achieved through the social skills, motivation and empathy part of the emotional intelligence core principles. An effective leader will never turn a blind eye to conflict and will do everything in their power to address the conflict as soon as it happens. To do this, you need to effectively tune into the emotions of the people who are involved in the conflict. Empathize with them, see where they're coming from. During conflict is when emotions tend to run high, and if you're not able to properly manage your own emotions, you won't be able to manage the emotions of others.

HOW TO BECOME AN EFFECTIVE AND AWARE LEADER

An effective leader is one that is not afraid of a challenge. Effective leadership is also not about bossing people around. It isn't just about telling them what to do. Effective leadership is about bringing out all the best qualities in all the people you work it, to get a team of people working together like a well-oiled machine. An effective leader breeds success. Effective leaders share in the responsibility and the workload of the team. They're not afraid to get down and dirty with the team, being one with the rest of them and taking on jobs that everyone else is doing.

. . .

As an effective leader, the responsibility also lies with you to let your team know you're always there for them no matter what. You need to let your people know that they matter to you. You need to nurture them, encourage them to grow in their way, empathize and be compassionate when you see that they are struggling. Emotional intelligence is your secret weapon to bringing out the best in your employees because it can help you connect with them in ways you couldn't imagine. This isn't just another boss-employee relationship. To be considered an *effective* and successful leader, you need to go the extra mile and look beyond that.

How do you use emotional intelligence to foster effective leadership and become more aware? By employing the following techniques:

- **Let Your Team Know They Matter** - People are emotional creatures. As a leader, if you want to be successful and effective, it is your job to listen to everyone's, and what they have to say. Make it your policy to encourage everyone to approach you and give them a chance to express themselves. Let them know they can come and talk to you about how they feel without judgment. Your job is to be encouraging, to empathize with them and make them feel supported. To make them feel like they matter.

- **Be Someone Who's Trustworthy** - You need to cultivate an environment of trust at all times when you are with their team. When a team can trust each other, they work much better together. When they know without a doubt, they can put their full trust in their leader to always have their best interest at heart, that makes for a happier, more positive team all around.

- **Forging Strong Connections** - Use the self-awareness and social skills aspect of emotional intelligence to help you foster stronger connections between you and the people you manage. Don't just connect for the sake of doing so, but build a connection that is meaningful, that shows the team members you genuinely care about them and their welfare. Reach out to them on a regular basis, congratulate them when they successfully meet their targets. Catch up with them regularly and talk about common interests. Ask them about their families, their hobbies, their passion. Build a relationship outside of just work matters.

- **Show Empathy** - There's a reason why this is one of the core principles of emotional intelligence. The people in your team have emotions and feelings, put yourself in their shoes and try to imagine what they would be feeling. This makes it much easier for you to see things from their perspective, to understand where they're coming from and why they're feeling the way that they do. An effective leader is one who can practice empathy and compassion with sincerity.

- **Listen Attentively -** When having a one-on-one conversation with a member of your team, listen to their voice inflections and the tone of their voice. Pay attention to the words they use, the points they emphasize on. Listen to the way they sound when they talk about how they feel. Self-awareness is what you need in this case. Practicing self-awareness (another EQ core principle) and listening attentively will help you connect with your people, and be empathetic towards them. It will help you be compassionate, understanding and nurturing in all the ways that they need.

- **Be Mutually Respectful -** Respect and encourage respect among every single person in the organization and team, because everyone has a role to play and their role contributes to the overall success. The most effective type of leaders are ones that provide a work environment where employees help each other and value the contributions that each makes. This can only be achieved by master emotional intelligence because without the crucial self-awareness, motivational and social skills needed, you're going to find it very hard to manage yourself and everyone else.

- **Take Time to Reflect On Your Feelings -** Leaders are sometimes so busy looking after everyone else that they forget to check in with themselves and their feelings. Part of being an effective leader with high levels of emotional intelligence is about being able to check in with yourself now and then. What have your feelings been lately? Reflect on them for several moments. This helps to avoid you falling out of touch with yourself and everyone else around you. Leaders have a lot on their plate, and they can be so busy trying to manage everything else that they forget stopping to take care of themselves is something they need to do.

- **Taking Breaks When You Need It** - Leaders are always expected to bring their A-game and be switched on all the time. It is easy to forget that leaders are people too, with feelings and emotions. They too, like everyone else, can burn out if they fail to take care of themselves. They too can be easily drained by having to manage all sorts of emotions. The emotionally intelligent thing to do is to stop and take breaks whenever you need them. It is perfectly okay to take some time to recharge your batteries. In fact, you should make it a point to do this to keep you drowning in your own emotions. Being a leader is challenging, and it can take a toll on you emotionally, mentally and physically. Whenever you think you need a break to recharge, take it and don't feel guilty about doing so.

As a leader with huge amounts of responsibility on your shoulders, you *need* emotional intelligence to help you sort through your feelings in healthy ways. Emotional intelligence teaches you how to regulate your impulses, so you don't act out emotionally and in the heat of the moment, because that's not what an effective leader does. That's how your people end up losing trust in you if you appear to be a leader who is unpredictable and acts out emotionally. EQ does make a *big difference* in the level of success you achieve because it trains you to focus on what matters. It teaches you to remain calm, focused and in control in the moments when you need it most. More importantly, it teaches you how to get a handle on the negative emotions that could threaten to disrupt your success. It teaches you to be mindful and to be attuned to the way that you're feeling at crucial moments. That is how emotional intelligence helps you become a more effective and aware leader.

8
THE ART OF EFFECTIVE COMMUNICATION

BESIDES A HIGH LEVEL OF EQ, THERE IS ONE OTHER quality that everyone should possess to help them thrive in the work environment and everyday life in general. That quality is effective communication. You could have all the most brilliant ideas, the best strategies and the best plans for success, but if you don't know how to communicate those ideas effectively, they are not going to be of much use to you. Even in everyday life, if you struggle to communicate, it can be a real challenge. It can be very stressful trying to get people to understand what you're trying to say and where you're coming from.

WHICH IS WHY THE ART OF EFFECTIVE COMMUNICATION is something you need to work on improving, along with your emotional intelligence. For communication to be considered effective and successful, your message must be understood clearly. The exchange of information that goes on between two or several individuals must be clearly understood by all involved, with little or no misunderstandings happening.

WHY EFFECTIVE COMMUNICATION MATTERS

How often have you thought about the way that you communicate? Give it some serious thought for a minute. Communication is a skill that many don't think twice about, but it is one of the most important skills you could have at your disposal. Effective communication matters because it helps us relate and collaborate with the people living in the world with us.

EFFECTIVE COMMUNICATION IS ALSO IMPORTANT because:

- **It Avoids Misunderstandings -** Misunderstandings increase the chances of conflict. This often happens when information is misconstrued or taken out of context. Why does this happen? Because there's a lack of effective communication going on. Misunderstandings can often lead to heated arguments, fights and severed relationships depending on the seriousness of the situation. If you have ever gone for weeks, months or maybe even years without speaking to someone because of a misunderstanding, you'll know exactly just how damaging this can be. Which further emphasizes why it is so important that we all work on improving our communication skills. We communicate with hundreds of people throughout our lives, every day and in the workplace. You need to be able to express your messages clearly so that it minimizes the chances that what you're going to say is going to cause problems for yourself and the people that you're speaking to.

- **It Helps You Form Powerful Relationships -** The connections that we make in life matter, especially in the career world. In fact, how well you're able to connect to other people is the foundation of all relationships. Everyone starts as strangers in the beginning, and it is through communication that those bonds are taken to another level. People start talking; you get to know each other, form connections based on mutual interest. All of this can only happen if you're able to express yourself well through effective communication. If nobody can understand what you're trying to say, it makes it harder to connect to you. For example, think of a time when you tried to forge a connection with someone who didn't speak the same language. Wasn't it much harder? That's a struggle you would have to deal with on a regular basis without the power of effective communication.

- **It Boosts Your Confidence -** Successful leaders and individuals alike seem to ooze confidence on every level. When they speak, people stop and listen, transfixed by what they're saying. When they speak, people absorb what they're saying, which is how they manage to captivate large groups of audiences. That's the art of effective communication at work. When you're able to communicate effectively, your confidence level is given a tremendous boost because you do not doubt at all that you can express and tell people exactly what you want them to know. You find that you are no longer shy and awkward when it comes time for you to speak because you exactly what to do and how to handle the situation. You know exactly what needs to be done. Success cannot be achieved if you're not able to convey yourself properly. If you're going to be a leader who is able to command large groups of people, the people must be able to understand you effortlessly.

- **It Gives You a Leg Up In Your Career -** Our workplace is where we spend the majority of our day. From Monday right up to Friday, morning to evening, our lives are focused on our careers and doing our jobs. If you aspire to achieve great heights in your career, effective communication, and emotional intelligence is the winning combination that you need. In the workplace, communication skills are just as vital as all the other skill sets you need to get your job done right. Without it, it's only a matter of time before you get overtaken by those with better communication abilities. Effective communication can give you a leg up in your career because it helps you form and maintain relationships, build rapport with the people who matter. It enables you to work cohesively with people from various departments and diverse backgrounds. It helps you effectively handle both easy and difficult clients, and even challenging situations. In the career world, it is all about how productive you are, and whether you're viewed as an asset to the company or the job that is going to put you ahead of everyone else. With a high EQ and effective communication skills at your disposal, you're already on your way to becoming a winner.

- **It Helps Promote Teamwork and Innovation at the Workplace -** When you're comfortable enough to communicate your ideas at work freely, it helps to increase the level of innovation experienced. This, in turn, increases the chances of good ideas and contributions being implemented at work to improve the workflow, draw in new clients and improve the company's daily operations as a whole. When effective communication flows freely in the workplace, it is easier to build teams which are productive and cohesive, who work well together to get things done. When colleagues and different teams are able to come together, work well and communicate effectively with each other, staff morale is given a boost, and there's generally a more positive vibe and feel at work. Instead of dreading your job, you might even come to love it because you feel productive, and you know that you're making contributions that are only serving to improve your reputation as an employee.

COMMUNICATION BARRIERS YOU NEED TO OVERCOME

For effective communication to take place, you're going to need to overcome the barriers that are preventing it from happening. Communication is complex. Sometimes, despite all your efforts, misunderstandings could still occur. During the communication process, there are sometimes barriers which tend to come up that can result in poor communication. These are communication barriers.

THESE BARRIERS ARE THE REASON YOUR MESSAGES TEND to become misconstrued or taken out of context. Some examples of communication barriers include:

- **Information Overload** - Not everyone processes information in the same way. If you distribute your information too fast and too soon, you could risk overwhelming the person you're speaking to because they don't have enough time to process what you're telling them.

- **Language Differences** - The world we live in today is more diverse than it has ever been. We come into contact with people from all sorts of different cultural backgrounds. While this is a wonderful thing, the different languages and accents can sometimes prove to be a communication barrier. Some words may be pronounced differently, or sentences become difficult to understand because of a different accent.

- **Being Distracted by External Factors** - Our mobile phones are perhaps the biggest distraction in our lives. General noise, other people talking, phones ringing, traffic honking, messages beeping into your mobile phone, even the urge to frequently check social media is a communication barrier because it distracts you from focusing on the message that you should be receiving.

- **Making Assumptions** - We've all been guilty of jumping to conclusions even before the person we're talking to has finished what they're trying to say. This barrier occurs when you decide to reach on a course of action without fully listening to all the information first. When you make assumptions, you're mentally blocking out the rest of the message without even realizing it, tuning out and not paying attention anymore because you've already jumped ahead to what you think should be done next. You run the risk of making even more mistakes this way.

- **A Lack of Self-Confidence** - Being shy and nervous can be viewed as a communication barrier because it makes the communication awkward. When you're shy, you tend to mumble, stutter or even forget a lot of what you intended to say.

- **Talking in A Hurry** - Rushing through the message puts you at risk of missing crucial information which needs to be communicated. When you speak in the hurried manner, the could stress out the person you're speaking to because they can't keep up with what you're trying to say.

HOW TO IMPROVE YOUR COMMUNICATION SKILLS

To start working on becoming a more effective communicator, here is what you need to start working on and taking into account:

- **Go Right to the Point** - Being concise and specific is the best way to get your message across in the most effective manner. Communicate only the essential points, and leave out anything that is unnecessary. People have short attention spans, and this technique is the best way to ensure all the important information is conveyed the way that it should be.

- **Focus on the Message -** Stay focused on the message. The more focused you are on what's important, the better you are able to ensure that the important information is clearly communicated with minimal room for misunderstanding. For example, at the workplace, if you were talking about a co-worker's performance, focus on the performance aspect alone and avoid discussing unrelated matters such as their personality or the way they are dressed as an example.
- **Keep Distractions at Bay -** If you know you're about to have an important conversation, put away anything that can serve as a distraction. Put your mobile phone on silent, put it away in your pocket, find a quiet space where you can speak. Do your best to give the person your full attention and request that they do the same.

- **Be an Active Listener -** Effective communication is not just about you speaking and making yourself heard, it is about learning to be an active listener too. Communication works both ways, and for both parties to fully benefit from the conversation, you must be an equally active listener. This is where the social skills and the empathy aspect of emotional intelligence come into play because you need to be attuned to the emotions and feelings of people around you too.

- **Speak with Clarity -** Speak clearly and confidently, and pronounce each word clearly. Avoid meek, soft tones and especially avoid mumbling or muttering your words because nobody will be able to understand what you're saying when you do.

Whether it is in your personal life or your workplace, there is no denying that communication is one of the most important skills you can develop. Great communication skills can make a world of difference. Your success in life is dependent on how well you can regulate your emotions, and your ability to effectively communicate well with others. This is how you build successful relationships. When you combine those skills with the emotional intelligence techniques you learned in the earlier chapters, there's going to be nothing holding you back from success after this.

CONCLUSION

Thank for making it through to the end of this book, let's hope it was informative and able to provide you with all of the tools you need to achieve your goals whatever they may be.

Your emotions guide every choice, every decision and every step that you make in life. As your self-awareness increases, you will slowly begin to notice it whenever you're faced with a choice to make. The good news is, you're now equipped with everything you need to know about what it takes to become a more emotionally intelligent person.

As you move forward from here and make the necessary changes needed to improve your EQ, use the strategies, tips, and techniques which you've gathered from this book as you see fit. The tools are here to help you, and you should use them in a way that works best for you. No matter what your ultimate goal may be for your emotional intelligence, this guidebook is here to help you every step of the way.

This is going to be a journey that's going to take time to see the changes manifest itself visibly in your life, so don't get discouraged or frustrated. You are progressing forward, even if you think you're not. Take it slow, pace yourself and don't rush. Take this time to work on strengthening yourself emotionally from within. Practice the strategies in your life every day, and eventually, you will get there. If it helps, focus on mastering one technique at a time before you move onto the next one.

Building and mastering your EQ is something which you will gain over time. It is a skill, a technique and a piece of knowledge which must be carefully honed, crafted and cultivated. Setbacks will happen along the way, but take them as learning curves, a challenge to overcome that is just going to make you better in the end. Most of all, be kind and patient with yourself. You're starting something incredible just by taking these first few steps towards improving your EQ. Whenever you need some help, you always have this guidebook to turn back to. Every tip and technique in here is meant to help you along with your process, so fully utilize it to your advantage.

Finally, if you found this book useful in any way, a review on Amazon is always appreciated!

HOW TO ANALYZE PEOPLE

Speed Read People, Analyze Body Language & Personality Types

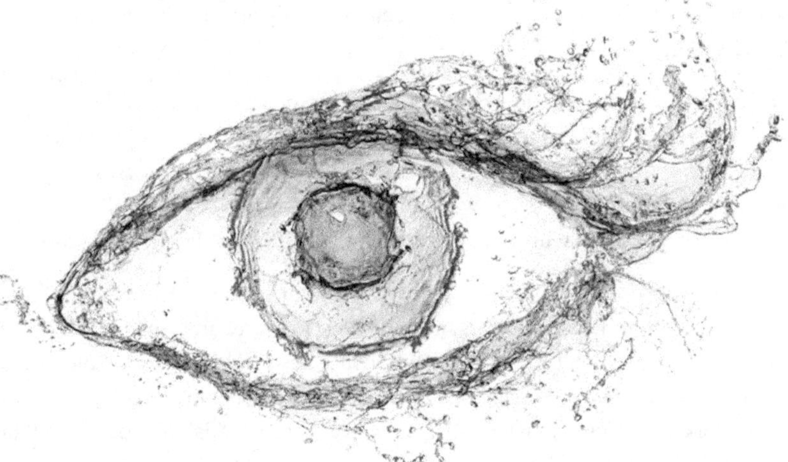

Edward Benedict

❀ Created with Vellum

INTRODUCTION

Learning to analyze people, their behaviors, and their personalities can be very helpful to you, as it can strengthen the relationships you have with them. This relationship can be with anyone—whether your partner, your colleagues, your bosses, your family, or even your acquaintances. But why analyze people? Firstly, if we could only read people effectively, we would know if they liked something or if they are feeling comfortable or if they are agreeing to what we said. Secondly, it helps create empathy in you—and when you have empathy, you can handle crises and negative situations efficiently. It also helps you create better bonds with people.

In a professional capacity, knowing how to read people can get you far in the career ladder, especially if you have the capacity to understand the needs and wants of your client or boss. Working on your ability to read and analyze people can greatly affect how to deal with them, and this is especially important with people with whom you have a relationship—whether personally or professionally. When you understand and empathize on how someone else is feeling, you can adapt the way you convey your message and communication style so that the person you are communicating with can receive this message in the best possible way.

But how do you analyze people? What signs should you be looking into? What words must you listen to? What other signs can you target to help you understand what someone else is feeling and thinking? When reading or analyzing someone, one of the first few things you must realize is that you need to get rid of your biases and whatever apprehensions you may have made or have on them. These notions are merely walls that contain old and limiting ideas.

People who have mastered the art of analyzing other people are trained extremely well to analyze the invisible and use their senses to look deeper into a person's embodiment, looking further than where the general attention goes to. You've probably heard that the eyes are the window into the soul. If that's the case, then words are the gateway into the mind. When analyzing people, you not only need to look at the way they react, their body language, and even their eyes—but you also need to consider the kind of words they use to describe, explain, elaborate, and communicate. In this book, we will explore the proven strategies and steps on how to read and analyze people using non-verbal gestures and body language. The information in this book will help you how to study someone's body language, decipher the various personality types there are, and determine how you can communicate with them on a level that engages them. This book will also look into how to spot lies and deception as well as identifying romantic cues from a person.

I

BODY LANGUAGE BASICS

BODY LANGUAGE IS ONE OF THE MANY WAYS THAT WE humans communicate—but while most people pay attention to words and actions, body language is rarely given attention to. What we say sometimes can be very different from our body language. We may sound happy, but our body language says otherwise—and according to experts, our body language takes up half of the way we communicate.

Figuring out how to peruse non-verbal communication viably can enable us to comprehend what somebody is attempting to express, if they are comfortable with the choices they make and if they are genuine about them. We also learn to communicate our messages effectively when we learn to read body language. It goes beyond just what words can put meaning in to.

HOW COMMON IS BODY LANGUAGE IN COMMUNICATION?

Believe it or not but body language takes up 55% of our daily communication. However, analyzing nonverbal cues isn't focused on just the broad strokes. These gestures indicate various things, and it depends entirely on context.

Nonverbal cues are extremely crucial when trying to read someone because, in many ways, you can detect if someone is lying or if they are enjoying a date or how they are as a person when they come in for a job interview. It is tied with finding some hidden meaning to decipher non-verbal communication precisely so you know whether the individual's words are expressing how they really feel.

Unfortunately, we humans are more inclined to lie than to tell the truth for plenty of reasons such as avoiding conflict, trying to impress someone and so on. Sometimes, we end up lying more than once in a short span of time and while they may necessarily not be big lies, we end up doing it anyway. We end up willingly partaking in deception because we rather hear a sweet lie than the bitter truth. In any case, non-verbal communication isn't as misleading as words—our bodies are horrendous liars.

WHAT IS BODY LANGUAGE?

It is our body's physical, non-verbal communication approach that is sometimes in-sync with the words that are coming out of our mouth. Body language can be anything from a stance, an eye-glance, a quick facial expression and even the biting of our lip.

You may have seen how some people speak very animatedly and they use mostly their hands to convey or emphasize their words. There are a lot of hand talkers who keep their hands in a steady movement to pass on their point, stress on information, or just to keep the conversation going.

This gesture and many other forms of body language often speak volumes. Make an observation of how a person's body language is:

a) When they speak

- Do they have slumped shoulders? Is their back rounded with their head hanging down? This could indicate that they are either shy or sad.

b) When you see a person walking into a room to address a team or a company

- Do they carry themselves stably? Do they have their head at eye level or held high? This can be interpreted as arrogance or confidence.

c) When you need to talk to someone

- Do they have their arms folded across their chest? Do they have their legs crossed? Are they glancing around or sighing? This could be understood as an unfriendly stance, or they are not open to what you have to say, defensive or standoffish.

It is truly fascinating what body language can do and how much we can perceive from it. Aside from being able to utilize it in judging the mood a person is in or their attitude, you can also make and create better relationships simply by observing them. These non-verbal communication gateways help create a deeper sense of bonding.

BODY LANGUAGE BASICS

Your main goal when it comes to reading body language is to determine if a person is comfortable in the situation that they are currently in. Once you have established this, the next thing is to process the context that they are in and look at other cues. Of course, this is easier said than done so we will go into the specifics in following chapters. Here are some common denominators for positive body language:

- Extended periods of eye contact
- Feeling at ease
- Looking down and away out of shyness
- Moving or leaning closer to you
- Relaxed, uncrossed limbs
- Genuine smiles

Here are some common denominators for negative body language:

- Feet pointed away from you, or towards, and exit
- The feeling of unease
- Looking away to the side
- Moving or leaning away from you
- Rubbing/scratching their nose, eyes, or the back of their neck
- Crossed arms or legs

One body cue and mean plenty of different things. While crossed arms can be construed as negative non-verbal communication, it can likewise propose that an individual is feeling chilly, awkward, disappointed, or closed off. When understanding somebody, it is pivotal to focus on a few prompts since one's demeanor can be deceiving. It is a must to look deeper to understand what is really going on and this means focusing on cues and also the context it is in.

Here are some common body language categories:

BODY LANGUAGE CATEGORIES

Body language can be separated into general classifications:

1. Aggressive – Threatening body language
2. Attentiveness – This shows that you are interested and engages.
3. Bored – This is the complete reverse of attentiveness, and it is usually represented by not making enough eye contact and constant yawning.
4. Closed – This is when someone shuts you off and is often shown having crossed arms and standing far away.
5. Deceptiveness – This is usually portrayed when a person wants to get away with a lie and displays nervous behavior, guilty and worry.
6. Defensiveness – This person who is defensive can look like they are protecting or withholding information.
7. Dominant – Dominant body language is used when someone wants to be in command and they usually stand tall, with their chest puffed out.
8. Emotional – When a person is emotional, they are greatly influenced by their current emotions and usually have varying moods.
9. Evaluation – A person portrays a sense of evaluation in settling on a choice without second thoughts.
10. Greeting – It happens when two people first come into contact.
11. Open – This is, of course, welcoming and accepting.

12. Ready – It tells people that you are open, willing and prepared.
13. Content and relaxed – This can be portrayed by a calm, happy and restful demeanor.
14. Passionate – This is often a romantic body language that expresses attraction and is flirty.
15. Submissive – This shows off the relenting side.

The body language described above is usually commonly communicated through a combination of postures and poses and is not singular to one. Again, a wide range of body positions has altogether unique importance relying upon the specific situation, the circumstance, and the social foundation. Take for example the pose of crossing your arms—in a meeting situation, this can be construed as simply someone being serious and focused.

It is extremely crucial to take context into consideration and if you want to learn how to analyze people, then you need to have a heightened sense of awareness of how your body acts and what it is saying when you talk to the people around you. Keeping these tips in mind will help increase your communication and comprehension skills, thus opening a more effective line of communication with your team, your partner, children, and friends.

2
UNDERSTANDING SELF

WHAT IS UNDERSTANDING SELF? THIS MAY OR MAY NOT be the first time you have heard of this—but in the exploration and learning of analyzing people, the understanding self is one of the elements that we need to discover.

Understanding self is a spiritual and philosophical question which includes an in-depth study and journey. For example, when you are shown the forest or the deep blue sea, it is entirely up to you on how deep you would like to journey in and the kind of experience you want to derive from your journey.

UNDERSTANDING ONE'S SELF INVOLVES AWARENESS

For any ordinary human being, being self-aware all the time, 365 days a year, 24 hours a day is impossible and quite frankly, unrealistic. There is a certain level of awareness as well as a moment of realization. To be self-aware for even 10 minutes is already a great thing.

WHY IS SELF-AWARENESS HARD?

Don't worry if you do not feel like you understand or have the right or correct understanding on self-awareness. In fact, nobody ever really does. However, it is not too hard to try to understand once you learn it because self-awareness is about understanding your own self so you can be an effective and positive member of the community, your family, your company and generally at life.

The moment we are born into this world, we are already fed with information about the rights and wrongs of the world we live in by our parents, media, the education system and the society we live in. We also tend to consume plenty of information from the internet which makes not only focusing hard but also identifying who we are as a person.

Our body's main function is to survive which means that our body will do whatever it takes to survive, stay alive and be comfortable as much as possible. So when thinking about or understanding self, there are two things we need to look into which are:

1. Ego – which is the state of mind that is the most powerful. Egoist states are what rulers and conquerors have and will go to great lengths to ensure that their empire remains. Ego is the element to want everything which is why some people start spending or investing to accumulate wealth for generations to come.
2. Self – An ego mind does not let you become self-aware because self-awareness is spirituality and this type of spirituality has nothing whatsoever to do with religion. Spirituality is a way of life whereas religion is a lifestyle. The body wants its pleasure whereas the ego wants power, wealth and control.

A good leader of a country or state will lead a life that is not excessive and really, to live a life that is the exact same one as the average human in that country. What is the point of living in a large mansion or palace when the people in your country life in small squatters? If the purpose of a leader is to serve, then they should not have the entitlement of the state.

One must differentiate between ego and self because ego will blind a person from seeking righteousness and truth.

UNDERSTANDING YOURSELF

The list below can give you an idea of how to understand yourself but keep in mind that this list is as fluid and torrid as the ocean and you should look at yourself as the ocean because the value of Self is as deep as the big, blue ocean.

1. Desires and interests
2. Your needs and wants
3. Passion
4. Identity – country, race, language, clan, community, sexual preference
5. Emotions
6. Awareness to thoughts
7. Ideas
8. Relationships
9. Your strengths and weakness
10. Skill
11. Knowledge
12. Expertise

Understanding self is a process or exercise that you need to do every day. It is about peeling off your superficial layers and getting lighter as you peel each layer away and feel the peace emanating from within. Understanding self also does not mean that you are forgoing your desires or ambitions whether personally or professionally.

Your motivation increases when you take on a task or project when you begin to understand yourself. However, do take note that it is not as easy as A, B & C.

As you go on the journey of self-discovery and seeking yourself, the truth about yourself will surface bit by bit. Think of it as mining diamonds. If diamonds can be found anywhere, they lose their value but because they are rare and exquisite, it is considered precious and demands a high premium. Self-Awareness and understanding self is exactly like the process of mining diamonds—it comes to you a little by little as you journey through life and discover a piece of you. You will value this piece more profoundly.

UNDERSTANDING SELF FOR YOUR CAREER DEVELOPMENT

Knowing yourself not only extends value to your relationships but it also enhances the partnerships and your ethics in your career. By being self-aware, it can help you make thoughtful career decisions and plan a career development path suitable for you. Pivotal as well for you is establishing your career goals and things that provide you with joy, fulfillment, as well as passion. Self-awareness also means pinpointing what kind of environments and work cultures that you thrive in because all of these elements will enable you to focus on a career path that has many opportunities that have the kind of environment and culture that will help you thrive, grow, and learn.

Some of us prefer routine with very minimal disruption. We like order, routine, going in at a certain time and leaving at a certain time because it enables us to pursue other passions and obligations. Some of us prefer an environment that is fast paced, full of energy and unpredictability.

Uncovering your Self

REALIZING YOUR TALENTS

To unlock what your talents are—if you don't know it already or having fully explored it—you can:

- Think about the significant achievements in your life and why you achieved it.
- Challenge what you have in life now.
- Question why these elements are significant.
- Rundown down what you have gained from them and how they impact you and the profession trajectory that you seek.
- Understand your personality classification.

Of course, someone's personality gets the biggest chunk in understanding self simply because your personality can provide the elements needed to establishing and perceiving why you have inclinations to act or respond with a specific goal in mind and help distinguish the sorts of workplaces you flourish in. To find out the classification that best describes you, it is always possible to look for tests such as the Myers Briggs Type Indicator. Doing this can help you understand yourself better and work towards refining your career goals so it is more aligned to what you like, what you can do, what you are interested in and where your passions life

UNDERSTANDING YOUR VALUES AND MOTIVATIONS

These are also indicators of a successful career development. We all get motivated based on various different things although money is the most common of all. But what other motivations would you consider as part of the factors for you strive to do better? What are these elements that you could consider form the foundation of your career success? Understanding these elements would help you find and stay in a job that you feel satisfied at the end of the day.

AUDITING YOUR CAPABILITIES AND EXPERTISE

Part of understanding one's self is also understanding and exploring what you are good at, where your strengths lie and what are your fortes. What aptitudes and characteristics do you have because of your examination, side interests, or even paid or intentional work involvement? If you want to find out, you can utilize the Vitae Researcher Development Framework (RDF) to map your current competencies, attributes, and capabilities.

UNDERSTANDING YOUR LEARNING STYLE

The path towards career development is paved with plenty of learning opportunities so identifying your most effective and procrastination-free learning capacity can help you pinpoint what kind of training or course you can and should undertake so that you can develop your capabilities and expertise efficiently and effectively. Again, you can use a variety of tools in determining the learning style that best suits you—and a powerful one is the Learning Style Questionnaire (Honey and Mumford, 1982).

THE IMPORTANCE OF UNDERSTANDING SELF

So what happens when you know yourself? Why is it so important to know yourself?

Here are some of the benefits:

- You are happier -It's a fact. You will be happier when you can express who you are in a song, in art, in music, in words. When you express your desires you will also be more likely to get what you want.
- You have fewer conflicts – These conflicts are more internal conflicts that you have with your inner self. When your actions outside are in tandem with your internal feelings and beliefs and values, you have lesser inner conflicts to deal with.
- You are better at decision making – Knowing self means you are also sure of yourself and this makes it easier for you to make better, informed choices about everything that happens in your own life. This can be anything from small decisions like what color to paint your walls too big decisions like who to marry. Your internal compass gives you a set of invisible guidelines that your mind processes to help you solve these issues.
- You gain better self-control – You have a better ability to resist bad habits simply because you know yourself better. You are also inclined to develop good ones. Self-control also helps you gain better insight to know which of your values and goals that activates your willpower.
- You rarely give into societal pressure – Knowing yourself also means your values are grounded and you know what your preferences are. You will be firm with your NO rather than let peer or social pressure give into you saying yes.

- Better tolerance and understanding – Your awareness of your own struggles and foibles make you more perceptive of other people's needs. You can also emphasize better with the problems and needs of other people.
- Vitality and pleasure – Being you in all its simplicity and truthfulness enable you to be more alive and also enables you to engage and experience life on a larger, richer and more exciting scale.

STOIC VALUES AND IDEAS IN UNDERSTANDING SELF

Value

The only one good thing is an excellent mental state which is rationalized by ethics and reason, and this is the main thing that can ensure an individual's everlasting bliss. Money, success, fame, and other material items may only give us temporary joy but make it hollow inside. There is nothing wrong with any of these – you need things like this to survive in this world and form a good life but excessive pursuit of these things will only lead to long-term damages. We will not feel a sense of fulfillment. Fulfillment and happiness can only be achieved through a rational state of mental excellence.

Emotions

Our judgments are the architects of our emotions. This judgment, is how we think something is good or bad that is going to happen or already happening. Oftentimes, our mistaken judgments are the cause of negative emotions. However, as we know in Stoicism, the only things we can control our own thoughts and actions. So keeping this in mind, these judgments are within our control which means so is our negative emotions. Stoicism, despite the popular opinion that it is an emotionless school of philosophy, is anything but emotionless. Stoicism principles are not repressive or denying anyone of their emotions. Stoicism instead views emotions are something entirely different. In following Stoic principles, you do need overcome negative and harmful emotions that are a result of mistaken judgment and at the same time, embracing the positive emotions. For example, you replace anger with happiness.

Nature

Living in agreement or in harmony with Nature is the Stoic principle of attaining the Good Life. We need to acknowledge that we are all but a small entity of the large universe. We are all small cogs in the big scheme of life and in order to live the Good Life is to live according to or in line with nature.

Nothing can be picked up from endeavoring to oppose these bigger procedures with the exception of displeasure, dissatisfaction, and frustration. While there are numerous things on the planet that we can change, there are numerous others we can't—and we have to comprehend this and acknowledge it.

Control

One primary principle that Stoicism rallies are the things in the life of what we can control and what we cannot control. Our thoughts, feelings, emotions, desires, and actions are all things that are within our control. The external processes, other people's reactions, the results, consequences, objects are all outside our control. Our unhappiness, most of it at least is a result of confusing these two categories – Thinking of the things that we have control but in reality, we do not. Thankfully, one thing that we happily do have control is the guarantee of a good, happy life.

The three popular Roman Stoics—Marcus Aurelius, Seneca and Epictetus offers a wide range of advice that is practical even for modern society. These writings were written with the sole purpose of helping people in their everyday lives and understanding self-worth. Seneca in the later years of his life, living quietly in his country estates, wrote two of his most famous books, the *Naturales Quaestiones*—an encyclopedia of the natural world; and his Letters to Lucilius, which details his philosophical ideas and thoughts.

Marcus Aurelius was also known as the philosopher king, until his death. He wrote the book Meditations as his own journal for self-improvement and guidance. Epictetus, born a slave but eventually rose to become a great Greek Stoic philosopher. His teachings and philosophy were written down and published by his pupil in books known as Discourses and Enchiridion.

3

CLUES TO REVEALING TRUE INTENTIONS - EYES

THE EYES ARE DEFINITELY THE WINDOWS TO OUR SOUL—don't you agree? When we see a person for the first time, our gaze automatically goes to their eyes—looking, searching, and wondering who this person is.

In all honesty, it is easier to evaluate a person's heart than their mind. We can effortlessly pick up on our friend's mood or sense why our partner has dismissed plans to meet even without them speaking a word. How do we know this? How do we know what is going on in their heads without even speaking a word to them? For close friends, our partners, brothers, sisters, and family members—we just know simply because we grew up with them or because we've known them for a considerable amount of time to know what floats their boat, so to speak.

But how do we get this special access to the human mind towards acquaintances or your colleagues? Recent research tells us that looking at people's eyes is one of the ways to get in touch with the human mind, hence the phrase "I can see it in your eyes." It is definitely poetic, and that's why you see it in so many music lyrics.

While it's all beautiful and romantic, the truth is that the eyes can tell a lot about a person because while people can somehow hide their emotions and check their body language, they can't change the way their eyes behave.

HOW DOES THE LANGUAGE OF THE EYES WORK?

When studying a person by looking in their eyes, firstly you need to do is subtly and not stare into their eyes. You need to maintain eye contact in a friendly manner and when you have established this, look into the changes in the pupil size.

A popular study published in 1960 says that the wideness or narrowness of pupils reflects how certain information is processed and how the viewer finds it relevant. The experiment was conducted by psychologists Polt and Hess from the University of Chicago, who analyzed both female and male participants when they looked at semi-nude images of both sexes. The study showed that female participants pupil sizes increased in response when they viewed images of men and for the male participants, the pupil sizes increased when they viewed images of women.

Hess and Polt in subsequent studies also found that homosexual participants looking at semi-nude images of men (but not of women) also had larger pupils. This is no surprise at all because pupils also reflect how aroused we are. Women's pupils responded to images of mothers holding babies. This goes to show that pupil sizes do not reflect how aroused we are but also how we find a piece of information relevant and interesting.

This idea was brought forward by Daniel Kahneman who led a study in 1966. Kahneman is now a Nobel-prize winning psychologist. His study required participants to remember several three to seven digit numbers and participants were to recall it back after two seconds. The longer the string of digits was, the larger their pupil sizes increased which also suggested that pupil size was also related to the information that the brain processing.

In looking for clues in the eyes of a person, the first step is to know what that person is thinking and to look deeply in their eyes.

Apart from the processing of crude information, our eyes can also send more sensitive signals that other people can pick up, especially if they are extremely intuitive. Another study conducted by David Lee began by showing participants images of other people's eyes and he asked them to determine what kind of emotions this person was experiencing. This researcher from the University of Colorado found that participants could correctly gauge the emotions whether it was anger or fear or sadness just by looking at the eyes.

The eyes also have the ability to reveal much more complex phenomena such as whether a person is telling the truth or if they are lying. For example, Andrea Webb conducted a study in 2009 which had one group of participants steal $20 from a secretary's purse and another control group was asked not to steal anything. This research led by the Webb and her colleagues from the University of Utah showed that pupil dilation gave away the thief. All participants were asked to deny the theft and the analysis of pupil dilation showed that participants who lied had pupils that were one larger by one millimeter compared to the pupils of participants who did not steal.

Our eyes also have the capacity to become a good indicator of what people like. To learn to read the signs, you would need to look at the size of the pupil as well the direction of gaze. Take for example someone choosing what they would like to eat at a restaurant. We are visual creatures anyway so our eyes are most likely darting between choosing the salad or the cheeseburger.

The other point to look into is decision making. When we are making a difficult decision, our eyes tend to switch back and forth between the different options in front of us and our gaze ends at the option that we have chosen. By observing these little details of where someone is looking, we can identify which options they choose.

Another way of studying this type of difficult trade-off is offering monetary bets to participants. A study conducted in Brown University by James Cavanagh was when participants were asked questions that involved difficult tradeoffs between probabilities and payoffs.

Participants were paid based on their decisions. The researchers were kind that the harder the decisions were, the more the pupils of the participants dilated. As the choices got harder, our pupils also got bigger.

The eyes also give away clues to if we experienced something unpleasant. Another study on eyes and its reaction was conducted in the University of Washington in 1999. The painful simulation was administered to the fingers of 20 participants and they were asked to rate this pain from tolerable to intolerable. The more intolerable the circumstances were, the larger the pupils of the participants became.

Although pain is a very different feeling than looking at images of seminude people, it still showed a change in pupil response. This shows that pupil size correlated with the strength of feelings and whether those feelings were positive or negative. So if you want to know whether a person is feeling bad or good, consider the context and look into their eyes.

SO WHAT DOES THIS MEAN IN TERMS OF NON-VERBAL COMMUNICATION?

Can we read everything just by looking at the eyes? Are the eyes the only signals we should concentrate on?

The thing is, the eyes are just one of the indicators or signals that we communicate with. When making high-stakes decision duh as whether a person is guilty of a crime, pupil dilation is not something you solely rely on to make a judgment.

We should also look into context. That said, we are more perceptive to the body language of the people we always come into contact with compared to total strangers simply because we can tell their regular facial expressions apart from the non-regular ones.

To make better assessments if feelings, we need to look at various other evidence or elements of body language and of course context. Because people cannot change how their pupils behave, the eyes are often used as a source of information to help create a better relationship simply because it enables us to empathize better. You may not be able to read a person's exact thoughts just by looking at their eyes but it still is a good perspective to study body language and read people.

☙ 4 ❧

CONTEXT - THE CUES THAT TELL IT ALL

In the previous chapter, we talked about how when looking at body language, taking note of the context was also crucial. For example, say, you are having dinner with a friend, and they start fidgeting or have their arms crossed, their body slumped, and their look seemingly bored. There are several possible explanations for this.

For one, they could be uncomfortable with the conversation topic. Alternatively, they could be uncomfortable because you're a loud eater, and they are not sure if they should tell you—or it just could be they are cold and feel uncomfortable sitting in the chair for too long. If you only looked at their body language and deduced that they are uncomfortable because of you, or what you are talking about, you will not get the right answer as to why they are uncomfortable. Body language will only tell you if someone *is* comfortable or uncomfortable—but it will not tell you *why*.

This is why you should look at *context*.

WHAT IS CONTEXT?

Context is the surrounding events and occurrences. It simply means taking into consideration the circumstances forming the current situation, the background events, idea or statement that is taking place or took place moments ago. Context enables the viewer or reader to comprehend the situation.

When looking at the context in body language, you need to be aware of three things:

1 – The conversation that is taking place – did something said in the conversation cause the person to become even more or less comfortable? Did their language change when you asked them a specific question or mentioned a specific statement? It could be something in the conversation that made them uncomfortable.

2 – The environment where the conversation takes place – Look around the area you are in when having this conversation. Is it in public? Is it in an open space? Are people around? Or is it in a private place where nobody can see the both of you? Both open or closed spaces can make a person uncomfortable depending on what is being discussed.

3 – The recent experiences of the person you are speaking to – This person's day may or may not have started with you talking to them. The previous day's experience may still be affecting this person. It could be that they had a rough day at work or they are not well or they are just stressed out.

APPLYING CONTEXT

When analyzing people, you need to take into account the context that they are in. Taking time to look at this element will enable you to identify potential causes of their discomfort. When you remove this discomfort, such as moving to a different room or speaking in more hushed tones changing the subject, you can see the difference it makes towards this person.

Take for example if their body language showed you some sense of discomfort when you start talking about a controversial topic. Change this topic and see if they look a little relaxed. If you still cannot pinpoint the source of their discomfort, just remember that the best way to find out is just to ask them.

Even if you do not know the source of discomfort, you can still attempt to make changes so that they are more comfortable. You can change the smallest things to create a different spark. For example, offering the person a drink before you give them some bad news or even asking about their day to make them feel more relaxed before starting an interview. While it is important to know the source of discomfort, simply just wanting to find out or even being away of their discomfort and trying to make it better would make the whole situation go a long way from bad to good.

IDENTIFYING CONTEXT

It will take some time to practice finding out context before you are comfortable with looking for it and also focusing on the conversation that is happening. But if you always think about context when a conversation is happening, you are one step closer to practicing context.

PURPOSE OF LOOKING FOR CONTEXT

The purpose of identifying context is to help you look for clues that will make the person you are speaking to more comfortable. When a person's body language shows you that they are uncomfortable, it helps that you look into context surrounding the conversation. This not only builds better rapport but it also helps you empathize better. Practice looking at context by consciously looking at your surroundings, the topic of the conversation and even your tone of voice.

Remember that even your body language plays a big part in identifying context, from the way you move, the tone of voice you use and even eye contact. It isn't just about the person's body language.

5
BEHAVIOR ANALYSIS

When talking about behavior analysis, we focus on using learning principles to bring behavioral change. This is actually a branch of psychology that aims to understand the unforeseen cognitions and focuses on the behavior of a person and not on the mental causes of said behavior.

Behavior analysis has extremely fruitful practical applications when it comes to mental clarity and health, especially in helping children and adults learn a new sense of behaviors or reduce certain problematic behaviors.

ANALYZING SOCIAL BEHAVIORS

The intentions behind certain actions of ours are commonly hidden. When a person is feeling angry or feeling depressed for example, their behavior portraying this feeling is usually very different such as they would keep quiet or go for a smoke to calm down.

Another example is also the kind of words used to convey dissatisfaction such as 'sure, go ahead' or 'fine' when actually we are not fine with the solution or the decision made. Empathy is a much-needed when it comes to analyzing social behaviors such as this because, at the end of the day, you want to understand and listen and not just hear to answer.

In analyzing behaviors, demonstrating trust and building rapport is extremely crucial because when you display empathy, you naturally break down any subversions and focus on the heart of the matter.

A rule to remember is that when you do experience emotions and feelings, you must know that people around you will not know about it unless they sense a change in your body language. When nobody understands or get it, there is no need to get angry—but of course, it is easier said than done. We get angry when nobody, especially someone close to us doesn't notice that we are angry.

BEHAVIOR IS LARGELY DICTATED BY SELFISH ALTRUISM.

Nobody is completely selfish and if we were to make such a claim, that would mean we are totally ignoring the acts of sacrifice, kindness, and love that goes around the world. However, most behavior does come out from the elements of selfish altruism.

It is a win/win situation when it comes to selfish altruism. It is a basic two-way road of you help me, I will help you. Here are a few scenarios where selfish altruism applies:

1. Transactions: If you were to purchase a car, both the seller and the buyer mutually benefit. The buyer gets the vehicle; the seller gets their sales. This is a primary form of selfish altruism between two people who do not have any kind of emotional bonds.

2. Familial: Our mind is designed to protect the people with whom we share our genes with. We have a higher tendency to protect these people and this sense of protectiveness depends on close friends to loved ones to siblings and family.
3. Status: People sometimes, not all the time, help someone as a sign of power. Sometimes, people offer assistance and help to boost their reputation and self-esteem.
4. Implied Reciprocity: Plenty of relationships are based on the fact that if I offer you with assistance one day, you would remember it and help me out as well one day when I need it.

Some certain behaviors are not part of the categories described above. For example, nameless heroes dying for a cause that does not directly benefit their country or bloodline. Another example is volunteers who devote their time selflessly towards missions and aids. But of course, these are just the smaller portion of the entire world community. The motives of people and what appeals to them is what you need to understand. When you do, you find ways to help people within these four categories. It's very rare not to expect people to give aid that does not benefit them in any form or way.

PEOPLE HAVE POOR MEMORIES.

Not everyone has a bad memory, but our minds have both long-term memory storage and short-term memory storage. For example, ever been introduced to someone at a party and then you just forgot their name the day after? People have trouble remembering things, especially something not relevant to be stored in their long-term memory. People are more likely to remember similarities that they share with you rather than differences.

When analyzing people, remember that people generally forget things so do not assume that they are disinterested with the information you have given or have malice against you.

PEOPLE ARE EMOTIONAL.

People have stronger feelings about certain things more than they let on but they can't show their specific emotions too much, especially negative emotions such as anger, outbursts, and depression simply because it is generally frowned upon by society. The rule is not to assume everything is fine just because someone isn't having an outburst. Sometimes the strongest ones are the ones that suffer most. All of us have some form of a problem, and these issues are normally contained. You necessarily do not need to call people out on their private deception, but what you need to do is be a little sensitive to those unseen currents and empathize with people because this gives you an advantage when you are trying to help.

PEOPLE ARE LONELY.

When you look at all these Instagram influencers having the time of their life or even celebrities going for numerous parties and ceremonies, the last thing you'd think is that they are lonely. The reality is, many people who seem like they have it all are actually quite lonely. People are sensitive to threats of being left out or ostracized or even having the fear of missing out. Loneliness and the desire to be among people exist in all of us, even if we are introvert. Analyzing this behavior is knowing that loneliness is very common among people and in this sense, you're not alone in feeling this way.

PEOPLE ARE SELF-ABSORBED.

Like it or not, people tend to be more concerned about themselves than about other people. Just look at social media and you can see how self-absorbed people are especially with an account full of selfies. People are more concerned more about themselves to give you any attention and for people to be lonelier, more emotional and feel different than they let on depends also on how you see the world. This perspective makes you independent and also proactive at the same time when you think about it. You become independent so you do not have to rely on anyone and you are more proactive so you have things to do and places to go on your own without depending on enjoying good times with other people. You place your own individual happiness in your own hand rather than in the hands of other people.

When analyzing people, just remember that in some ways or another, they all think and act like you in varying degrees.

6
WHAT IS VERBAL COMMUNICATION?

VERBAL COMMUNICATION IS A FORM OF communication that uses languages and sounds to convey a message. Verbal communication serves as a channel to express your ideas, desires, and concepts—and it is extremely crucial to the process of teaching and learning. Verbal communication is used in tandem with nonverbal forms of communication—however, as humans, we use verbal more than any form of communication when talking to people.

DEFINING VERBAL COMMUNICATION

When people look at the written word, they often relate it to the action of talking. No matter what civilization we come from, humans have always used verbal communication as a means to exchange thoughts and ideas and messages. Verbal communication is always spoken communication but written communication is also a form of verbal communication. For example, when you read this book, you are decoding the writer's point of view to learn more. In this chapter, we will explore the various elements that define verbal communication and how it affects our lives.

THE BASICS

As we know, verbal communication is all about the written and spoken word. It refers to the words we use when we speak or write whereas nonverbal communication is all about communication that takes place using other forms of communication other than words and body language is one such way that we humans use to communicate through gestures and well, silence too.

Here is a great table that helps simplify the understanding of both verbal and nonverbal communication.

Verbal Communication

Nonverbal Communication

Oral

Spoken Language

Laughing, Crying, Coughing, etc.

Non-Oral

Written Language/Sign Language

Gestures, Body Language, etc.

TYPES OF VERBAL COMMUNICATION

Public speaking and interpersonal communication are the most common types of verbal communication. Public speaking generally refers to any kind of communication done verbally to a group of people whereas interpersonal communication refers to an exchange that takes place involving a group of people that are simultaneously talking and listening.

Professor Robert M. Krauss from Columbia University says that signs and images are the essential flags that establish verbal correspondence. Words go about as images, though signs are optional items that help the hidden message and incorporate things with the manner of speaking and even outward appearances.

THE PURPOSE OF VERBAL COMMUNICATION

It is important no doubt, as without verbal communication, you wouldn't even be reading this book. But apart from that, verbal communication has plenty of purposes chief of it being to relay and convey messages to at least one of the receivers. It incorporates everything from one-syllable words and sounds too complex sentences and dialogs that depend on both feeling and dialect to create the ideal result and impact. Verbal correspondence is utilized to ask, advise, contend, examine, present and spread subjects of different sorts. In teaching and learning, verbal communication is extremely important. It also bonds and builds relationships and of course used wrongly, destroys and breaks relationships too. While every human on earth communicates in one form or another, the language we speak is a human phenomenon that enables us to convey our messages in a more precise way that any other forms of communication used by other beings such as animals.

THE CHALLENGES OF VERBAL COMMUNICATION

Challenges do happen as we all know with verbal communication especially when we are trying to express ourselves. Misunderstandings happen because we use poor word choices, arguments may arise when two or three people have clashing perspectives and when faulty communication techniques are used, sometimes the messages conveyed is understood wrongly and all of these causes a breakdown in communication. Also, knowing and speaking different languages also become a barrier to communication can cause confusion, which is why nonverbal communication is used.

PREVENTING COMMUNICATION BREAKDOWN

While confusion and misunderstanding do occur and it cannot be avoided completely, we can, however, choose to communicate effectively to lessen these disrupt. Always think before you speak is one golden rule, also consider the message you want to convey before speaking about it and also take into consideration the recipient's point of view. Not everyone is going to agree with you. Also paying attention to nonverbal cues and body language will help you craft what to say and how to say it—depending on the situation at hand. Always enunciate and speak your words clearly when you communicate.

While everyone has a different style of communicating and perceiving messages, you can only control what comes out of your mouth so only you can craft and convey your message as well as possible to ensure those listening to you understand what you are trying to say. Using nonverbal actions in your communication can also greatly affect the way the message is understood and perceived.

A SYSTEM OF SYMBOLS

Symbols are also worth exploring in this chapter of verbal communication. What is symbolled? Nelson & Kessler Shaw describes symbols as ideas, thoughts, emotions, objects and even actions that are used to decipher and give meaning. Symbols represent or stand for something. It serves as a symbolic representation of the idea of a sentence we want to say and also sometimes for an object.

Characteristics of Symbols

- Symbols are Arbitrary – The symbols used are arbitrary, and they sometimes have no direct relations to the ideas that represent or the objects we want to describe. However, using symbols is considered successful communication especially when we reach an agreement on the meaning of these symbols.

- Symbols are ambiguous – Symbols have several possible meanings. For example, a Blackberry in today's world can be anything. It can be the fruit or it can be a mobile phone. Or take Apple for instance – it can be a fruit or a computer or if someone says they were on a date with someone really cool, does that mean that person is an awesome person or they are cold? Or if someone says they are gay, does that mean they are happy or they are homosexual? Meanings towards symbols change over time because of the changes happening in the world today, the shifting social norms, the advances in technology. We are all able to communicate in symbols because of the finite list of possible meanings and these meanings relate to the members of a given language agree upon. Without this agreed-upon symbolism, we share very little meaning and context with one another.

- Symbols are also abstract – They are not material or physical. A specific dimension of deliberation is a fundamental component in the way that images just establish of thoughts and items. This abstraction enables us to use phrases such as 'the public' to mean the people from a certain state or place rather than having to be distinctive about the people in a country based on their diversity. For example, the non-wizarding world in Harry Potter is called 'muggles' rather than explaining the separate culture of muggles. Abstraction is useful when you want to convey an intricate concept in a simple, straightforward way.

❦ 7 ❦

COMMON PATTERNS OF INTERPRETING BEHAVIOR

HUMAN BEHAVIOR IS A COMPLEX THING. BECAUSE OF ITS complexity, reading and analyzing people is not as easy as it sounds—but neither is it hard simply because as human beings, we exhibit more or less the same kinds of mannerisms and behavior when we experience a certain emotion or action.

SO WHAT EXACTLY IS BEHAVIOR?

Essentially, scientists categorize human behavior into three components:

- actions
- cognition
- emotions

ACTIONS ARE BEHAVIOR.

An action is regarded as everything that constitutes movement and observation whether using your eyes or using physiological sensors. Think of actions as a form of transition or even an initiation from one situation to another. When it comes to behavioral actions, these can take place at different scales and they range from sweat gland activity, sleep or food consumption.

COGNITIONS ARE BEHAVIOR.

Cognitions are described as mental images that are imprinted in our minds and these images are both nonverbal and verbal. Verbal cognitions are such as thinking 'Wow, I wonder what it's like to wear a $2000-dollar designer dress' or 'I have to get the groceries done later' all constitute verbal cognition. However, imagining things, in contrast, is considered nonverbal cognition, such as how your body will look after losing weight or how your house will be after a repaint. Cognition is a combination of knowledge and skills and knowing how to skillfully use them without hurting yourself.

EMOTIONS ARE BEHAVIOR.

An emotion is basically any brief conscious experience that is categorized by an intense mental activity and this feeling is not categorized as a coming from either knowledge or reasoning. This emotion commonly occurs or exists on a scale starting with positive vibes such as pleasurable to negative vibes such as being unpleasant. There are other elements of physiology that indicate emotional processing—such as an increase in respiration rate, retina dilation, and even increase in heart rat—all a result of increased or heightened arousal. These elements are usually invisible to the naked eye. Emotions, similar to cognitions also cannot be noticeable to the naked eye. These can only be noticed through tracking facial electromyographic activity (fEMG) indirectly which monitors the arousal using ECG, analyzes facial expressions, respiration sensors, galvanic skin response as well as other self-reported measures.

EVERYTHING IS CONNECTED

Cognitions, emotions, and actions run together and simultaneously with one another. This excellent synergy enables us to understand the events, activities, and happenings that are happening around us, to get in touch with our internal beliefs and desires and to correctly or appropriately respond to people that are in this scenario.

It is not that easy to understand and determine what exactly is the effect and cause. For example, when you turn your head, which is an action and seeing a face familiar to you, this will cause a burst of joy, which is the emotion and is usually accompanied by the realization which is the cognition. In other words, it is through this equation:

Action = Emotion (joy) + cognition (realization)

In some other scenarios, this chain of effect and cause can also be reversed – you may be sad (experiencing an emotion) and you proceed to contemplate on relationship concerns (you go through cognition) and then you proceed to go for a run to clear your mind (you take an action). In this case, the equation would be:

. . .

EMOTION (SADNESS) + COGNITION (I NEED TO GO FOR A RUN) = action

CONSCIOUS + UNCONSCIOUS BEHAVIOR

CONSCIOUSNESS IS AN AWARENESS OF OUR INTERNAL thoughts and feelings and it also has to do with proper perception for and the processing of information gathered from our surroundings. A big portion of our behaviors is through the guided unconscious processes that surround us. Like an iceberg, there is a huge amount of hidden information and only a small fraction of it is obvious to our naked eye.

OVERT + COVERT BEHAVIOR

OVERT BEHAVIOR FOCUSES ON THE ASPECTS OF behavior which can be observed by the naked eye. These behaviors are such as body movements, or as some would call it–interactions. Physiological processes such as facial expressions, blushing, smiling and pupil dilation may be subtle but it all can still be seen. Covert expressions are thoughts or cognition, feelings which are emotions and responses that are not easily or visibly seen. These subtle changes in our body's responses are usually not seen by the observer's eye.

IF WE WANT TO OBSERVE COVERT RESPONSES, THEN physiological or biometric sensors are usually used to help in observing them. As mentioned earlier on in this chapter, usually

EEGs, MEG, fMRI or fNIRS are all used to look out for physiological processes that showcase covert mannerisms and behavior.

Rational + irrational behaviors

Any action, cognition or emotion which is guided or influenced by reason is considered rational behavior. Irrational behavior, in contrast, is any action, emotion or cognition that is not objectively logical. For example, people who have extreme phobias are considered as having irrational fears, which are fears that are cause them to behave a certain way.

Voluntary + involuntary behaviors

When an action is self-determined or driven by decisions and desires, this is often categorized as voluntary actions. Involuntary on the other action would be actions that are done without intent, by force or done in an attempt to prevent it. People who are in cognitive-behavioral psychotherapy are often exposed to problematic scenarios involuntary as a form of therapy so that they can help get through this fear with the help of the therapist at hand. Now that we have a form of understanding of human behaviors, here is how we can interpret these behaviors. Keep in mind that these are just the surface or basic ways that interpretation can be done as there are more other complex and detailed ways.

#1 Establish a baseline

. . .

When you read people, you would notice that they all have unique patterns and quirks of behavior. Some people look at the floor while talking, or they have a habit of crossing their arms, some clear their throat ever so often while some pout, jiggle, or squint even. These behaviors are displayed for various different reasons – as we concluded in chapter 1, it could be they are uncomfortable or it just could be a habit. However, these actions could also mean anger, deception or nervousness. When reading people, we first need to form a baseline by understanding context and also what is normal behavior for this person.

#2 Look for behavior deviations

When you have established baseline behaviors, your next goal is to pay close attention to the inconsistencies that show up between the baseline mannerisms and the person's words and gestures. Say for example you've noticed that your teammate usually twirls their hair when they are nervous. As your teammate starts their presentation, they start to do this. Is this common behavior in your teammate's mannerisms or is there more than meets the eye? You might want to do a little bit more digging and probe a little bit more than you normally would.

#3 Start noticing a collection of gestures

A solitary word or gesture does not necessarily mean anything but when there are a few behavioral patterns start forming, you need to pay attention to them. It could be that your teammate starts clearing their throat in combination to twirling their hair. Or they keep shifting. This is where you need to proceed with caution.

#4 Compare and contrast

So we go back to the teammate again and you've noticed that they are acting more odd than usual. You move your observation a little closer to see when and if your teammate repeats this behavior with other people in your group. Make an observation on how they interact with the rest of the people in the room and how their expression changes, if at all. Look at their body language and their posture.

#5 Reflect

This reflection isn't about meditation rather it is to reflect the other person's state of mind. As human beings, we have mirror neurons that act like built-in monitors wired to read another person's body language simply because we also have these mannerisms as well. For example, a smile activates the smile muscles in our faces whereas a frown activates the frown muscles. When we see someone that we like, our facial muscles relax, our eyebrows arch, our blood flows to our lips making them full and our head tilts. However, if your partner does not mirror these set of behavior, then it could be that they are sending a clear message which is they are not as happy to see you.

#6 Identifying the resonant voice

You might think that the most powerful person is the one that sits at the head of the table or the one that is standing in the front. That is not always the case. The most confident person always has a stronger voice and they are more likely the most powerful one. Just by looking at them, you can deduce they have an expansive posture, they have a big smile and a strong voice. However, make no mistake that a loud voice is not a strong one. If you are presenting to an audience or pitching an idea to a group of people, you would normally focus on the leader. What happens when the leader has a weak personality? They will depend on others to make a decision and they are easily influenced by them. So when pitching or presenting to a group, identify the strong voice and you'll have a stronger chance of success.

#7 Observe how they walk

People who shuffle along or lack a flowing motion in their movements or always keep their head down while walking lack self-confidence. If you see this exhibited by a member of your team, you might be inclined to make extra effort to recognize their contribution in order to build this person's confidence. You might also need to ask them more direct questions at meeting so that they are inclined to offer their ideas out in the open as opposed to keeping them quiet.

#8 Using action words

Words are usually the closest way for people to understand what is going on in another person's mind. These words symbolize the thoughts that are running through their mind and in identifying these word, you also identify its meaning. Say for example if your friend says 'I decided to make this work', the action word used here is 'Decided'. This solitary word shows that your friend is 1 – not impulsive, 2 – went through a process of weighing the pros and cons and 3 – Took time to think things through. These actions words offer insight into how a person processes a scenario and thinks.

#9 Look for personality clues

Each and every one of us human beings has a unique personality, and these rudimentary classifications can enable us to assess and relate to another person. It also helps us read someone accurately. In looking for clues, you can ask:

- Did this person exhibit more introverted or extroverted behavior?
- Do they seem driven by significance or relationships?
- How do they handle risks and uncertainty?
- What drives them or feeds their ego?
- What kinds of mannerisms does this person exhibit when they are stressed?
- What are the kinds of mannerisms shown when they are relaxed?

By observing a person long enough, you can be able to pinpoint their base behaviors and mannerisms and set apart the odd one out.

CONCLUSION

It takes time to read people accurately. No one can identify a person's thoughts, feelings, and emotions just by looking at them and the singular mannerism and behaviors they exhibit. As we know, it could be something or nothing at all and it also depends on the context of the situation. Of course, there are exceptions to the rule but by keeping the basics of analyzing people and the principles with which you have built your powers of observation, you will eventually have greater control in reading other people, communicating with people effectively and understanding their thinking.

8
HOW TO SPOT INSECURITY

WHEN SOMEONE IS BEHAVING IRRATIONALLY, YOU HAVE to remind yourself that this could be because they are acting out of a certain emotion, or it also could be that their insecurity is behind this false sense of bravado. When you notice this, you will more likely procure a sense of empathy for these people who act arrogantly or rudely due to the fact that what they are trying to do is covering their insecurity.

Their insecurity can be about anything—looks, power, money, smartness, getting better grades, and so on—and most of these insecurities creep out from a sense of material value. Sometimes, insecurity can be justified—but most of the time, it is not. Insecurity manifests differently, and it can range from the inability to accept that they've done a great job or accept a compliment to as far as not wanting to wear a swimsuit to the beach.

FACTORS DETERMINING GOOD AND BAD

None of these traits helps us to behave virtuously. There is a fine line between being insecure and being a brat. Here are some identifying factors that can help you separate the good and the bad:

1. Self-kindness is not self-judgment.

Compassion towards someone who is insecure is being understanding and warm to them when they fail, or when we suffer or at moments when we feel inadequate. We should not be ignoring these emotions or criticizing. People who have compassion understand that being human comes with its own imperfections and failing is part of the human experience. It is inevitable that there will be no failure when we attempt something because failure is part of learning and progress. We will look into how failure is a friend in disguise in the next chapters. Having compassion is also being gentle with yourself when faced with painful experiences rather than getting angry at everything and anything that falls short of your goals and ideals.

Things cannot be exactly the way it should be or supposed to be or how we dream it to be. There will be changes and when we accept this with kindness and sympathy and understanding, we experience greater emotional equanimity.

2. Common humanity and not isolation

It is a common human emotion to feel frustrated especially when things do not go the way we envision them to be. When this happens, frustration is usually accompanied by irrational isolation, making us feel and think that we are the only person on earth going through this or making dumb mistakes like this. News flash —all humans suffer, all of us go through different kinds of suffering at varying degrees. Compassion involves recognizing that we all suffer and all of us have personal inadequacies. It does not happen to 'Me' or 'I' alone.

3. Mindfulness is not over-identification.

Compassion needs us to be balanced with our approach so that our negative emotions are neither exaggerated or suppressed. This balancing act comes out from the process of relating our personal experiences with that of the suffering of others. This puts the situation we are going through into a larger perspective.

We need to keep mindful awareness so that we can observe our own negative thoughts and emotions with clarity and openness. Having a mindful approach is non-judgmental and it is a state of mindful reception that enables us to observe our feelings and thoughts without denying them or suppressing them. There is no way that we can ignore our pain and feel compassion at the same time. By having mindfulness, we also prevent over-identification of our thoughts and feelings.

DISCOVERING COMPASSION

You're so dumb! You don't belong here loser! Those jeans make you look like a fat cow! You can't sit with us! It's safe to say we've all heard some kind rude, unwanted comments either directly or indirectly aimed at us. Would you talk like this to a friend? Again, the answer is a big NO.

Believe it or not, it is a lot easier and natural for us to be kind and nice to people than to be mean and rude to them whether it is a stranger or someone we care about in our lives. When someone we care is hurt or is going through a rough time, we console them and say it is ok to fail. We support them when they feel bad about themselves and we comfort them to make them feel better or just to give a shoulder to cry on.

We are all good at being understanding and compassionate and kind to others. How often do we offer this same kindness and compassion to ourselves? Research on self-compassion shows that those who are compassionate are less likely to be anxious, depressed or stressed and more resilient, happy and optimistic. In other words, they have better mental health.

IDENTIFYING SOMEONE WITH INSECURITY

Based on what was discussed above, when we are able to identify when a person is acting out of insecurity can enable us to protect ourselves from engaging in a mindless power play and feel insecure ourselves. People who are insecure tend to spread their negativity and self-doubt to others as well and here is how you can identify them and decide whether to show compassion or to show them the exit:

#1 People who are insecure try to make you feel insecure yourself.

You start questioning your own ability and self-worth and this happens when you are around a specific person. This individual has the ability to manipulate you and talk about their strengths and how they are good in this and that and in a way try to put you down. They project their insecurities on you.

#2 Insecure people need to showcase his or her accomplishments.

Inferiority is at the very core of their behavior and for people like this, compassion to tell them that they are not what they think in their heads is just a waste of your time. They feel insecure and to hide it, talk about their accomplishments, not in a good way but constantly brag about their amazing lifestyle, their wonderful shoes, their huge cars, and their elite education. All of this is done to convince themselves that they really do have it all and you have none.

#3 People who are insecure drops the "humble brag" far too much.

The humblebrag is essentially a brag that is disguised as a self-derogatory statement. In this social media age, you can see plenty of humblebrags who complain about their first-world problems such as all the travel they need to do or the amount of time they spend watching their kids play and win games or even the person who complains about having a tiny pimple when the rest of their face looks flawless. Social media is ripe with people who are narcissistic and this is not worth your time. Do not feel any less just because someone shows off how much of traveling they need to do.

#4 People who are insecure frequently complain that things aren't good enough.

They like showing off the high standards that they have and while you may label them as snobs, it might be a harder feeling to shake off because you might be thinking that they are really better than you although you know that it is all an act. They proclaim their high standards to assert that they are doing better than everyone else and make you feel less of yourself and more miserable. Pay no attention to people like this.

CONCLUSION

It does make sense that people who have better self-esteem and compassion as if you are happier and optimistic about your own future without having to worry about what insecure people have to say. When we continuously criticize ourselves and berate ourselves because we think other people are winning at life, we end up feeling incompetent, worthless and insecure ourselves which is what these people want us to feel. This cycle of negativity is vicious and will continue to self-sabotage us and sometimes, we end up self-harming ourselves.

BUT WHEN OUR POSITIVE INNER VOICE TRIUMPHS AND plays the role of the supportive friend, we create a sense of safety and we accept ourselves enough to see a better and clear vision. We then work towards making the required changes for us to be healthier and happier. But if we do not do this, we are working ourselves towards a downward spiral or chaos, unhappiness, and stress.

9

HOW TO SPOT ROMANTIC INTEREST

If we had the definite guide to spot a romantic interest, Tinder would go broke. That said, it is not hard to identify the telltale signs if someone is interested in you. Granted that some people are oblivious to it—but if you really do focus, you'd come to the realization if that person is indeed romantically interested in you or if they are just being flirtatious.

Usually, that special someone starts with a casual acquaintance, which leads to friendship—and before you know it, you look at this friend in a different light and keep thinking about them. Do they feel the same way you feel? Identifying if someone is interested in you romantically requires the careful and skillful interpretation of signals and actions.

WAYS TO FIGURE OUT IF SOMEONE IS ROMANTICALLY INTERESTED

Here are 15 ways to figure out if someone is romantically interested in you or if they are just flirting for the thrill of it:

#1 Their conversations with you

Conversations, meaningful ones are one of the ways a person shows a deeper interest in you and what you do. Do they keep asking you questions in an attempt to keep the conversation going? Pay attention to the questions they ask because it can tell you if they are genuinely showing interest in the things you do and like. A good and long conversation about your likes, dislikes, favorite music and so on is a classic sign of someone genuinely liking you and your company. If you are enjoying the conversation and the other person is engaging in it without looking bored or yawning, this is a sign that both parties are equally interested in each other.

#2 They keep bumping into you.

Call it fate but this can also be a sign that they like you and they are engineering any possible opportunities to meet you. This is sweet but also can be creepy if it becomes too much like stalking. If you feel that this person is following you or you suddenly feel uncomfortable, listen to your gut feeling and make a report. Stalking is serious and dangerous. However, if it bumping into you happens to be at places like the cafeteria or the lunchroom or neighborhood coffee place and not specific places like your gym that you've been going to for years, your house or anyway specific and private – make a complaint.

#3 They discuss future plans.

Another sign that someone could be romantically interested in you is if they plan for more dates or start talking about the near future because they clearly see you in it. It isn't about plans of getting married or buying a house but merely simple things like a concert in your area that they'd like to take you or even a friend's party in a week's time that they'd like you to come with. They have these upcoming events and they'd like you to be part of it.

#4 Five more minutes

If someone is interested in you, chances are they would like to spend a few more minutes longer with you. They don't mind adjusting their schedule just so they can spend an extra 5 more minutes to talk to you or even spend that extra 5 minutes on the phone just so they can continue talking to you. The fact that they do this is also an indication that they have romantic feelings for you.

#5 Reasons to spend time together

'I'm in the area—want to grab a bite?' or 'Oh you're having a cold? I can make a mean chicken soup—I'll bring it over' or even 'What are you doing right now? Want to go have dinner together?' Make no mistake that these could just be that the person likes spending time with you simply because you are a cool person to hang out with but if these reasons keep piling up and it only involves just the two of you, it is probably a big sign that this person likes you.

#6 Observe their body language.

If someone likes you, they mirror your body language and your movements. They sit in closer, they lean in, they smile when you smile, they find ways to touch you (not in a creepy way) like brushing against your shoulder, putting a strand of your hair behind your ear – all these are classic flirtation signs and if you are uncomfortable, say so but if you are enjoying it, this person is clearly into you.

#7 The compliments are mountainous.

Complimenting someone excessively can be a sign of ass-kissing or just trying to be nice. But if this person compliments you sincerely, it could be that they are interested in you. Look out for verbal cues such as complimenting your fashion choice or the way you style your hair. It could be that they are just being friendly, but them dropping compliments every time you meet is a big sign of them being interested in you.

#8 They remember the little things.

THE CLOSER YOU GET TO KNOW SOMEONE—THE MORE information you divulge to them. Your romantic interest will pick up a lot of interesting things about you and save it in their long-term memory and these things can be your favorite color, your favorite ice cream flavor, the first movie you watched together, where you first met – all of this is an indication that this person is genuinely interested in you.

#9 CONVERSATION STARTERS

SOME PEOPLE ARE SHY AND ARE NOT BIG TALKERS SO while this is something to take note of, you cannot be the only one initiating contact all the time. If someone is willing to connect despite them being shy, that means they really do want to talk to you. Having one-way initiations for everything is a definite NO that the other person doesn't like you and do not see the need to spend the time to talk or even meet you but if they initiate contact as much as you do, that is a sure sign that they are into you.

#10 Other people are off-limits.

Take note of when a person talks about someone else—do they talk a lot about other girls or guys when they are with you? Or is the conversation focused on just you and your person? What a person says in a conversation and how they refer to other people in their social circle can give you real clues into whether they are romantically interested in you. Talking about going on a date with a girl or guy is not really a good indication that this person likes you.

Trusting your feelings and your intuitions in all these possible scenarios above is the best bet. Remember that different people do different things to show someone they care or that they are interested in them and cultural values, upbringing, and societal norms also play a big part in identifying these signs so nothing is set in stone. All the signs described above are a good telling sign that a person is interested in you especially if they like spending more and more time with you. Even if you are not sure, you can exhibit signs that you are interested in them so that they will also have an idea but to be on the safest side, telling someone that you like them and you'd like to get to know them better and even start dating is the best way forward to prevent any miscommunication or misunderstanding between two people.

Of course, the game of love is not as straightforward and as simple as it is. It takes a little bit of dating experience to figure out if someone is into you or not or you can just do the good old fashion trial and error, get your heart broken, kiss all the toads till you meet your prince or princess charming.

10
HOW TO SPOT A LIE

Body language is an important part of communication, and both visual and verbal elements of it should align with the message you are sending out—otherwise, people will find it easy to see that you are being deceptive. There are definitely clues in behavior that you will be able to identify if a person is telling a lie or even just shielding the truth. Nobody likes a liar, and nobody likes being lied to. It is heartbreaking to know that someone is lying to you, especially if it is a partner. If it is in a professional setting, all trust is gone out the window with even one tiny lie. Lying and the extent of it makes and definitely breaks relationships—depending on what the lie is.

SCENARIOS OF LYING

As much as we want to say we always tell the truth, the realities of human communication are complex. Here are some scenarios of lying:

1 – Some lies are intended as a courtesy or are habitual.

For example, when you say 'I'm fine' when someone asks how you are doing and while you may not be fine, you just say it anyway to prevent them from asking you more questions or to be involved in more conversation. Most adults lie plenty of times, every single day and while this is fine, some lies though will get you into trouble.

2 – Some forms or lies are even expected.

It has become so habitual to lie in our culture that we become to expect it. Legal strategies used is a scenario of when 'plausible deniability' is expected and customary. We always face scenarios such as cross-company relationships and also adherence to nondisclosure agreements. Certain situations require fast thinking and practice to keep to your commitments while staying honest about the information we want to protect. So when asked 'What is your weakness?' you tell a fib that makes a negative trait a positive one.

3 – Lying by deflecting

On a regular basis, we are bombarded with people who by nature or through training avoid showing off excessive body language and deflect core questions and thus, flood their audiences with irrelevant information or use deceptive forms of truth. Take politicians for example. So while a deception can be easily spotted in action, it is much more difficult to spot a deception with a person who is fundamentally dishonest.

KEY ELEMENTS IN SPOTTING A LIAR

So while there are these various forms of lying that is done on a daily basis, what if there is a person that you really want to know if they are lying or not? According to Susan Carnicero, a CIA officer, one can usually tell if a person is lying in 5 seconds. So if you want to analyze someone or read someone, here are some key elements that you need to pay exceptional attention to know how to spot a liar.

#1 Analyzing versus speculating

As we talked about in chapter 1 about how when a person crosses their arms, it could mean that they are uncomfortable or it just could mean that they are cold or it's just a habit of theirs. Assuming that crossed or folded arms is a signal of deceptive behavior is just speculation. You should instead analyze whether this behavior or mannerism is a result of the question asked. Knowing the first sign of deceptive behavior will happen in the first five seconds of the question asked will enable you to determine if that question was the one that produced the folded arms. This first clue of deception could even happen while the first question is being asked, which goes to know that this person's brain is moving much faster than the words coming out of the interviewer – it is a sign that they are subconsciously trying to frame their response. You should also look for clusters of behavior and whether these clusters are a direct response to the question and not just a nervousness bout.

#2 Managing your bias

Believe it or not, people who are being deceptive can give you truthful answers. They give you true information thus increasing your belief that they are telling the truth and simultaneously, lessen your ability to identify when they are in fact lying. To prevent this, you need to focus on filtering out the fluffy, truthful responses they give. So really focus on what the fluff in so that you won't be caught by surprise thinking that this person seemed honest the entire time.

#3 Recognizing when someone is being evasive

When a person is being deceptive, they usually create fluff and give long explanations of their answers without actually addressing the issue. They are adept at deflecting and redirecting their responses such as 'Have I ever been accused of doing this before?', 'Do have a reputation for doing good?'. When someone goes on and one for a good 10 minutes and never answers the question this is a sign that they are lying.

#4 Watching out for signs to deny

One of the most important things you need to listen to is the direct denial of an accusation. When a person is guilty, they will verbally create fluff, not getting to the point, not answering the question and attempt to justify the situation by saying things like 'not likely' or 'not for the most part' or the common favorite 'not really'. A person who responds to the question of 'Did you do this?' with 'This is not really the way we do things around here' instead of a definite 'NO, I did not', that is a big sign of deception.

#5 There will be signs of aggression.

Well when someone gets angry at the question being asked, it is 100% an indication that they are guilty. They may exhibit signs of aggression such as attacking the interviewer or they would also attempt to flip the situation by accusing the questioner of bias or discrimination. "Don't you see what he has done? Don't focus on just me!' or 'It's your fault for not keeping it this way, not mine' may be some ways of deflecting from answering the question. They exhibit anger, disgust or even go on to the blame game in response to the question asked.

#6 Convey versus convince

You ask a question and instead of a yes or no answer, the person launches into an amalgamation of how they are a good person, they have been a good employee, how long they've worked and have had no issues, how they have a good reputation – This person is providing an unsolicited statement to defend themselves instead of just answering the very direct question with a very direction answer. Disqualifiers added to their statements such as 'You know I won't lie to you' or 'You trust me, don't you?' or 'to be perfectly honest with you' or the crowd favorite 'Quite frankly are all attempts to prevent themselves from answering. They are subconsciously trying to cover up their lie and may also use race or religion to justify such as saying 'I swear on the bible' to create a compelling and convincing argument.

#7 Look out for nonverbal signals.

If you see an inappropriate amount of concern for a situation or the lack thereof or even a smile or a smirk in response to a question like 'Did you kill that man?', these are all nonverbal clues you need to pay attention to because they can be extremely subtle but very useful in catching a liar. These nonverbal clues extend to include jumping in to answer a question fast or even a pause. They also have a habit of not being able to look at the questioner in the eye or in contrast, stare with aggression to the questioner. They may even say 'No' but be nodding a 'Yes'. A person can even touch their face or nose or even cover their mouth or face because this is another subconscious way of hiding a lie. The stress of deception can also cause the skin to turn cold and start itching or even flush – notice when they suddenly scratch their ears or nose. Look out for anchor point movements such as the changes in the arms or even the feet. A foot could be dangling but suddenly tapping nervously or even pointing at a different direction.

Summary

All of these situations are important to watch, and you must also watch the cluster of behaviors and activity as opposed to zoning in on only one behavior. Spotting whether someone is telling a lie or the truth can be hard at first, and it requires training to efficiently tell if someone is, in fact, lying. Wrongly accusing someone can be disastrous not only to them but also to your reputation—so depending on the situation, look out for the body language, understand your baseline, and properly look for nonverbal clues.

CONCLUSION

At the end of this book, you are now better at analyzing and reading cues as well as become more adept at understanding yourself and the people around you. Knowing how to analyze people effectively is crucial in the business world as well as the social world, the political world, and the socio-political world. In fact, knowing how to do this the right way helps in just about any aspect of life.

If you're in the marketing department or a designer or presenting a project proposal or even meeting a patient—it is extremely important and valuable for you to recognize signals and cues of the people you meet. Through reading this book, it will help you get more accustomed and comfortable in analyzing people—however, never stop practicing to look for nonverbal and verbal cues, as this is what helps give you a lead.

Not only will this give you a better headway in life, but it will also help you create more meaningful and long-lasting relationships. It makes you a better friend, a better partner, a better co-worker, or even a better boss just by knowing what cues and gestures people use to convey their innermost thoughts—especially when words fail them.

By learning what non-verbal gestures mean, you would be able to break the code that would lead you into learning more about the people around you and empathize with them. At the same time, hopefully, this book has enabled you to improve your relationship with your friends, colleagues, partner, and family by learning how to communicate better through the right non-verbal gestures.

COGNITIVE BEHAVIORAL THERAPY

Rewire Your Brian by Overcoming Anxiety, Depression, Phobias, and Eliminating Negative Thoughts

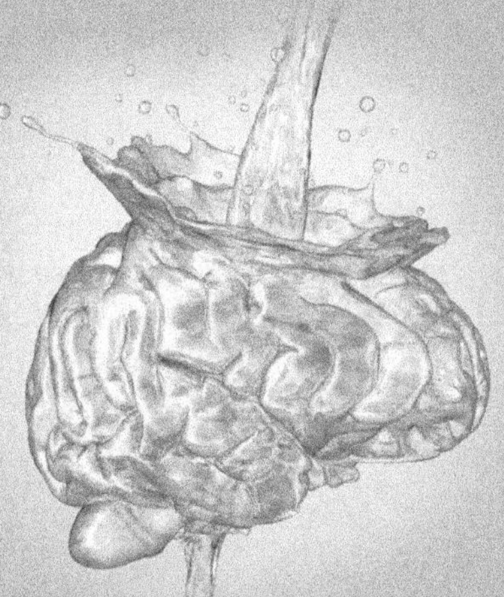

Eric Skinner

❀ Created with Vellum

INTRODUCTION

Congratulations on downloading *Cognitive Behavioral Therapy: Rewire Your Brain by Overcoming Anxiety, Depression, Phobias, and Eliminating Negative Thoughts* and thank you for doing so. The bad news is that approximately 40 million people between the ages of 18 and 54 are currently dealing with some form of mental health issue that is more intense than that which is experienced by their peers. The good news is that this issue is manageable without the use of pharmaceuticals and one of the most effective ways of taking control of your mental state is through the use of cognitive behavioral therapy.

Cognitive behavioral therapy is a version of psychotherapy which aims to alter negative thought patterns for the better and the following chapters will discuss a wide variety of ways to do just that. First, you will learn all about cognitive behavioral therapy and the many ways it can benefit those who are in your situation. With the basics out of the way, you will learn more about the issues that cognitive behavioral therapy deals with most effectively so that you can be prepared to get started putting them behind you once and for all.

From there, you will find a wide variety of starter exercises to help you start dealing with you issues in the moment, as well as a detailed look at mindfulness meditation, what its good for and why you should already be practicing it. Next, you will find a discussion of the bad habits in your life and why getting rid of them will likely do your mental state a world of good along with specific chapters focusing on exercises devoted to cleansing the mind of negative thoughts, depression, phobias, and anxiety. Finally, you will find tips for sticking with it in the long-term and ensuring you remain successful throughout.

With so many choices out there when it comes to consuming this type of content, it is appreciated that you've chosen this one. Plenty of care and effort went into ensuring it contains as many interesting and useful tidbits as possible, please enjoy!

I

INTRODUCTION TO COGNITIVE BEHAVIORAL THERAPY

COGNITIVE BEHAVIORAL THERAPY (CBT) IS A FORM OF psychotherapy that seeks to analyze why you feel certain ways and how you see certain situations. Because anxiety is a reaction to these things, and because it results in distorted thinking and perceptions of reality, CBT shows patients a healthy, more realistic way to think. At its core are a few simple beliefs. The first is that thoughts influence actions and behaviors. This is usually represented on a diagram in a cycle. It illustrates that if we can change on component of the cycle then we can change all three. It also shows how these things are all interconnected rather than independent of each other.

The second concept is especially important as it relates to anxiety (even though CBT can treat many forms of mental illness). Anxiety's non-stop obsession with what can be makes us feel like we've lost control over our lives and everything around us. But that isn't the problem. The problem is that it tries to make us take control of everything to protect ourselves. CBT teaches us to accept what's beyond our control and to recognize and hold on to what is. This is largely done through introspection.

CBT works on the assumption that thoughts, behaviors, and feelings are all constantly interacting and influencing each other. Thus, the way a person thinks or interprets a given situation will ultimately determine how they feel about it and thus, how they will react to it.

For example, consider a pair of individuals who both recently failed to do as well as they would like on a difficult and important test. The first person thinks that if they were smarter they would have done better on the test which must mean that they are stupid. They feel anxious about the idea of future tests and depressed about their prospects for the class overall. As a result, they develop a negative opinion of themselves while at the same time not taking any positive actions when it comes to improving the ways in which they prepare for future tests as they now believe that their lack of basic intelligence is the root of the problem.

On the other hand, the second student, who received the same low grade, remember, feels anxiety at the thought of what the grade will mean for their overall GPA, but is able to get past it by reframing the situation to understand that they simply underestimated the difficulty of the test of the distribution of the material, and thus did not prepare properly. While this leads to feelings of disappointment, and maybe a little more anxiety, it also, ultimately, leads to a scenario where future behavior can be improved to ensure that the grade on future tests improves as well.

The important takeaway here is that the thoughts that you have are a useful means of interpreting the world around you, along with the things that you experience. Everything that you hear, touch, see, smell and taste all provide data that allows your brain to determine what is happening at any given point and time. This is why CBT focuses on the creation of new, positive, habits as these will allow you to more easily interpret the experiences you have in the most positive, and productive ways possible.

This is the case as part of any thought is going to involve making assumptions about the stimuli you are going to be presented with. For example, assume you see someone walking towards you holding a knife, while this will not automatically mean that this person means you harm, it is perfectly reasonable to assume that they could be dangerous until you are presented with a reason to believe otherwise.

Unfortunately, when anxiety comes into play these assumptions can also be extremely harmful as they will just as likely cause you to assume that the person walking towards you is holding a knife when in reality they are just reaching for their phone.

Due to the fact that each of us is constantly taking in far more information than we can realistically process, a vast majority of the thoughts that you have in response to everyday occurrences are going to occur automatically without any conscious brainpower actually being used to generate them. These are known as automatic thoughts and those with anxiety often experience that anxiety bleed over into their automatic thoughts, causing an increased level of anxiety overall.

A long history of usefulness

Several of the exercises discussed in this chapter have proven so effective that they have been in use for thousands of years going all the way back to the ancient Greeks. The Greeks knew that logic was of vital importance when it comes to determining which beliefs are accurate and which need to be looked at more closely and why this process was so important when it comes to living a happy and fulfilling life. This idea remains as useful to CBT practitioners today as it was then which is why seeking out negative thoughts and actions remains of upmost importance.

Behavioral therapy and cognitive therapy: The type of CBT that is practiced today can actually trace its roots back to behavioral therapy which was first formalized in the 1920s and came into the public eye with the famous experiment done by Pavlov on his dogs. This led to the formation of a hypothesis which states that automatic behaviors can be trained based on external stimuli and that the process could also be used for therapeutic purposes by a scientist by the name of Mary Cover Jones. Jones began using this new type of therapy as a means of treating phobias in children. Behavioral therapy continued to grow in popularity throughout the 30s and 40s until it was one of the go-to therapies when it came to helping those with a wide variety of anxiety, depression and phobia disorders.

At the same time, a therapist named Aaron T Beck was working as an associative therapist when he had a sudden breakthrough regarding the very nature of thought itself. Specifically, he came to understand that not all thoughts are formed by the unconscious mind which means that some thoughts actually cause the feelings they are supposedly in response to. This realization ultimately led to the creation of cognitive therapy as Beck began to learn more about automatic thoughts.

CBT is formed: While behavioral therapy was great for helping certain specific neurotic disorders, there were still some issues that it wasn't particularly great at handling. Thus, as cognitive therapy started to gain additional traction, behavioral therapy started to be used less and less frequently. However, as both types of therapy were already focusing on various behavioral patterns of their patients and as they also focused more on the present than other types of therapy some therapists started using aspects of the two interchangeably.

This continued for a time until two therapists, Dr. Barlow and Dr. Clark decided to conduct tests to see where the ideas of behavioral therapy stopped and the ideas of cognitive therapy began. With their research in hand, they were able to develop a never-before-seen approach to treating panic disorders and create cognitive behavioral therapy at the same time.

Stages of CBT

The goal of CBT isn't to listen to each and every issue that you have going on in your life in an effort to diagnose you with a fancy sounding illness, it is to get to the root of the biggest problems in your life and find ways to make it easier for you to deal with them on a daily basis. The goal, then can either be to change the way you think or determine where specific maladaptive behaviors are located and work to squash them specifically.

The best way to go about doing so is through the use of a cognitive behavioral assessment which is made up of five key steps. First, you are going to want to determine the primary behaviors that are in play. Next, you are going to want to determine if the behaviors in question are either good or bad before then taking a look at the negative behaviors that you have uncovered in order to determine their frequency, duration, and intensity. From there you will want to determine the most beneficial course of action you can embark on in order to correct any relevant negative behaviors. Finally, you will want to determine how effective the treatment is and make changes accordingly.

Therapeutic alliance: This process is going to be overseen by a therapist, which means the first step to completing CBT successfully is find a therapist that you can form what is known as a therapeutic alliance with. This alliance is built on a relationship of mutual trust and respect, that can then be leveraged to generate solutions for the problems that are created as a result. This doesn't happen immediately, of course, and instead, every CBT experience starts with a session where you and the therapist get to know one another in an effort to decide if the relationship is going to be a good fit for everyone to ensure that you get what you need from the process.

During the initial sessions, the therapist will also assess the patient's mental and physical state in order to more quickly get to the root of the current problems. The goal for the end of the first session should be for both parties to determine if they can create a positive working relationship to effectively deal with the issues in question. This alliance is a crucial part of a successful CBT experience which means that the patient needs to take a serious look at how they feel about the therapist to ensure that they are comfortable opening up to them as this is the only way that true change can occur.

If you are starting a CBT therapy session and do not feel comfortable with the therapist that you have chosen it is important to break off the new relationship and find someone that you do feel comfortable with. CBT is all about building positive habits to replace the negative and stifling ones and this can't be done if you can't think of you and your therapist being on the same team. If something about the situation seems as though it is not working out, don't be afraid to go back to the drawing board and try something else instead, the therapist may even be able to give you alternative suggestions.

Control your thought process: After you have successfully formed a therapeutic alliance with a therapist you are comfortable with and determined which problems you are going to be focusing on, the next thing you will start working on are numerous different ways to control your own thought processes. In order to do so, you will need to understand what causes you to think the way you do. As such, the early sessions you attend will likely include some delving into your past to determine how, if at all, it actually relates to the problems you are currently experiencing.

CBT assessment

CBT has never been terribly interested in cataloging every single issue that a given patient is dealing with in order to give them a label that has been officially sanctioned. Instead, CBT has always been far more interested in what these issues mean for the big picture with the belief that this is the only way to ever successfully get to the root of the problem. Once the true problem has been revealed, the goal then either becomes to reevaluate how the patient responds to negative thinking or possibly change the way they view specific situations in hopes of negating negative habits or remove the power from relevant triggers.

To wit, a common cognitive behavioral assessment contains five unique steps including noting key behaviors, analyzing the behaviors, putting the negative behaviors under a microscope in an effort to determine frequency and severity, and decide the best way to move forward.

While the exercises outlined in the following chapters will all be more effective at treating certain issues than others, this doesn't mean that you are guaranteed to find what you are looking for inside as everyone is different. However, there are a number of questions you can ask yourself as a means of deciding if CBT is the right fit, right now.

- Do you like to focus on the present more than the past?
- Do you feel that talking about what is going on in your life

is more important than talking about things that happened to you as a child?
- Do you feel as though you are largely focused on achieving your goals as effectively as possible?
- Do you prefer talking to an active therapist as opposed to a passive one?
- Do you prefer structured therapy over open sessions?

If you can safely answer yes to most of the questions outlined in the proceeding chapters then you may very well find that CBT is the type of therapy you have been looking for. While the exercises outlined in the following chapters will likely help you deal with your personal issues, it is important to understand that starting CBT with a therapist first can help give you a proper perspective on the exercises you do undertake to ensure you get the most out of the time you put in. Furthermore, if you feel as though you are dealing with a life threatening situation then it is important that you reach out for professional help immediately as opposed to trying to go it alone.

Maximize the CBT experience

If you like the sound of CBT so far, then there are a wide variety of different things you can do to help you get off to a great start.

Know what to expect: While there will always be some things you won't be able to prepare for when it comes to CBT, there is still plenty of research that you can do in order to ensure that the therapist you end up with is a good fit. This means you will want to do things like check out their online reviews and also look more closely at their professional site to see what types of issues they deal with most regularly. If you are looking for a therapist for a child, for example then a therapist who typically works on adult couples is likely not going to be the most effective choice. When in doubt don't be afraid to ask around, you will be surprised how many people you know who have an opinion on the topic.

Be prepared for change: Based on the issues you are dealing with, it is entirely possible that it is not currently a good time to introduce a lot of new change into your life. Nevertheless, if you plan on introducing CBT into the mix you need to be prepared for it to pull you completely out of your comfort zone. This is also why it is so important for you to commit to your CBT sessions fully once you start so that you have enough time to start truly seeing the effects of what you have done before you decide one way or another if you are interested in keeping things up in the long-term.

A big part of this step means that if you feel as though CBT doesn't seem to be working for you right from the start that you try a variety of different exercises with an open mind before completely abandoning all of the work you have done up until this point. For example, if you have only been tentatively working towards a CBT breakthrough then it is entirely possible you will have more success if you fully commit and go for broke. In fact, studies show that simply by making a commitment to the change that is a part of CBT can make you 30 percent more likely to succeed at it in the long-term.

This doesn't mean that you should plan on remaining in active patient sessions forever after all if you can't create your own positive habits after a few months, it is unlikely that you will be able to no matter how long you struggle. This is nothing to be ashamed of, of course, it is a simple fact of life that not all types of therapy are going to be the right choice for all types of people. This is not to say that it might not just take you a little longer than most, of course, and it is important to always consider the context of your situation before you make a change to your timetable for success.

2
KNOW YOUR ENEMY

Anxiety

Everyone experiences some type of anxiety at one point in their lives. When you get up to speak in front of a group of people do you get a bit sweaty? Do you blush when you meet someone new and forget what to say? If you're called on in class, do you feel nervous because everyone is looking at you? These are all situations that most people will face at some point and it is common to have the symptoms that I described. When you talk quiet and get nervous, do you blame it on your shyness? Shyness and social nervousness are quite normal. Overthinking and feeling nervous at a point in your life could be described as anxiety, but it does not mean that you suffer from social anxiety.

Being shy is not the same as having a social disorder. Social anxiety disorder, also known as social phobia, is an intense fear and nervousness that you are being judged by others to the point that it effects your life in certain situations. Most of us can just take a deep breath and get through it, but when you experience social anxiety it seems like an impossible task. You are so fearful of what people are going to say or think or feel about you that you literally suffer to the point of feeling ill.

Imagine this situation. You are tasked with doing a presentation in class. As soon as you learn of the assignment, you start to get nervous. This nervousness becomes an obsession; you think about all the eyes that will be on you and fear that everyone will be judging you negatively. In your eyes, there is no way that this can be a positive situation. You continue to think about it to the point where it starts to cause you physical and emotional illness and you can't even focus on doing the project. When the day comes to do the project, you are so sick to your stomach that you cannot even make it to the class and you are willing to take a failing grade in order to avoid doing it. Then you start to worry about your teacher confronting you and how it will feel.

The anxiety needs to be severe enough that you would classify it as interfering with your daily life and it must include physical symptoms such as fatigue or stomach issues. If your physical symptoms aren't that severe, then the biggest indicator that you may notice is that your anxiety is affecting you in ways that lead to undue dysfunction or suffering in your day to day life.

Another key indicator that you might have an anxiety disorder is if you find yourself lying awake at night agitated, or worried about specific issues that need your attention, regardless of whether or not those issues are serious in the grand scheme of things. Roughly 60 percent of all generalized anxiety sufferers experience these types of symptoms. Another common sleep-related issue is that when you wake up you are immediately wide awake, your mind racing, and you feel as though you are unable to calm yourself down.

Another easy to miss symptom of an anxiety disorder is near constant muscle tension. This one might be hard to find for yourself, especially if you have been living with the condition for a long time as it can manifest in different people in different ways. This could be anything from balling your fists to clenching your jaw or holding an extreme amount of tension in your shoulders. It can also be difficult for others to diagnose for you, as a majority of those with generalized anxiety disorder feel uncomfortable with intimate touching to some degree.

Panic attacks can be a confusing symptom, simple because not everybody who has an anxiety disorder experiences them, and not everyone who has a panic attack will automatically have an anxiety disorder. Rather, if you tend to experience panic attacks on a regular basis, and your triggers don't seem to be linked to specific fears, then there is a reasonable chance that an anxiety disorder may be the root cause.

Finally, it is important to keep in mind that anxiety is a tricky foe to master for many reasons, not the least of which is that it rarely comes alone. A vast majority of anxiety diagnoses are accompanied by other types of issues as well, with depression being the most common. In many ways, many mental health issues can stem from the same source and thus treating one can treat them all.

The reasons why anxiety develops this way in certain people is not entirely understood, though there are many reasons as to why certain people will experience anxiety. For example, if a person experiences something that was particularly traumatic or stressful, their anxious response to triggers that stimulate the memory of those challenging experiences might cause anxiety. This type of stimuli can also trigger PTSD, so it is important that if this is what has caused anxiety, you are clear as to whether it is truly anxiety that is being dealt with or if it has progressed to PTSD.

It is also believed that consistent exposure to stress and overwhelm can cause anxiety in people, which can escalate to problematic anxiety over time if they are not able to relax their minds. This likely happens from consistent exposure to cortisol and adrenaline, which are the two hormones responsible for generating feelings of stress and anxiety in people who are experiencing them.

Alternatively, being in a volatile relationship with someone can also result in someone experiencing anxiety as they may be trained by their abuser to live "on edge" all the time. This anxiety is used to the advantage of the abuser who relies on their victim to be anxious all the time so that they can easily swing them off balance and abuse them further, without having the anxious victim fight back.

There are truly many reasons as to why a person may develop anxiety, but regardless of how it has developed, problematic anxiety can be troublesome and challenging to ward off. It is believed that more than 40 million people live with anxiety worldwide. Living with anxiety can be life-changing, as it can cause negative consequences in virtually every area of your life if it becomes overwhelming or out of control. For that reason, it is important that anyone who is experiencing anxiety seeks support in dealing with their symptoms so that they can hopefully be treated and resume living a normal life.

Depression

While everyone feels a little depressed now and then, there is a serious difference between feeling down in the dumps from time to time and feeling a level of complete and utter despair that is so severe that it seems as though it is never going to end. Depression can make it virtually impossible to enjoy the good things in life, or even remember that the good things in life exist at all. When you are in the clenches of a depressive episode, even making it through to the end of the day can be a Herculean feat. The good news is that things can get better, and recognizing the symptoms, and connecting them to yourself is a great first step.

Officially, depression is a common and debilitating mood disorder, that is far more than simple sadness. Rather, depression changes the way that your mind processes common events and activities, altering the way it functions, and you feel, in the process. If left untreated it can interfere with your ability to work, eat, sleep, and generally enjoy any facet of life. The feelings of hopelessness that it brings along can be so intense that it can seem impossible to believe that any relief is in sight.

If you do feel as though you are battling depression, the first thing you will want to do is to pay closer attention to your moods and emotions. If you are truly suffering from depressing then your brain will have a hard time regulating your emotions properly which means you may find yourself dealing with extreme levels of guilt, hopelessness, despair, numbness and more. You may also feel as though you are worthless in general, though if you look for the source of these feelings you will likely come up empty handed as well. You will also likely be more irritable than normal, which can result in a shortened temper and an increase in verbal or physical altercations.

Depression often comes in degrees with several different types that we should be aware of. These different types may have many similarities but you will also find they each have their own unique symptoms that set them apart.

Major depressive disorder: This condition can be identified when at least five of the following symptoms are present:

- An overwhelming feeling of sadness
- A loss of interest in normal everyday activities
- Decrease in appetite

- Insomnia/hypersomnia
- Psychomotor agitation
- Chronic fatigue
- Feelings of worthlessness
- Excessive guilt
- Recurrent thoughts of death or suicide
- Diminished ability to think

Any of these symptoms that last for more than two weeks or create a major divergence from normal behavior could be considered as the development of a major depressive disorder.

Persistent depressive disorder (dysthymia): This is characterized by an overwhelmingly sad mood that is persistently present for the majority of a two year period (1 year for children and adolescents). They should also have at least two of the following symptoms:

- Poor appetite
- Overeating
- Insomnia/hypersomnia
- Fatigue
- Low self-esteem
- Poor concentration
- Feelings of hopelessness
- Has trouble making decisions

The symptoms of a persistent depressive disorder may be the same as that of a major depressive disorder but are generally milder. There are various kinds of depressive disorders that could be remedied by CBT. The symptoms are often very similar in their degrees of intensity. If you recognize some of these symptoms in yourself or in someone you know, it is strongly recommended that you seek a professional diagnosis, and start treatment as soon as possible so you can get back to living a normal and productive life.

Additional symptoms: Appetite changes: depression can show itself through your eating patterns. Sometimes you may eat too much and other times you may eat far less. Both cases of extreme eating patterns indicate depression. Additionally, your depression may even be more pronounced when you stick to one type of food.

- Lack of focus: a depressed person would hardly concentrate on the task at hand. They just waste time, avoiding what needs to be done and for this reason, they hardly achieve their important goals. If you find yourself without any focus and just spending your time on unhealthy pastimes, you might be a depressed person.
- Uncontrollable negative thoughts: when you are going through the motions of life, you can't help running into negative thoughts. However, if those negative thoughts take center stage in your life so that every waking moment you are engulfed in some form of negativity, that's a huge sign that you are battling depression.
- Irritability and aggressive behavior: again from time to time we will run into situations where people will test our limits, and our aggression will manifest; that's totally okay. However, if we are in a constant state of aggression, seeking someone to destroy, it shows that we are trapped in a negative thinking pattern.
- Drug abuse: actually, this is one of the biggest indicators that someone is struggling with depression. When life becomes unbearable, we tend to seek ways of escaping, and drugs and alcohol offer an escape from reality, albeit a short one. As it happens, drugs only make one numb to their reality for a limited time, and when the effects wear

off, the full weight of reality sets in, and it takes an even bigger dose of drugs and alcohol to numb the pain, and it goes on and on without end.

- Reckless behavior: depressed people seem to exhibit some reckless behaviors which stem from their negative thoughts. They might injure themselves or engage in activities they know too well are dangerous.
- Unexplained aches: another indicator of depression is a presence of unexplained pain and aches throughout the body. Your body should be in optimum shape at all times as long as it hasn't endured physical abuse.

Treatment: When it comes to depression treatment, cognitive behavior therapy is one of the best known and empirically supported treatments for depression. CBT is believed to work so well when relieving the symptoms of depression as it produces changes in cognition which fuel cycles of negative feelings and rumination. Cognitive Behavioral Therapy is so protective against those episodes of acute depression, that it can even be used in place of the anti-depressant medications in some instances.

It has also shown a lot of promise as an approach for assisting with the handling of postpartum depression and as an adjunct to the medical treatment when it comes to bipolar patients. Similarly, preventive cognitive therapies as paired with antidepressants have been found to assist the patients that experienced reoccurring depression. It may also interfere with maintenance for unhealthy body weights, reduce feelings of isolation and assist patients to get more comfortable around trigger foods situations which are exposure therapy.

Phobias

Panic disorder is a type of mental health disorder characterized by reoccurring and unexpected panic attacks. Panic attacks are sudden periods of intense fear that may include heart palpitations, shaking or trembling, shortness of breath, feeling of choking, chills or hot flashes, fear of losing control, fear of dying, numbness or tingling in extremities, or a feeling of impending doom. These differ from typical anxiety symptoms in their extremity. A panic attack is so severe that it may be paralyzing to the sufferer during the, thankfully limited, duration of the attack. The symptoms may be so intense that one may check themselves into a hospital out of fear of having a heart attack.

A panic attack differs from anxiety in that an anxiety attack often comes after a stressor whereas a panic attack has no stressor and can be completely unprovoked. An anxiety attack is a gradual buildup of stress related to something perceived as threatening whereas a panic attack can happen completely out of the blue. One who has panic disorder may find themselves avoiding places, people, and situations over fears that they may trigger a panic attack.

The cause of panic disorder is unknown, but it often runs in families. It is unknown if that is a result of genetic or environmental factors. Smoking, psychological stress, and a history of child abuse may intensify the symptoms of a panic attack or increase their frequency.

Treatment for panic disorder is the exact same as for generalized anxiety disorder and consists of cognitive-behavioral therapy and medication including benzodiazepines or beta blockers.

When this is left untreated, these sorts of issues can lead to phobias. There are two types of phobias, agoraphobia, and specific phobia. The Agora was a market and meeting place in ancient Greece and is the root of the word "agoraphobia". Agoraphobia is not the fear of public places itself but is the fear of being unable to easily and safely escape public places.

Agoraphobia affects around two percent of the population. Like most anxiety disorders, it affects twice as many women as men. Other phobias, such as fear of germs (bacteriophobia), and other disorders, such as obsessive-compulsive disorder or post-traumatic stress disorder, may complicate and/or intensify the symptoms of agoraphobia.

Fixed mindset

While this might seem hard to believe, for some of you anyway, heading out into the world each day with the understanding that success is possible as long as you put in the time and effort to find it will, in fact, lead to more success over time. This is what is known as a growth mindset, and you can be sure it is one of the things all successful people have in common. What's more, most had it instilled in them at a very young age. This occurs, because at some point, every child is either told that they succeeded because they worked hard, and hard work pays off, or that they succeeded because they were naturally gifted.

Those who are told they have a natural gift, often develop what is known as a fixed mindset, which has the negative benefit of their brains being the most active when people are telling them how great they are. On the other hand, those who were told that they succeed thanks to hard work develop in such a way that their brains are the most active when they are overcoming a challenge, which has far more productive uses at every stage of life. Additionally, those with a fixed mindset often spend more time worrying about what others think about them then their actual success, which is why growth mindset individuals always end up winning out in the end.

Growth-oriented mindset

- Appreciates constructive criticism
- Inspired by the success of others
- Treats obstacles as tools for learning
- Appreciates challenge
- Understands that effort and success are linked
- Focused on the long term

Fixed Mindset

- Does not listen to feedback
- Finds the success of others threatening
- Believes effort and success are not linked
- Gives up when presented with roadblocks
- Prefers to avoid challenging situations
- Prioritizes looking competent over subtle skill

A large part of this is due to the fact that those with a fixed mindset often prefer to avoid challenges as they find obstacles in their path discouraging as they challenge their belief that they succeed effortlessly. On the contrary, those with a growth mindset find it easier to focus on the long-term results of their actions because they naturally equate effort to success. They typically enjoy a good challenge because they see obstacles in their path as an opportunity to learn. They also appreciate constructive criticism and find the success of other inspiring.

Furthermore, the two differing mindsets also respond differently to setbacks that the occur on the path to success. Those with a fixed mindset believe themselves to have a set level of ability which means that if they cannot surpass an obstacle on the first try, there is no reason for them to try again because nothing about the scenario will ever change. It doesn't take much to see how this type of reductive mindset can make it difficult to start working your way out of a difficult situation as it can make it seem like there is no point in even getting started. On the other hand, those with a growth mindset always appreciate a good challenge for the opportunity to overcome it and learn from the experience.

Neuroplasticity: By this point, it should be obvious to you whether you have a growth or a fixed mindset and why it is so important to prioritize the one above the other. Luckily, in this case, knowing really is half the battle as it is only by knowing that you are burdened with a fixed mindset that you can start making real progress towards changing it for the better. As luck would have it, the human brain changes noticeably and visibly throughout its life-span, based on the stimuli that it receives on a regular basis. As such, it doesn't matter how deeply seated a given idea, trait or characteristic is, given enough of the proper stimuli there is nothing that cannot be overwritten.

At its most basic, the human brain functions as neurons travel along preexisting neural pathways taking a path of least resistance to ensure that thoughts move as quickly as possible. As new neural pathways are formed, they are worn-in with use which means that in order to change from a fixed to a growth mindset all you need to do is to commit to practice growth mindset inducing behaviors as frequently as possible. This doesn't mean the process is going to be easy, however, as unfortunately, the fixed mindset pathways are going to be some of the most well-worn of them all. It will be possible, however, and that possibility is what you are going to need to hang on too as tightly as you can and use that thought as a lifeline when your natural inclination to give up kicks in.

Success takes time: One of the most important parts of successfully retraining your mind to support a growth mindset is to understand the importance of the old adage "fake it 'til you make it." It is important not to undertake the task of completely changing your mindset with the assumption that it will happen overnight. Building up new neural pathways and using them enough that they become a habit isn't easy which is why it is important to set easily achievable goals and use that success to trick yourself into believing that whatever it is you are working towards is actually close at hand. This extra mental boost will help you continue struggling along until the next milestone provides another boost.

For example, if you wanted to build up a habit of working out regularly start out with an easily achievable goal of exercising for as little as ten minutes at a time. After the small goal becomes routine, upping the difficulty factor won't seem nearly as intimidating as it did before. With enough repetition you mind will no longer associate the success derived from the effort with just whatever task you initially aimed to master, instead it will more broadly equate the level of success with the amount of effort put forth.

The following mantra can help when the fruits of your labor are not yet in sight. "Nothing is promised, if you want something, claim it". You aren't promised a promotion you have to claim it, you aren't promised a thinner waistline, you must claim it, you will never be promised success and happiness, you have to do whatever it is you have to in order to claim them.

☙ 3 ❧
STARTER EXERCISES

CBT IS FILLED WITH A WIDE ARRAY OF EXERCISES THAT you can use combat anxiety. These are initially taught and practiced during therapy sessions but are designed so that they can be practiced alone at home or, in many cases, anywhere you find yourself.

The flexibility of these exercises is important because they have a duality. Because many of the help you when you need them (say, during a bout of panic) they can be practiced as part of a daily regime of as needed. Ideally, you would do both.

The thing to keep in mind, as always, is that development of these skills (and the benefits they reap) takes time and practice. If you know going in that you won't do things perfectly the first time, or that you'll instantly feel better on your first attempt, it will be much harder to be discouraged when you have setbacks. And be aware of this: there will be setbacks. That's a simple fact of life. But it's how you react and overcome that determines your eventual success.

This section discusses common, simple discussions as well as two advanced techniques.

Breathing: CBT teaches us that our thoughts influence our feelings and behaviors, but they also affect our physical well-being. Treating anxiety requires a physical component as well as mental. Think of your last anxiety attack and how you physically felt. What changed? What went awry?

Of the many physical symptoms of anxiety disorders, poor breathing may be the most damaging. How we breathe directly impacts how everything else in our body functions. When we're anxious our breathing may slow to a crawl or jump to a rapid pace. If we're either getting too little or too much oxygen it can worsen the other symptoms, creating a snowball effect.

The good news is that learning to control our breathing is easy and for many is the first step to recovering from anxiety. The simplest exercise is called "four-seven-eight." It works like this: find a place where you can sit comfortably. With your back straight, take a deep breath for four seconds. Hold that breath for seven seconds. Then, slowly breath out for eight seconds. Repeat the process for a minute or two, keeping careful track of time that your breathing in, holding, and breathing out. Some people find it helpful to close their eyes during four-seven-eight, though it isn't required.

As you do this you should notice everything slowing down, such as your heartbeat, and you'll become more relaxed. You may not see this results at first, however, because it may take longer than a few minutes. Such a short time frame is recommended at first because people sometimes find it difficult or even uncomfortable to hold their breath and/or breathe out for the required periods of time. But it does get easier with time.

Breathing exercises help to reign in the physical symptoms of anxiety disorders. It's a tool that can be implemented anywhere at any time, making it powerful despite its simplicity. However, one of the biggest problems those new to the exercise have is focusing. It can be difficult to time the breaths when you have worries running through your head and you can't shake them, or if you immediately go back to them once the exercise has stopped. Preventing this requires focus, which leads directly into the next item in our tool belt.

Keeping a journal: Your thoughts are a continuous stream; there's no waking moments where you aren't thinking about something. It may not also be in the front of your mind but thoughts are always present and always moving. As the adage goes, "I think, therefore I am." It's difficult to recognize everything that passes through our heads as it is. Throw anxiety into the mix and it becomes impossible to follow everything.

A journal is a great way to track your anxiety. By putting your thoughts on paper you'll give them tangible form. Though similar to a diary, your journal isn't for just a record of your daily happenings. It's closer to an operating table where you'll examine, dissect, and explore your distressing thoughts. This is helpful in several ways:

Better self-expression. How often have you tried to explain your issues to someone only to feel like they didn't fully understand what you were saying? It's difficult to articulate worry or sadness, especially at the moment. But no one will have a better understanding of your thought processes than you do. By laying it out on the page you can practice how you can communicate it to others. In therapy sessions, you can even read your entries to your therapist.

Self-reflection. As we become more aware of ourselves and our thought cycles it can become easy to let thoughts get lost in the blur. If you have a written record of your thoughts it acts likes a map of sorts. You can see what sort of thoughts you had on any given day and see how they changed overtime, creating pathways and patterns that you can recognize. This recognition will help you develop plans for going forward.

Progress. It's also beneficial to have the journal of your thoughts because it shows how much progress you make on your journey to recovery. But of equal value to these positives are seeing where you come short. If you're honest in writing all the highs and lows you'll have examples of moments that need improvement. When you reflect on these moments you can better discover and understand your personal issues and work on better handling them in the future.

Affirmations: Affirmations or mantras, positive sentences which are repeated throughout the day, are a great place to start. Affirmations are written down while mantras are repeated either aloud or in your head and both make it easier to block out any negative static that your fixed mindset has to contribute in a given situation.

Common mantras and affirmation include thing like:

- I can follow my path to happiness no matter how rocky it may be
- Success is measured in forward progress
- Through hard work, I can attract the love and success I deserve
- I am strong enough to overcome any obstacle
- I can find fulfilment through dedication and perseverance

When you are first stating out with this practice, it is natural to feel foolish, or as though you are wasting your time. While these thoughts are perfectly natural, if you make the mistake of acting on them, then you will be allowing your fixed mindset to assert its dominance and prevent you from making positive changes in your own life. When you are feeling especially dispirited and as though you aren't making any forward progress, it is important to power through these feelings as they are just your fixed mindset fight back. The longer you don't interact with these thoughts, the less likely they are to return.

To ensure you don't bite off more than you can chew all at once, it is recommended that you start off with an affirmation or mantra that is fairly close to your current mental comfort zone. Starting with something small will make it easier to rewire your brain in a positive direction when compared to starting with something serious right off the bat.

Once you have chosen a mantra or affirmation that is right for you, it is important that you utilize it to the fullest. This means you will want to ensure that it is the first thing you think in the morning when you wake up, and then once and hour, on the hour, throughout the rest of the day, before making sure it is the last thing you think before you fall asleep at night. When working through it, ensure that you really focus on the words, to the exclusion of all else.

Progressive muscle relaxation: The progressive muscle relaxation technique is useful at the moment when you are experiencing particularly harsh flair ups of anxiety. It involves working to tense and then relax specific muscle groups in a row as a means of distracting yourself from your anxiety for long enough that it short circuits the mental loop that caused it to flare up in the first place. This is largely due to the fact that it is difficult for your body to remain in a tense state that is full of anxiety while specific parts of the body are indicating that they are perfectly relaxed. This means that if you feel as though an anxiety attack is heading your way, a period of forced relaxation may be just what's required to stop it before it gets too serious. This exercise can be especially effective if your anxiety makes it difficult for you to sleep through the night.

While you will eventually be able to use this exercise without a moment's hesitation when you are first getting into the swing of things you may find better success if you find someplace quiet to practice from to start. To begin, all you need to do is to pick a specific part of the body and then shift your entire focus to it. This step is going to remain the same regardless of the muscle groups you are focusing on.

As an example, if you wanted to begin by using your left hand, you would then hold it out in front of you in such a way that it is easy for you to focus on it to the exclusion of all else. Then, while slowly breathing in and out you are going to want to tense all the muscles in your hand as thoroughly as you can, for anywhere between five and 10 seconds. When you tense, it should be hard enough that your hand begins to feel uncomfortable by the time you reach your goal. While doing so, you are also going to want to focus on all of the tension you are feeling in general and focus it through your hand.

After you have finished tensing, you will then want to abruptly change course and relax the muscles you were focusing on (in this case your hand). After you have finished tensing you will want to relax those muscles completely, feeling all of the tightness float out of your muscles, and from your mental state as well. You will want to go completely limp for this exercise to be effective, before then focusing on the difference between the two states.

This comparison is where the real results come into play as it will force your body to realize that it is now in a relaxed state, which means that the anxiety you are feeling can't exist, so it has to abate. You will want to remain in your relaxed state for between 15 and 20 seconds before moving on to the next muscle group if your anxiety has not yet abated.

Find your triggers: Every person has a trigger, something that will set them off and often results in their emotions taking the reins and causing a lot of issues. They may have been fine doing stuff and then that trigger will push them to be angry, mad, upset or something else. Often those emotions take over control so much that they will end up doing things that they regret later on. One of the biggest things that you need to do when getting started with CBT is learning how to recognize these triggers so that you can avoid them and keep your emotions under control.

There are going to be times, no matter how hard you work against them when your emotions are going to appear. Someone says something that makes you angry, your stress levels get high, or something else happens. That is normal and as a human, you are going to experience these emotions no matter what other mental issues you may be dealing with.

Remaining in control of your personal issues is not about never feeling emotions, it is more about how you deal with those emotions as soon as they arise. When you feel anger or happiness or sadness, take a moment to recognize that you are feeling those emotions. It is not a bad thing to feel anxious on occasion; the bad part is when you react in a negative way to the anxiety or when it becomes oppressive. Being able to recognize the feelings that you are having and figuring out why they show up will help you to start gaining some of the control that you are looking for.

When going through your day, you are going to want to take note of the major and minor interactions you have during the day, along with anything else that triggers feelings or issues that you have previously linked to your mental health issue. For each one, you are going to want to rate the overall success of the action or interaction, how it made you feel, any issues relating to depression that it triggered, what you did about them and how you feel you might improve in the future. If this is not the first time an event has occurred, make note of how you may have changed your approach compared to previous events and how that changed the results overall.

It is important to be extremely thorough, especially at first, though eventually, you can likely taper off to just covering the ongoing issues that you are still struggling with. This does not mean that you should waste time criticizing what you did or how you failed to live up to a plan, focus on the facts, not opinions.

Once you have gathered a few weeks of data, you can start actively working out ways that you can start improving the common interactions that you have the most trouble with. You should be able to start seeing patterns in your data as well as, hopefully, clear things that you can change to improve the overall outcome for the better.

Once you have managed to make a list of your triggers, the next thing you are going to want to do is everything in your power to ensure you remove them from your general line of sight until you have a replacement behavior ready to go. While you will rarely be able to remove absolutely all the power a given trigger has, you should be able to lessen it significantly, with practice. It is important to keep in mind that the early days are likely going to be tough going, but each time you successfully withstand a serious temptation it will get a little easier.

Regardless of your goals, if you aren't already maintaining a schedule where you can eat regularly, then it is important to make doing so a priority. Not only will eating at regular periods help you to feel better, but it will also ensure that your brain has the fuel required to make good decisions. Specifically, studies show that those with low blood sugar are three times more likely to make poor decisions based on a lack of resolve than those whose blood sugar was on point. Don't let something as simple as a lack of food lead to a relapse into behavior you are trying to avoid. Rather, make it a point of keeping healthy snacks on hand to ensure that you are always able to keep a clear head no matter what.

If you typically have a difficult time avoiding triggers, despite your best efforts, you may instead find it effective to mix up your daily routine to give new habits the time they need to take root. With these changes in place, you will find it is much easier to avoid whatever it is that you are trying to avoid, rather than staring at the hole it left in your schedule day in and day out. When it comes to creating a new, and improved, lifestyle, it is important to not bite off more than you can chew all at once. Instead, you are going to want to focus on adding to one aspect of your life before moving on to the next.

4
MINDFULNESS MEDITATION

One of the major underlying factors of a persistent negative mental state is being bombarded by thoughts that cause worry. While everyone worries and experiences stress, it becomes dangerous if you can't move on from those feelings. For those suffering from an anxiety, depression or phobia disorder it's simply not enough to "snap out of it" because the thoughts are so frequent and so loud that they are pulled back in no matter how we try to distract ourselves. The trick is to find your anchor--to find your center.

Meditation is a skill everyone's heard of but many people really don't understand. In the West, we often think of meditation as a spiritual or mystical practice, and while it's true that meditation has uses in various religious practices in its most basic form it is a simple thought exercise. Mindfulness meditation teaches us to focus and occupy the space between our thoughts rather than on those thoughts specifically. As we come to recognize these peaceful moments we can use meditation to come back to them. It's a great tool made even more powerful by the fact that it can be done anywhere in any situation. All it takes is practice.

STUDIES HAVE SHOWN TIME AND TIME AGAIN THAT those who practice meditation are better able to manage stress, and studies focusing on a wide variety of mental health disorders have shown direct positive improvement. Simply put, meditation has a real, measurable effect. However, to reap these benefits you need to meditate regularly, not just when you're in the midst of an unfortunate mental episode. Think of it as a muscle: the more often you use it, the stronger it becomes.

Start this way: FOR JUST A FEW MINUTES, TAKE A SEAT. IT need not be in a chair, nor do you need to sit with your legs positioned in a specific way. Simply sit down with your back straight. Put your hands in your lap and close your eyes. Then, breathe slowly. When you do, focus all of your attention on how breathing itself feels. Really fixate on the senses: the air entering and exiting your nostrils or mouth; the expansion of your lungs, how cold or warm the air is. When these few minutes are up, open your eyes and examine how you feel physically and mentally. Try this once a day, extending the time a little bit each day.

Practice mindfulness at all times: ONCE YOU GET THE HANG of the basics of mindfulness meditation you will find that there is practically nothing you can't do that doesn't lend itself to being mindful. The following are some of the easiest ways to get into the habit of practicing mindfulness meditation around your home, but you can also practice at work, on public transportation, or even while driving. With a little extra practice, the wide variety of times you can easily slip into a mindful state are sure to surprise you.

MINDFULNESS TEACHES AN APPROPRIATE WAY TO respond to the circumstances of life, whether they are pleasant or unpleasant, and it also allows a person to become more aware of emotions and thoughts. Mindfulness can allow for emotional regulation, distress tolerance, and interpersonal effectiveness. Mindfulness skills include witnessing the present circumstances without judgment, describing the present situation, and completely participating in the present circumstances in a one-minded way while concentrating on effectiveness. Medical professionals impart in their patients these mindfulness skills through techniques such as skills training and individual therapy.

MINDFULNESS SKILLS

The "What" Skills: Mindfulness, as it pertains to cognitive behavior therapy, contains two skill sets, "what" skills (acceptance) and "how" skills (change). The "what" skills begin with observing, a vital skill of mindfulness. Making observations from the mind allows a person to be able to witness a difference between self and thoughts; a person is not limited to their thoughts, so it is important to not allow thoughts to command mentality and to comprehend that thoughts come and go. This permits a person to start to hold the power of selecting where to allocate attention.

THE SKILL OF OBSERVING ALSO ALLOWS A PERSON TO contemplate his mind between thoughts, which is a quieter location in which a person can recognize a fresh capacity to be entirely present in a particular instance. When a person is not observing, that person is inclined to feel obliged to any thought that may appear, but when a person observes he is capable of seeing the temporary character of thoughts and control over attention can be reclaimed. A person's observations of the mind can impart powerful training of that person's capability to release what does not help him.

ADDITIONALLY, A PERSON IS ABLE TO OBSERVE HIS physical existence, which places emphasis on attention to the body rather than thoughts. Mindfulness is fastened on observation of breathing, perceiving the physical feelings of breathing in and out, which guides the mind away from unwelcome thoughts and combines a person's body and mind.

THE SECOND MINDFULNESS SKILL IS DESCRIBING. IF A repeated thought creates pressure, stress, or any other physical or emotional sensation, it is important to take note of it. When a person describes what he has observed, it assists that person in processing and understanding present feelings and thoughts. A person has the capability to be watchful of what sensations a particular thought gives that person without adhering or giving value to the thought. Rather, the person should merely describe the thought in order to understand it better, then watch the thought disappear.

PARTICIPATING IS THE FINAL "WHAT" SKILL OF mindfulness. Clearly stated, participation is executing the exercise of the other two mindfulness skills. Participation is the action of a person selecting to observe his thoughts, describe them and understand them completely, and apply non-attachment. Participating in mindfulness signifies involvement of a person in the action of transferring the focus of the mind, softly, once a person comprehends that the mind has become sidetracked. Participating contains giving the self authorization to provide and obtain the benefits of mindfulness through supplying time and space for mindfulness in life.

The "How" Skills: THE "HOW" SKILLS OF MINDFULNESS begin with being non-judgmental. The start of observing a person's emotions and thoughts impartially begins with pledging to be nonjudgmental about those thoughts. No thoughts are good, bad, unwanted, or welcome; they are simply thoughts and exist as equals. Being able to let go of judgmental opinions provides a release to an individual by letting go of stress which can contribute to suffering. Judgment is part of human nature, so individuals will most likely be tested by this skill of mindfulness.

IT IS IMPORTANT TO RETURN THE MIND TO THE PRESENT moment when it becomes noticeable that the mind has become sidetracked and started judging thoughts. Mindfulness is meant to be a holiday of sorts from judgmental thoughts, which means a person should not judge himself if he falters in his mindfulness. A person must treat himself with sympathy and consideration and begin again.

THE SECOND SKILL IS BEHAVING ONE-MINDFULLY BY concentrating on one objective at a time, which is the stark contrast to multi-tasking. Participating in responsibilities one-mindfully strengthens a person's capability of refraining from multi-tasking and handling one action at a time. Mindfulness meditation utilizes one-mindfulness by allowing the person to concentrate his mind and release his mind from distractions such as checking an e-mail or answering a cell phone.

When a person's mind is concentrated on one specific task and the skills needed to complete that task, completion of that task is more likely to be faultless.

The final mindfulness skill is acting effectively through the application of mindfulness concepts. Effectiveness implies that a person has progressed and reinforced the muscles of the mind. Practicing effectiveness through mindfulness allows a person to become more conscious of the area between that person's actions and thoughts.

Rehearsing mindfulness also allows a person to improve his effectiveness at decreasing judgment of himself and others and to release emotions which deter that person from developing his sense of sympathy and consideration. A person can fortify his resilience through effectiveness when the mind becomes sidetracked and there is a need to return the mind to its original state.

Group mindfulness strategies

Some of the cognitive behavior therapy activities are comprised of mindfulness through group therapy. This method utilizes mindfulness in order to decrease social anxiety in patients afflicted by various mental health disorders and involves eight members gathering for two hours every week for 12 weeks. At the beginning of each group meeting, the members participate in an exercise dedicated to mindfulness and a conversation about the advantages of the exercise. A few of the exercises encompassed in this therapy plan include the raisin exercise, the body scan, mindful seeing, and mindful listening, all of which promote mindfulness in the members of the group.

Raisin exercise: THE RAISIN EXERCISE INVOLVES THE therapist to offer a food, preferably one with an interesting smell, texture, or taste such as a raisin, to each member of the group and requires the members to act as if they have never experienced that particular food before. Each member then studies the food and observes the look, feel, smell, and taste of it, an exercise whose purpose is to carry the mind to the current instance. If the group member is focused on the food in his hand, then he is most likely not focusing on the worrisome aspects of his life as well.

Body scan exercise: THE BODY SCAN EXERCISE INVOLVES very little equipment and causes the group member to be attentive to each portion of the body, starting with the toes and working up through the feet to the legs. The scan then takes the mind from the pelvic region, through the abdomen and chest, and into the back, followed by the hands and arms. The scan is completed by running through the neck to the head and face. A typical body scan utilizes five steps, beginning with the group members resting flat on their back, feet apart and palms up; however, the members could also complete this exercise while sitting in a chair with their feet on the ground. In the second step, the therapist requests that the members stay still during the length of the exercise and only move as their body as it becomes a necessity.

. . .

STEP THREE IS THE BEGINNING OF THE BODY SCAN, guided by the therapist, and requires the group members to become aware of the rhythm of their breathing without changing it. This leads into the fourth step, which is providing attention to each portion of the body and how it feels, including how the clothing rests against the body and how the body rests again the floor. The final step completes the scan as the therapist asks the group members to become aware of the sensations in the body, both positive and negative.

Mindful seeing: THE MINDFUL SEEING EXERCISE SIMPLY requires a window, and its purpose is to develop a healthy imagination in each group member. The members look out the window and find a view on which to focus, then observe the attractions outside of the window. Instead of categorizing the sights by name, this exercise drives the members to perceive aspects such as patterns, colors, and textures, like the motion of leaves in wind or the hues in the wings of birds. It is important for the group members to remain observant and aware of the attractions outside the window without becoming critical and fixated.

IF THE MIND BECOMES DISTRACTED DURING THE exercise, the group members are expected to find a shape or color outside the window that is capable of bringing the mind back around to the task at hand. While this exercise typically only takes a few minutes, it opens the mind up to new discoveries and extends the imagination of each group member.

Mindful listening: THE MINDFUL LISTENING EXERCISE AIMS to create a sense of stillness and self-regulation inside each group member. In order to accomplish this, the group members must bring to mind something that causes stress and something to which the member is looking forward, then each member will share his thoughts with the rest of the group. Each member must discuss the feelings behind a negative thought and a positive thought and should also become aware of the sensations felt while each member is sharing his thoughts. The exercise finishes with discussion groups based around a set of questions, such as asking about any judgment felt while experiencing the other group members' stories and the feelings throughout the body while sharing and listening.

Individual mindfulness strategies

While some patients thrive in a group setting for therapy, many patients feel anxious and stressed at the thought of participating in group mindfulness exercises, and therefore, individual therapy may be the way to go. Many individual exercises exist which can produce mindfulness practices in a patient, such as the self-compassion pause, self-inquiry meditation, the five senses exercise, the mini-mindfulness exercise, the mindful walking down the street technique, and the three minute breathing space.

Self-compassion pause: THE SELF-COMPASSION PAUSE exercise, which uses awareness of thoughts and feelings to induce mindfulness, is ideal for patients who lack a sense of self-respect and compassion within themselves. The exercise begins with a simple observation of where awareness lies within the patient, whether in the body or on emotions and then works to achieve a feeling of compassion within the patient by perceiving actions and thoughts through mindfulness. The patient must then initiate physical contact with himself, whether through a hug or a hand over the heart or another method and then inhale and exhale with deep breaths. After this step, the patient will recognize his suffering without becoming overwhelmed with negative emotions, which allows the patient to practice mindfulness and recognize his feelings as real and painful while accepting this fact with compassion.

Self-inquiry meditation: THE SELF-INQUIRY MEDITATION exercise is often used during meditation to achieve enlightenment and begins similarly to the self-compassion pause exercise, with the patient observing their awareness of the body or emotions. The patient then finds a comfortable position in which to sit and settles in the mind and body while releasing all thoughts and clearing the mind of what is typically burdening it. The patient will take this time to focus on the sensation of being "you" by asking himself questions about who he is and of what his inner self consists.

IF THE MIND BECOMES SIDETRACKED DURING THIS exercise, the patient should bring thoughts back around to himself by asking who is experiencing the distracting thought. This exercise may be practiced as long as is wanted by the patient, and while it may be difficult for the patient to focus on himself, self-inquiry is an important technique which brings awareness to the self and releases the mind from everyday distractions.

Five senses exercise: THE FIVE SENSES EXERCISE SIMPLY focuses on how the patient experiences each of the five senses. First, the patient must observe five things through the sense of sight, preferably something the patient would not normally perceive, such as a shadow in the corner or a crack in the sidewalk. Secondly, the patient must observe four things through the sense of touch, such as the sensation of clothing resting against the body or feet resting on the floor.

NEXT, THE PATIENT MUST OBSERVE THREE THINGS through the sense of hearing, specifically something in the background, like the chattering of squirrels or the noises of traffic from the street. Then, the patient must observe two things through the sense of smell, whether unpleasant or pleasant, such as the scent of a restaurant or the smell of a garbage truck down the road. Finally, the patient must observe one thing through the sense of taste, whether by taking a drink, eating a piece of food, or simply tasting the air. This is a relatively short exercise which can be very effective at bringing the patient to a mindful state.

Mini-mindfulness: THE MINI-MINDFULNESS EXERCISE, which also can take a short duration, contains only three steps. The first step is for the patient to bring awareness to the sensations of the moment through acknowledgement of thoughts and feelings while also letting them elapse. For this step, the patient should sit comfortably and try to take his mind out of auto-pilot. The second step calls for the patient to become aware of his breathing for one minute, perceiving the patterns and movements of each breath, and the final stage asks the patient to become aware of his environment, both of the surroundings and of the body. These steps should take the patient to a state of mindfulness throughout the rest of the day and expand the patient's general awareness.

. . .

Mindful walking: THE MINDFUL WALKING DOWN THE street exercise focuses on becoming aware of thoughts and emotions without feeling the need to solve or hide them and teaches impulse control. The patient begins the exercise by imagining a scene where the patient is walking down a street he recognizes and suddenly sees a person he knows. The patient imagines waving to the person, but the person does not react and continues to walk. The patient must then ask himself to what extent he perceived his thoughts and emotions during the imagined scene and must reflect on those thoughts and emotions and how they affected the patient.

Three-minute breathing: THE THREE MINUTE BREATHING space exercise breaks down the three minutes into different sections, each of which uses different techniques to promote mindful behavior. The first minute is occupied by the patient asking himself how he is doing at the current moment, with the particular focus put on thoughts and emotions that appear and putting those thoughts and emotions into words. The second minute focuses on the patient becoming aware of his breath, and the third minute is spent putting attention on the movement and sensation of the body as the patient continues to breathe. This quick exercise can be difficult, but it is important for the patient to remember to let thoughts simply pass through the mind.

Informal mindfulness strategies

Along with group and individual exercises facilitated by a medical professional, many daily informal cognitive behavior therapy exercises using mindfulness exist which can help patients with anxiety and other effects of borderline personality disorder. One exercise involves perceiving a leaf for five minutes, where the patient picks up a leaf, holds it in his hand, and pays attention to it for five minutes, observing the shape, patterns, textures, and colors of the leaf. This exercise teaches awareness of the current moment through mindfulness of a particular object.

Eating for four minutes: ANOTHER BENEFICIAL EXERCISE IS mindfully eating for four minutes, which is similar to the raisin exercise used during group therapy. The patient chooses a non-messy food and observes the sensation of the food in his hand, including the color, weight, and texture. Next, the patient observes the smell of the food, and finally, the food may be eaten. While slowly eating the food, using a great deal of concentration, the patient should observe the texture and taste of the food. This exercise can also allow the patient to create new encounters with well-known foods.

Observation of thoughts: ANOTHER EXERCISE IS THE observation of thoughts for 15 minutes, an exercise which increases awareness of the patient's thoughts. In order to accomplish this, the patient lies down or sits in a comfortable position and releases all the tension from the body through focusing on breathing, the sensations of the body, and thoughts. The patient should not be judgmental toward the thoughts that cross his mind, but instead, let them pass through his mind, and if a distracting thought appears, the patient should acknowledge the thought and move back to the original thoughts.

ANOTHER INFORMAL ACTIVITY IS THE MINDFULNESS bell exercise, which lasts five minutes. This exercise utilizes a video to allow the patient to be aware of the current moment. The patient listens for the cue in the video and concentrates on the sound until it has faded away entirely. Another exercise which applies a video is the stare at the center exercise, which uses a shifting pattern with multiple colors to promote deep thought and focus. The patient should become fixated on the center of the pattern and let his mind freely wander while staying in the current moment.

Practice mindfulness meditation to start your day out right: No matter how rushed you feel you are in the morning, you can find a few minutes to practice mindfulness meditation if you make a concentrated effort to do so. The easiest way to do so is by taking a few extra moments to really savor your favorite morning drink be it coffee, tea or even soda or an energy drink. What's more, if you shower in the mornings as well, you can string together a group of mindfulness meditation sessions practically from the moment you wake up until you reach your workplace. From there, if you do it right you can be mindful throughout your day right up until it is time for bed.

THE MORNING MINDFULNESS MEDITATION SESSION IS one of the easiest to get the hang of as the first cup of an energizing beverage of the day is naturally more potent than those that follow it as your body has had all the hours you were asleep to get the caffeine out of your system ensuring that the first jolt is the most powerful that you are going to feel throughout the day.

For the best results, you are going to want to wake up with the idea of mindfulness on the brain. As you wake in the morning take a few extra moments to consider the thoughts that are already racing through your head and consider why they are there without interacting with them directly. If your thoughts are all about the day ahead, make a concentrated effort to push them aside until you have successfully finished your morning mindfulness meditation routine.

If possible, go ahead and slip into a state of mindfulness directly after taking stock of your mental inventory. Once you are properly adapted to the moment the next thing that you are going to want to do is to pay special attention to the preparation of your drink of choice. While there is certainly going to be more to be aware of if you are grinding coffee beans and filling an espresso machine, even pulling out a teabag or taking a cold drink from the refrigerator has plenty of sensations to offer when it comes to locking you in place in the moment.

Strategies for Depression, Anger, and Anxiety

Some cognitive behavior therapy exercises which use mindfulness focus primarily on issues such as depression, anger, and anxiety. These mindfulness activities can be helpful in coping with these powerful emotions, managing the thoughts feelings which enter the patient's mind, and decreasing rates of relapse in patients who use them.

Sorting boxes exercise: The sorting boxes exercise deals specifically with depression and involves muscle relaxation and breathing strategies, similar to the body scan activity and three minute breathing space exercise. The patient pays close attention to his breathing without attempting to change the pattern of it and becomes aware of all emotions, sensations, and thoughts which enter the mind. The patient must then sort those emotions, sensations, and thoughts in three "boxes" which have been labeled accordingly in the mind. The patient continues to sort everything into the boxes until the mind has been cleared. This exercise has proved useful in successfully clearing the mind of worries and helping to create a focus on the current instance of time.

Reliving anger: A BENEFICIAL ANGER MANAGEMENT exercise begins with sitting comfortably and closing the eyes while observing how the body rests against the chair or floor. The patient takes a deep breath and exhales quickly, then focuses all thoughts on a recent time when the patient felt anger at specific circumstances. All other feelings, such as sadness or guiltiness, should be omitted as the patient relives the feelings of anger that were experienced in the particular situation.

THE PATIENT SHOULD THEN OBSERVE THE SENSATIONS that overtake the body while feeling anger, such as feeling hot or cold or tension in the chest. The final stage of this activity is to bring compassion to the experience of anger and release the feelings of anger by saying goodbye to them. This activity should help decrease instances of chronic anger in the patient.

Ten attitudes: AN EXERCISE WHICH HELPS WITH FEELINGS of anxiety utilizes mindfulness through 10 attitudes: intention, beginner's mind, patience, acknowledgement, lack of judgment, non-striving, reliance on the self, allowing, the compassion of the self, and balance. The patient begins by realizing the intention to work with anxiety through a mindset that focuses on new stances and ideas on anxiety. The patient must use patience in order to persevere and acknowledgement in order to form acceptance.

It is also essential for the patient to remain nonjudgmental in his thoughts and to accept an experience without trying to change the situation. The patient must put trust in himself that he can handle emotions, even when allowing himself to feel anxiety. Lastly, the patient should show compassion towards himself in all situations and realize that life is bigger than the current situation which is causing anxiety.

5

EXCISING BAD HABITS

WHAT GOOD ARE HABITS FOR BATTLING NEGATIVE mental states? That's a fair question. Many of the exercises we've discussed thus far are intended for repeated use and not just for when you are in the midst of dealing with your personal mental issues. However, in order for almost all of them to be successful, you need to ensure that you practice them regularly which means that your basic life habits are in order as well.

FURTHERMORE, IT TURNS OUT THAT SIMPLE THINGS LIKE eating better, exercising regularly and getting more sleep also make it easier to deal with whatever else is currently on your plate. With that in mind, this chapter looks at ways you can excise common bad habits so you can focus on what matters most.

Sleep better: SLEEP DOES WONDERS FOR THE HUMAN BODY, but too much or too little leaves us unable to think clearly. Our reaction time slows and our memory clouds. Which is to say nothing of the lack of energy that naturally results from too much or too little sleep. All these things drag us down and worsen anxiety. The cure is balance. Doctors recommend that adults get seven to nine hours of sleep a night. Of course, anxiety makes it difficult for us to sleep. Beyond using the exercises we've already gone over; better sleep helps you fight back. There are quite a few things you can do to achieve this end.

Loads of sleep studies have shown that when we use electronics can disrupt our sleep. The effects of light from monitors and television screens affect our bodies much longer than we'd normally think. A good sleep hygiene practice is to unplug from screen time an hour before bed. It may also improve your mood all around if you're an avid user of social media: studies have shown that those who use social media frequently feel more isolated, even in actual social settings. Your sleep may also improve simply because you'll be processing less information before hitting the hay. This is particularly true for news junkies.

To make good sleep habitual you need to set a schedule so your body knows what to expect when. The amount of sleep is just as important as when that sleep takes place. Set a specific time when you'll be in bed and when you'll get out of bed. The latter is easy: use an alarm. In time you'll wake up before the alarm even goes off. The latter can be harder to accommodate for depending on your living situation. But if you're willing to make the changes it will pay off. On a similar note, try spending less time when you're awake in your bed itself.

. . .

A STRICT SLEEPING SCHEDULE WILL ALLOW YOU TO BE tired when you are supposed to and wake up feeling refreshed. You want to pick a time that you can have about nine hours of undisturbed sleep for example 10 pm to 7 am. You want 9 hours because it may take an hour for you to fall asleep. If anything comes up that is not urgent and involves you ruining your sleep schedule then decline it.

Some sleeping schedules may also be reversed and this can cause a lot of problems. The problems with this is that you will only be awake during nighttime and most people are awake in the daytime so you will not be able to make plans with your friends and other important things. Unless you have a job that requires you to work overnight shifts then you should try to fix your sleeping schedule immediately.

THERE ARE THREE DIFFERENT METHODS THAT WORK best for resetting your sleeping schedule these methods will also work if your sleeping pattern is just off by a few hours and you want a quick fix. The first method is to stay up until you are scheduled to sleep. This may be difficult because it involves you to be awake for over 24 hours, but if you can handle it then this is the fastest method.

THE NEXT METHOD IS ALSO PRETTY DIFFICULT BECAUSE it involves not getting adequate rest for one night and continuing throughout the whole day until you are scheduled to fall asleep. Basically how this works is that right before you fall asleep you want to set an alarm to wake you up in three or four hours. Once you wake up you must stay awake for at least 16 hours before you fall asleep. By doing this you are reversing your regular sleeping schedule by four or five hours and once you are on track you can start having a full night's sleep.

THIS LAST METHOD TAKES THE LONGEST BUT IT IS ALSO the easiest out of the three. It's easier than the other two methods because it doesn't require you to stay up for hours and hours with little sleep. To do this method you want to either try going to bed one or two hours earlier or later then what you are used to. So say for example you usually go to bed at 1 am and you wake up at about 9 am, and your goal is to be in bed by 8 pm and wake up at 5 am.

THE FIRST DAY YOU DO THIS METHOD YOU GO TO BED two hours earlier then what your used to so, in this case, it would be 11 pm. Then the next day it would be 9 pm. Then from here, you can just go to bed an hour earlier to make it 8 pm which is your goal. Depending on how far your original sleeping schedule is compared to your goal will determine how long this process may take.

Get More Active: IT'S WELL KNOWN HOW PHYSICAL activity relieves stress. But research has proven time and time again that exercise also battles anxiety the same way it battles depression. According to the Mayo Clinic, exercise releases endorphins to create a natural "high" of sorts. On top of this exercise signals the immune system to halt production of chemicals triggered by anxiety that worsen your symptoms. Though unproven, it's believed that the elevated body temperature resulting from a rigorous workout has a therapeutic effect on the nervous system. Regular exercise can improve your health all around.

. . .

BUT A LOT OF US SIMPLY DON'T LIKE THE IDEA OF IT, and that's a major hurdle. Whether it's the idea of gyms or feelings of inadequacy, we just don't want to get off our duffs and do something. This is where framing how we think comes in really handy. Exercise doesn't have to mean "exercise" with weights and machines. Exercise is merely a physical activity. Anything that you can do that gets you moving qualifies. Anything as simple as a walk around the block or a swim in the pool is enough. And if you frame it this way, it's easier to think of ways to incorporate other people into what you're doing, making it a social event, too, filling that emotional need.

IF YOU LIVE AN INACTIVE LIFE STYLE OR HAVE BEEN inactive for a long period of time, you'll want to start small before going all out. Your end goal should be to engage in some form of physical activity every day, but when you start it's helpful to aim for every other day instead, just to get in the swing of it. It also isn't necessary to total exhaust yourself, either.

YOUR DEPTH OF SLEEP AND AMOUNT OF REST YOU GET plays a role in the energy you have over the course of the day. The higher your level of physical activity, the better your sleep. When higher physical activity and better sleep are two goals you are working towards, the two will naturally complement each other, magnifying their benefits.

IF YOU HAVEN'T EXERCISED IN A WHILE YOU CAN consider the following a basic introduction to the types of exercises you can get started with in an easy and (relatively) painless fashion.

First and foremost, however, it is important to keep in mind that everyone's body is different which means that what is right for you, might differ from what is suggested here. Have a clear idea of what your body is always trying to tell you, and never push yourself further than you feel comfortable with. It is always better to play it safe today, and train tomorrow then push too hard today and have to sit out for a week or more with a torn muscle instead.

It is important to always take the time to warm up before any strenuous activity as getting started directly without warming first is a great way to seriously hurt yourself in the process. Warming up properly will also help to raise your overall core temperature which helps make your muscle more elastic and more willing to benefits from the exercise you are doing. Additionally, taking the time to warm up properly will ensure that the maximum amount of blood flow is getting to and from the heart which will further help you successfully push your body to the limits. Regardless of the reasons, start every workout, no matter how minimal, with a good warmup first.

While it is natural to want to always push yourself as hard as possible, in reality, a training regimen that involves alternating intensities is actually more effective in the long run. Not only will it help you to continue exercising regularly without injury, but the variation is also better when it comes to producing reliable muscle growth. Finally, it gives your body extra time to recover from the more intense workouts while not simply sitting around doing nothing. This means that your intense days can actually be more intense because you know you will have a rest before you have to do it all again.

JUST LIKE IT IS IMPORTANT TO ALWAYS WARM UP BEFORE you exercise, it is equally important to take a few extra minutes at the end of your workout session to cool down properly with a little light cardio and some additional stretching. Not only will this prevent your muscles from cramping up on you later, but it will also actually help improve their growth because the cooldown ensures that they are receiving an appropriate amount of blood to maximize growth.

STARTING WITH BASIC YOGA EXERCISES IS A GREAT LOW-impact way to get started. As a physical practice, yoga can offer many benefits, and one of the best aspects of yoga as a physical practice is that there are variations of each pose that anyone can do.

HERE WE WILL TAKE A LOOK AT THE BASIC STRUCTURE of a sun salutation. After learning this sequence, you'll have a better understanding of not only what a sun salutation is, but also how to do the foundational poses that are often found in a yoga class. Of course, a sun salutation is only the starting block. There are so many other wonderful poses that yoga can offer you.

- Tadasana: The first pose of the sun salutation is known as mountain pose or This pose itself it quite simple. You stand with both of your feet on the ground at the top of your mat. Your hands should be by your side, with your palms facing away from you.

- Urdhva Hastasana: Technically, this pose is referred to as, "upward hands pose" pose, so it may just be easier for you to refer to it as urdhva hastasana. After your hands are by your sides, you raise them over your head. Some people think of this part as the actual "saluting" of the sun during a sun salutation. The arms go over the head, with the palms facing towards one another.

- Uttanasana: After your arms are over your head in urdhva hastasana, the next pose is known as "uttanasana" or forward fold. Often, people will bring their hands from overhead through their heart's center so that the palms touch, before they hinge at the hips and fold forward.

- Chaturunga Dandasana: In English, Chaturunga Dandasana can be translated to mean "four-limbed staff pose". After you've lifted the gaze, found a flat back and have lengthened your spine, the next step in the sun salutation is to shoot your legs back into a plank-like position and bend the elbows so that you're in a low push up.

- Urdhva Mukha Svanasana: The next pose in the sequence is known in English as "Upward-Facing Dog" pose. After moving into your low pushup, you will begin to straighten your arms into this position on the inhale.

- Adho Mukha Svanasana: The downward facing dog is performed on the exhale following the inhale from upward facing dog. Instead of having the hips and pelvis bent towards the floor, the hips rise up so that your seat is high in the air.

Improve your eating habits: We live in the golden age of convenience. It does make our lives easier—until it reaches our diet, that is. Grocery stores are brimming with pre-made meals and frozen dinners. Fast food restaurants are everywhere. When we're hungry it's easy to reach for one of these options and not think much of it. After all, they're quick and cheap most of the time. All the better! But what they say is true: we are what we eat. And what goes into those does more than curb our appetites.

What we consume fuels our body, but what that fuel is takes its toll on our physical and mental state. Some things found in food and drinks can make anxiety symptoms worse. Complicating matters further is that many of these things are found in what many consider "comfort food," the things we turn to when we want to feel better. At the time, we're consuming them we feel better because we're responding to a need, but when the moment passes the real effects take hold. Building a better diet to combat anxiety requires you to eliminate or reduce unwanted elements and replacing them with healthier alternatives.

THE BIG BAD IS CAFFEINE. AS A STIMULANT, IT RAISES your heartbeat and can cause shaking, which exasperate the feelings of anxiety. Caffeine is so prevalent in drinks that we hardly think about it. When we do it's usually as some sort of anti-sleep agent, which is true to a degree, but how it does this is harmful. Using caffeinated drinks as a "pick-me-up" for low sleep nights tells your body the lie that it doesn't need as much sleep as it actually does. Soda and coffee offer little to nothing in terms of positive returns and should be the first things to be kicked to the curb.

FRIED FOODS ALSO POSE A MAJOR RISK, AND NOT JUST TO your physical well-being. Fried foods are more difficult for your body to digest, making it harder overall for your body to digest anything. The stress this causes you makes your anxiety symptoms much worse.

DAIRY FOODS, WHILE NOT OVERLY DANGEROUS, NEED TO be closely moderated. Here's why: dairy can spike adrenaline levels, which feeds anxiety. This category is all-too-often overlooked because dairy, in general, is good for you.

IN ADDITION TO CUTTING DOWN THESE ELEMENTS, there are some types of food that may help to fight anxiety:

VEGETABLES ARE A MUST. THEY'RE RICH IN VITAMINS

and minerals. While this doesn't sound special in and of itself, you have to remember that those with anxiety disorders and depression usually aren't getting enough of even the most basic nutritional needs. Vegetables are a quick way to stock up and replenish.

Of course, one can't talk about vegetables without also bringing up fruit. Much like their leafy counterparts, fruits are brimming with the "good stuff" your body craves. But fruit's real role in your diet is to provide natural sugars. Processed food and soft drinks tend to use processed sugar. The sudden rush of energy amplifies the physical symptoms of anxiety by a tremendous amount. Stick to fresh fruit (and veggies, too) to ensure that you're avoiding needless additives.

A surprising but a simple fix is to increase your water intake. Dehydration drags your body down and can trigger feelings of anxiety. Shoot for eight glasses a day.

By now you should have noticed that the dietary recommendations fall in line with general healthy eating guidelines. That's no coincidence: your physical well-being and your mental well-being are directly linked. When your body gets the proper nutrition your mind balances out, too.

When you first begin transitioning to a healthier diet, you may find that you routinely get cravings for specific types of foods that are now off of the table. One of the biggest reasons that many people fail to start a new diet once they have committed to it is they don't account for just how addictive many types of processed foods really are. Don't fall victim to the lure of unhealthy options, have a plan in place by keeping the following list in mind. The next time you get a craving, consider countering it in the following ways.

- Replace chocolate ice cream with chocolate flavored fat free Greek yogurt.
- Replace an ice cream sundae with frozen yogurt topped with fruit.
- Replace cheese doodles with non-processed cubes of actual cheese for a snack full of healthy fats.
- Replace chips and dip with vegetables and hummus.
- Replace a candy bar with a healthy protein bar.
- Replace potato chips with a small amount of air popped popcorn.
- Replace a cheese burger with a soy or black bean patty.
- Replace other salty favorites with healthy nut options instead.

If you are heavily committed to processed foods, then you are in for an unfortunate couple of weeks. The high levels of fat and sugar that are found in most processed foods these days make many of them literally addictive. This means that when you commit to cleaning out your refrigerator and going cold turkey with healthy alternatives you will feel the physical symptoms of withdrawal, the same as those detoxing from harmful drugs or alcohol. As such, you can either prepare for an unpleasant week or so whereby your body can experience flu like symptoms, or you can go cool turkey and try and wean yourself off of the unhealthier parts of your diet slowly to make the transition less painful.

6

EXERCISES FOR COMBATING NEGATIVE THOUGHTS

NEGATIVE MENTAL STATES TYPICALLY PERPETUATE themselves through negative thinking. You worry so much that you can't stop worrying. So, there's something to be said about bad habits and how they change our lives. Think back to the explanation of self-talk for a moment. Recognizing that you're beating yourself up and substituting those thoughts and words with positive reinforcement forces you to recognize just how often you have those thoughts. But if you think a little deeper there's more to it: what brings those thoughts on? What are you doing, saying, or thinking before those thoughts take hold? What situation were you in? When you go over these answers, take note of how often these triggers occur. Are they the result of situations you find yourself in every day?

Let's use an example everyone can understand. We all want to exercise more, right? But lots of us jump into it right away with only the end goal in mind and get discouraged when things turn out to be more difficult than they had first expected. Let's say that you want to start running a mile a day, and you haven't been running regularly for a while, if ever. In this instance, you aren't conditioned for it and shooting for that one-mile goal will be an uphill battle. That's why it's beneficial to break it down into smaller pieces. Depending on your fitness level you may start by running a quarter mile every other day as a means to ease yourself into it. Once you've done this for a while it feels easy for you, try running a quarter mile every day. When that challenge is conquered add more distance. Keep adding until you've reached your ultimate goal of one mile every day.

Behavioral activation: The theory of behavioral activation states that negative life events, over a prolonged period of time, can lead to scenarios where individuals do not experience enough positive reinforcement for a prolonged period of time. This, in turn, can lead to additional unhealthy behaviors such as social withdrawal, unhealthy drug use or erratic sleeping patterns. These patterns might provide some amount of temporary relief but are ultimately just generating a greater number of negative outcomes.

When utilizing behavioral activation, you will want to find something you know you are good at, and also find a way to demonstrate your skill on a regular basis. The positive reinforcement that you receive will then, slowly but surely, transfer over into other aspects of your life as well. This, in turn, will make it easier to replace your avoidance behaviors with something more productive and rewarding.

If you feel as though you don't have any worthwhile skills at all, don't sell yourself short, everyone has skills that set them apart. Just because your skills aren't flashy or generally appreciated by the masses, doesn't mean there isn't a niche out there that will appreciate everything you are able to do. Searching out niche forums online is also a good way to find a way to display your talent in such a way that the right people are around to appreciate it.

Remember, this doesn't have to involve you getting up on a stage and doing a thing, there are any number of ways you can be appreciated. For example, if you are excellent at planning and organizing events, then find a local charity and volunteer your time for their next big fundraiser. You'll help make the event a success, raise a bunch of money for a good cause and feel great about yourself as a result. Likewise, if you are a great cook, you don't need to go and become a professional chef, all you need to do is invite a number of friends over for a nice meal.

Finally, after you find an activity that actively serves to boost your overall confidence level, the final step is to keep it up on a regular basis. While being showered in praise once likely won't do all that much for your anxiety on its own, eventually you will be surprised at what having confidence in one area of your life is going to do for your overall mindset. Once you find the right positive outlet for your skill, you will find that making positive enforcement a regular part of your routine can just as easily make your anxiety a thing of the past.

Seek out new reasons for positive thoughts: Creating positive associations is a cumulative process which means that every time you entertain a negative though you are hampering the overall potency of any potential positive associations that come out of the situation. To ensure that stray negative thoughts don't ruin your overall positive experience, there are several different things you can try.

First, if you find that you routinely start off new situations with negative thoughts about the things you are going, the places they take you or the people you are doing them with, then you may find it useful to instead train their minds to pick out a handful of positive things about every room they enter. Not only will this make it easier for you to create positive associations overall, but it will also stop your mind from starting off every new situation from a negative perspective. Furthermore, it will help to train your mind to look at every new situation through a filter of its positive aspects instead of its negative ones.

Another good way to build up similar habits is to take a set amount of time out of your day, each and every day, to work on cognitively reframing the issues that are bothering you at the time. This exercise is especially helpful if you have a partner to bounce positive affirmations off of because you will be able to feed off one another's positive energy which will be especially helpful on the days that one, or both, of you, really isn't feeling it and needs a little something extra to make it through the day.

Look at core beliefs: The thoughts that you have in any situation are always going to be influenced by what is known as your core beliefs. These are going to be thoughts that you hold in a much higher regard than anything else you come across, so much so that they can be thought of as the lens that determines how you perceive the world. For those with a high level of anxiety, their core beliefs may look some like:

- The world is generally a dangerous place
- Everything will always work out for the best
- People are mostly good
- I am unlovable

Your core beliefs are not something that you come to overnight, rather they develop over a prolonged period of time based on the experiences that you have had in your own life. Unfortunately, just because you drew a specific conclusion from a certain experience, doesn't mean that it is the right one. Indeed, it could be the completely opposite lesson from how the world works. While having core beliefs that are a little out of whack isn't normally that serious, for those with a high level of anxiety, their beliefs can make the world seem far more dangerous and complicated than it really is.

Your core beliefs can be thought of as a series of filters that each of your thoughts, even your automatic thoughts must pass through, and pass muster with in order for them to be passed along to interact with emotions and actions. For example, if you have a core belief that tells you that you are unlovable, then even if you spend the day with a friend and have a lovely time, you will find yourself questioning the legitimacy of the friendship and whether the other person is simply spending time with you because they feel sorry for you; you are, after all, unlovable so there must be some ulterior motive in play.

Faulty core beliefs often lead to negative thought patterns that are collectively known as cognitive distortions. These then often end up reinforcing existing negative emotions and thoughts. These are often especially common in those with elevated levels of anxiety and tend to manifest themselves in a variety of harmful ways.

Common cognitive distortions include:

- Minimization or magnification: This type of cognitive distortion leads to the minimization of positive events and the exaggeration of negative events such as seeing your achievements as meaningless and your mistakes as being extremely earth-shattering.
- Catastrophizing: This type of cognitive distortion is very common in those with anxiety and leads to those who utilize it to only see the worst potential outcome for a potential situation.

- Overgeneralization: This type of cognitive distortion leads to the mistake of making broad generalizations of a situation based on a single event.
- Magical thinking: This type of cognitive distortion leads to an association between events that are otherwise unrelated.
- Personalization: This type of cognitive distortion leads to an assumption that you are responsible for things that are actually beyond your control.
- Mind reading: This type of cognitive distortion leads to the assumption that it is possible to determine the beliefs and thoughts of others despite adequate evidence.
- Fortune telling: This type of cognitive distortion is also common in those with high levels of anxiety and it assumes that a situation will turn out poorly despite any concrete evidence to support that assumption.
- Emotional reasoning: This type of cognitive distortion is based on the assumption that your emotions accurately reflect the way things actually are.

If you were able to view the world through the perception filters of another person you would likely be able to pick out their cognitive distortions without even trying. For example, if you were friends with the student who felt stupid after failing the midterm you would easily be able to see why this was not the case. Nevertheless, even when directly confronted with your own cognitive distortions you are likely going to find them much more difficult to overcome, which is likely why they persist at all. For most people, if they don't make a conscious effort to see through their own distortions they will remain in place indefinitely no matter how much they actually differ from the real world.

If you feel as though you are one of these unlucky individuals, there are multiple different ways that you can go about breaking through your own cognitive distortions, regardless of how long they might have been influencing you, through a process known as cognitive restructuring. These techniques can be used both daily, in an effort to maintain a positive mindset, and also during times of extreme duress when you find yourself unable to avoid your triggers. With enough time and practice you will be able to start seeing the seams between your cognitive distortions and the real world, and eventually, you will be able to tell them apart completely.

In order to restructure your thoughts, the first thing that you are going to need to do is to become aware of when your thoughts are distorting the truth of the matter. While cognitive distortions can come in a wide variety of shapes and sizes, the one thing they will have in common is that they will try and force you to see the world differently than it truly is. As such, the way to ensure that this ceases to be an issue is to become more aware of when they are affecting the way you respond to specific situations.

Once you are more aware of when cognitive distortion is occurring, you will then be able to more easily respond to the situation in a way that is productive, instead of simply being along for the ride. To start, you simply need to ask yourself how else you could be thinking about whatever it is that is going on. You may also find it helpful to consider what the worst-case scenario in the current situation could be. With that in mind, you will likely find that you start to feel better when you consider how likely that scenario is to actually occur.

Socratic questioning: Based on the teachings of the ancient philosopher Socrates, the goal of this exercise is to use a basic group of questions to explore the complicated beliefs that underline these types of assumptions. Using this method should help you to determine if you are responding to a situation accurately or if you are viewing the situation through the filter created by a cognitive bias. Once you are aware of your inaccurate thoughts it will then be much easier to pay them no mind.

To ensure this is not the case, ask yourself the following questions:

- Am I reacting the way I am for a specific reason, or is it just a force of habit?
- Am I looking at a complex situation in a way that is overly simplified?
- What evidence supports this thought?
- Am I basing this thought of facts, or is it simply based on feelings?
- Is this thought realistic based on any available evidence?

When working your way through these questions, it is important to take your time and really think about your answers, not simply rush through to say you gave them. Keep in mind that, when explored fully, these questions can really help you, but only if you take the time to consider the situation accurately in the first place. This means you may need to spend a few minutes on each question in order to ensure that you come up with the best answers possible. With practice, the amount of time required will likely decrease, and you will also feel the need to use the process less frequently as your answers are often going to come out the same.

Seek out negative thinking traps: By now it should be clear to you that your thoughts affect not only the way in which you see yourself but the world around you as well. While this normally isn't much of an issue of concern, if your anxiety has progressed to the point where you have developed the types of thinking traps, or cognitive distortions, discussed in chapter 1, then this exercise will help you to excise them from your mind once and for all.

This exercise is going to use coping statements to help you to convince your mind that you are able to deal with the situations that your cognitive distortions see as untenable, to the point where they fade into the background. When it comes to ensuring that they help, it is important that your coping statement be as personalized to your situation as possible.

If your anxious thought is that you are never going to improve at a skill or activity that you want to improve at, then you could replace this thought with a more productive thought such as:

- I have made changes before and can do so again.
- I have a support system in place that will help me through this difficult time.
- I have to simply take things one day at a time.
- Don't beat yourself up, at least you are trying.

Other useful coping statements include:

- Just go for it.
- Taking time for myself is perfectly acceptable.
- My anxiety does not define me.
- Food is fuel.
- I am smart, health and strong.
- I am capable of making good choices.
- My life is mine to do with as I will.
- Practice makes perfect.
- In 10 years' time, this will not matter.
- I deserve respect.
- My thoughts do not define my reality.
- The worst-case scenario practically never occurs.
- My best will be good enough a vast majority of the time.

- Being anxious will not prevent me from tackling this situation head on.
- I have time for me.
- I deserve a break.
- Practice, practice, practice.

7
EXERCISES FOR COMBATING DEPRESSION

MMT: THERE ARE MANY WAYS TO HELP SOMEONE ADJUST their negative behavioral patterns with CBT. In multimodal coaching, the emphasis is placed on the distinct dimensions of the human personality:

Behavior

- These are the traits that an individual may present
- Effect: Positive or negative influence our emotions
- Sensation: Automatic sensations in our bodies like sweating, heart racing, tension, etc.
- Imagery: Mental pictures
- Cognition: Our thought processes
- Interpersonal: Relationships

These aspects can be easily remembered by using the acronym, BASIC ID. While all people experience these same dimensions in one form or another, it also has room to address the uniqueness of each individual. You can think of it in the same way music is composed. Music is always composed of the same notes on the scale yet, no musical pieces are exactly alike. The same is true for the billions of people who have these seven dimensions in their personality, you may find some that are similar but none of them are exactly the same.

The goal of the MMD is to help the individual make the changes necessary to move them from their current personality to become a more progressive and better individual. It is not likely that any of us will reach our full potential, however, by applying the MMD model, it can help us pinpoint the areas in our personality that may need adjusting and help us make those changes.

In this type of therapy, the patient is asked a series of questions relating to these modalities to help determine exactly what kind of help they need. For example:

- Behavior: What behavior would you like to see more or less of?
- Effect: What emotion do you want to change?
- Sensation: What sensations would you like to eliminate or would you like to experience more?
- Imagery: What would you prefer to see in your mind's eye?
- Cognition: What thoughts would you like to have? Which ones would you like to start or stop?
- Interpersonal relationships: What kind of changes would you like to make socially?
- Biological intervention: What health habits or physical issues would you like to overcome?

The answers to these questions will help the therapist and patient determine a set of goals, a course of action, and a timeline. What follows is an example of how MMT might be used to help someone who is dealing with depression.

- Behavior: If the client is having trouble getting out of bed on a regular basis, and as such has grown disconnected from many facets of their life, then MMT would suggest setting daily goals as a means of connecting with the world once more.
- Affect: Assuming that the client's issues with depression were based on incorrectly based feelings of guilt at the death of a parent (through no fault of the client), then the MMT therapist would likely probe the triggers that are associated with the guilt.
- Sensation: If the depression is having the opposite effect on the client and is actually causing them to have difficulty sleeping, then the MMT therapist will likely recommend a variety of relaxation exercises including proper breathing techniques and mindfulness mediation, possibly even self-hypnosis, to help ensure that they get a good night's sleep.
- Imagery: If the client is experiencing issues with their self-image that is leading to their depression, or if they are having trouble viewing the future in a positive way; then the MMT therapist would work to help them to replace the negative thoughts they are experiencing with positive alternatives instead. This would be done through a variety of CBT-based techniques.
- Cognition: If the client is using their depression as a filter through which to view the rest of the world, then this is a classic example of a cognitive distortion and the therapist would then offer up alternative methods by which to view the situation without having the bias stuck to it.
- Interpersonal relationships: As the client in this example is missing out on interpersonal contact as a result of their depression, the MMT therapist would focus on ways to remind the patient of the importance of their support

group as well as offer up assertiveness exercises and other ways to initiate positive social interactions.
- Dependence: If the client is known to use prescription or nonprescription drugs to make themselves feel better, then MMT will make it a point to monitor and moderate use until a more permanent solution can be found.

While all types of CBT are more effective with the help of a mental health care professional, you can start practicing multimodal therapy for yourself by taking stock of your current situation and determine if you are experiencing any negative behaviors, emotions, sensations, dependencies, imagery, attitudes, thoughts or beliefs or a deterioration of interpersonal relationships. After you have found the results, you must trace them back to the cause. Once the cause has been found you can determine if it is something that can be handled by yourself, with your personal support group or with the help of a mental health care professional.

Conceptualizing your behavior model: The first step in helping to control your depression is recognizing what the behaviors are that are preventing you from experiencing more positive emotions in your life. By identifying these cycles you can pinpoint the exact behavior that is resulting in you not feeling better in your day to day life, thus giving you the opportunity to change that behavior. The easiest way to identify what your exact cycle is involves an activity log and consistent journaling in this log. You want to jot down nearly every activity that you are doing, what emotions coincide with that activity, and anything else that particularly stands out to you in that moment. By doing this over several days you will begin to see patterns in your activities, just like you would in your thought records when you are tracking your thoughts.

After you have developed a log over several days to give you your starting point, you can begin to identify the exact cycle that you seem to go through. For example, say you have been feeling depressed and you feel as though you have no drive or motivation to begin doing anything in your life. If you were to look at your log you might notice that you are feeling tired, so you decline invitations to go out and do things. Each time you decline an invitation you feel bad which causes you to have even lower energy levels, leaving you less likely to go out and do anything in the near future, too. This leads to a constant cycle of lowered energies because you are no longer taking the time out of your day to do things that bring you joy and lift your spirits.

From the example above, you can see that the pinpointed problem is the fatigue or lowered energy levels causing said individual to avoid going out and doing anything in their free time. You need to pinpoint exactly where your problematic behaviors lie, too, to give you a stronger understanding of what is causing you to experience your current emotional symptoms. Then, you can begin to develop a plan for how you are going to combat those problems in order to increase your positive feelings and decrease your negative or frustrating ones.

Consider your relationships: If something is toxic it means that it is poisonous, which goes to show that it is not good for you – it will only end up bringing you a lot of harm. Toxic connections are just like poison, they do you more and no good at all. They can be in the form of relationships, friendships, family ties, and even work situation.

If you are not sure whether you are in a toxic relationship – there are signs that can look out for in order to figure out whether the relationship is good for you.

Are you feeling drained in the relationship? Is the lack of trust? Is there a lot of negativity in the relationship? Does it make you unhappy? Are there constant challenges? Is there never-ending criticism? Is the relationship stagnant? These are just a few questions that you can ask yourself concerning the relationship. If your answer to these questions was yes, then you are more than likely in a toxic relationship.

If you want to change how you think you also need to change the people around you who are causing these kinds of thoughts inside of you. In your journey to full recovery, you cannot leave any stone unturned. If you continue keeping connections that still cause stress and depression in your life you are likely to suffer from a relapse.

Even though leaving people that you are used to hanging around is hard since you are not sure of what will happen next, you should ask yourself what value they add to your life. Nobody wants to be alone in fact, it is never easy for some, and for this reason, some people choose to be in relationships that are bad for them. Why is it so important to break this kind of ties?

Think of it this way, you are better off alone than in bad company. Being alone is not the same as being lonely. No matter the ties that you have with the party, you should not let yourself be ill-treated. Leave the bad relationship. After you do that, it is always good to look back and see the signs that you missed before getting into the relationship but you ignored them. This will mainly apply to romantic relationships.

8
EXERCISES FOR COMBATING PHOBIAS

UNSURPRISINGLY, FEAR LIVES AT THE HEART OF EVERY phobia. But it isn't the usual, healthy fear that everyone feels from time to time. Whereas healthy fear prompts us to make a decision and fades as we move forward, anxiety creates a fear that persists long after the trigger is behind us. It sticks to us like a shadow, and as time passes by it worsens until it's well beyond our control and has come to dominate our lives.

What many people find when they begin CBT is that when they stop to analyze what triggers their phobias and what thoughts said phobias produce, the fear is often both irrational and out of proportion. It's a tremendous relief to be sure, but how do we get to a point where we can even see the distortions that clearly?

Let's talk about the distortion first. As mentioned previously,

Fear, to a degree, is a healthy response to the things and situations we perceive as dangerous. It may influence a decision we make for a brief period of time but once that decision is made it's gone. The prolonged fear through phobia follows us around because our attention is fixated on the trigger moment; we never give ourselves the chance to put the fear behind us. As a result, we feel as though we need to be constantly on guard. And as we keep thinking about it our brain scrambles to find more and more ways for what we fear to become a reality, limiting how we choose to live our lives.

Even more damaging is how we eventually find other things to become afraid of: “Well, this may not happen, but what if this does?” Because of the cyclical nature of our thinking, we seek these things out even though they make us totally miserable. It's almost like an addiction, and in short order, we have a list of reasons to be afraid that's increasingly more removed from where we started. To get on with living we need to take a step back and put them in proper perspective. Generally, you can do this by trying one of the strategies outlined below.

Play the script until the end: This strategy involves examining what the worst case scenario is in a given situation. It is especially helpful for those dealing with intense fear and anxiety. This exercise is beneficial in helping you determine what your underlying fear outcomes are. The idea behind this technique is to conduct a thought experiment or a ‘rehearsal” in your mind. You set out to imagine the worst possible outcome to a situation, and then let the event play out in your mind. By doing this, you can learn that no matter what happens, things will likely turn out okay.

To start you will want to articulate what you're afraid of. Is it a consequence of something you think you've done? Is it how you perceive others will feel about you, and if it is, be honest with yourself and put it down on paper. The benefit of having your fear in a tangible form this way cannot be understated.

Now write how you think this could come to reality. This part proves to be difficult for some, but it's also very revealing to how you think. How does what you fear become reality? Explain it in fine detail. Connect as many dots, as many as there may be.

Finally, how realistic is the result? Let's say that, for example, you have a phobia regarding being around large groups of people and you avoid going out with friends. One of your fears could be that they'll learn of something embarrassing you did years ago and will think less of you because of it. How would they learn about it? Obviously, you don't want to tell them, so it must be some other way. Does someone else know?

Perhaps an old friend you haven't seen in a long time was present. They could resurface ad decide to tell everyone. It's entirely possible, sure, but how possible is it? This is where the details of the previous step come into play. How many dots did you have to connect to make your fear reality? This is a useful way to gauge how plausible your fears may or may not be. Of course, because of the way your phobia distorts your thinking, you may find it difficult to see things as they really are. This is when an outside perspective—like that of a professional therapist—can be useful.

Situation exposure hierarchies: This exercise involves putting all of the things that you find yourself avoiding because of your current issues on a list, and then rate each on a scale from 0 to 10 in terms of how much trouble the list item causes you. For example, someone with severe social anxiety might place asking someone out on a date at the top of his list with a rating of 10, but asking for someone to hold the elevator might be at the bottom of the list with a rating of 2.

It is important to be thorough when you make your list so that you don’t have any serious jumps between numbers. The end goal of this exercise is to slowly work your way from the bottom of the list to the top so that each new activity slowly adds to your overall level of discomfort. The idea is that by the time you have mastered the activity you will have become used to that level of your specific stressor, so you can more easily move on to the next. As such, it is important to not get ahead of yourself and try and bite off more than you can chew at once. A slow and steady buildup is going to be far more effective than a dramatic spike all at once. Journaling is sometimes combined with exposure therapy so that you can record and understand how you felt during the exercise, and how you managed the feelings that you had.

An example of exposure therapy would be if you were afraid of bees and wasps and you eventually worked your way up to being able to put yourself in the vicinity of them to illicit the fearful response. Then, as you are in their presence and the fear begins to arise, you recall information about bees and wasps that remind you about how positive they are to the environment and about how unlikely it is that you would be stung by one. As you continue to remain in their vicinity and allow the fear to run its course.

Interoceptive exposure: Interoceptive Exposure is another technique used to treat panic disorder and anxiety. It involves exposure to feared bodily sensations that simulate how they feel during a panic attack. The purpose is to then challenge the unhelpful and automatic thoughts that have been associated with these sensations, and to be able to manage them in a controlled environment. During interoceptive exposure, individuals learn to maintain the sensation without panicking and learn that the symptoms and feelings that they are experiencing are not, in fact, dangerous or threatening.

Therapists use this exposure to physical sensations as a way to simulate a panic attack in order to change the experiences associated with the attacks into more benign experiences. Physical symptoms associated with panic attacks include excessive sweating, elevated heart rate, dizziness, trembling, and chest pains.

Clients who suffer from panic disorders avoid situations that might cause panic attacks. An example of such avoidance is a person gets into a car accident. Each time the person drove after that they were afraid of having an accident, which caused them to have anxiety. Due to the anxiety even small experiences while driving cause panic attacks. The person avoids driving all together to avoid the panic attacks. However, avoiding the situation only makes it worse.

In order to lessen the effects of the panic attack, the interoceptive exposure method imitates the physical symptoms of a panic attack. This can be done by holding the head down between the legs and pull up quickly to produce a head rush. Other examples are to breathe very quickly to induce hyperventilation or spin around in a chair to mimic dizziness. Repeated exposure to the physical symptoms makes panic attacks easier to deal with when they do occur.

Interoceptive exposure should only be done with the help of a licensed therapist. Clients unfamiliar with the technique could hurt themselves by attempting to reproduce the panic attack on their own and are unlikely to get any therapeutic value out of it. Before starting interoceptive exposure the client should discuss with the therapist the methods he or she plan to attempt.

To practice dealing with the issues that particular sensations call forth, practice the following.

Breathing

- Rapidly breathe in and out, taking full breathes each time (1 minute)
- Hold your nose and breathe through a straw (2 minutes)
- Hold your breath (30 seconds)

Physical exercise

- Run in place (2 minutes)
- Walk up and down the stairs (2 minutes)
- Tense all the muscles in your body (1 minute)

Spinning or shaking

- Spin as fast as you can while sitting in an office chair (1 minute)
- Spin while standing as fast as you can (1 minute)
- Shake your head back and forth before looking straight ahead (30 seconds)
- Put your head between your legs and then stand up quickly (1 minute)
- Lie down for a minute and then stand up quickly (1 minute)

Unreality

- Stare at yourself in a mirror (2 minutes)
- Stare at a blank wall (2 minutes)
- Stare at a florescent light and then read something (1 minute)

Nightmare exposure and rescripting: Nightmares are unavoidable. Individuals are likely to have bad dreams if they are dealing with heavy issues in their lives. This is a technique that is used by in CBT to help the individual to replace the feelings they had after having a nightmare. If the nightmare caused intense fear in the person, the emotions can be redirected into something that is more positive.

In order to arouse the feelings you experience in relation to your nightmares, you must first begin to recall them in as much detail as you possibly can. As you do, the emotions accompanying the nightmares should begin to arise once more, typically overcoming you sometimes in a rather intense manner. With these emotions now stirring up once again you can identify what emotion you would rather experience and develop a new image associated with your desired emotion. After moving back and forth through the process of awakening the emotions relating to the nightmares and then rescripting them with new desired emotions and images you train your mind to adjust its focus each time the nightmare is aroused. Typically, what will end up happening during your sleep then is that if the nightmare begins to start up your mind will naturally switch to the preferred emotion and image that you have rescripted it with. As a result, you should no longer experience disturbing nightmares anymore.

Note that when you are dealing with nightmare rescripting it can take time since nightmares themselves typically happen when you are asleep, therefore it can be challenging to tap into them with your conscious mind. You might need to continually use the rescripting method for several nights over before you find complete freedom from your nightmares. If you do not experience instant relief you need to continue practicing your rescripting process until the nightmares begin to go away. Trust that as long as you stay committed they will disappear in due time and you will no longer have the disturbing or distressing experience of your nightmares.

❧ 9 ❧
EXERCISES TO COMBAT ANXIETY

Rational Emotive Behavior Therapy: Rational Emotive Behavior Therapy: The theory behind this type of exercise is that humans do not act rationally in many situations. Logic is not always a part of our make-up. Computers and machines all perform their functions rationally. They take in data, analyze its logic, and provide an acceptable output. Humans, on the other hand, receive millions of tiny little inputs every day, process them very differently from machines, and instantly produce a wide variety of outputs, some of them may fit in a lot of things but many others do not.

REBT was designed to train us to think more rationally to change our dysfunctional behaviors. Its goal is to break down our natural instincts to think irrationally and stop us from making unreasonable assumptions to make realistic assumptions instead. This could change our inappropriate and destructive behavior to much more positive ones. Since most of our negative thoughts and assumptions come from the irrational side of our beliefs, we react to them in inappropriate ways.

It is believed that most of our behavioral problems stem from these irrational assumptions and beliefs, thoughts that are not grounded in reality are the cause of our negative behavior. Addressing this issue, the ABCDE model of emotional disturbance was implemented.

When our goals and desires are blocked or inhibited by a particularly negative event in our lives, we hold ourselves back from accomplishing what we set out to do. This can lead to the development of these irrational beliefs. For example, an individual may apply for a job and prepares diligently for the interview. On the day of the interview, they take extra care to ensure that their appearance is perfect and they are ready to give the best impression possible. However, after all that effort, the hiring manager decides to give the job to someone else.

The logical conclusion is that, for some reason, you weren't the right fit for the job but someone with an irrational belief, they may conclude that the hiring manager was out to get them. Regardless of the type of negative thought that is reached, its foundation lies in the realm of unreality and can embed itself deep in the mind, triggering negative emotions and unacceptable behavior later on. To combat this type of thinking, the ABCDE model can help.

- Activating Event: An inciting event is identified, which triggers the irrational belief. This could be any number of negative experiences including an argument with someone, a car accident, or the loss of a job. It is the trauma of this event that compels the mind to create a new irrational thought or belief.
- Belief: Once the belief has been created, the mind will automatically revisit it every time a similar negative event occurs. Each time the mind goes back to the belief, it is reinforced causing the person to get stuck in a spiral of

negative behavior without ever really understanding why it happened in the first place.

- Consequences: The belief will trigger the consequences of their irrational thoughts. Some consequences could be emotional as in the case of guilt or shame while others could behavioral as in overeating or some form of substance abuse. The underlying emotions for these behaviors could be depression, lack of self-confidence, or hostility.
- Dispute: The dispute phase of the program is when you learn to challenge that belief system and see it as irrational. You begin to recognize it as the root of your problems. At this stage, you learn to argue with your subconscious mind and dispute your negative beliefs. You will be asked to come up with convincing proof that will successfully contradict your imprinted way of thinking.
- Effect: You could also call this phase reinforcement. Once you have had your internal debate and successfully convinced yourself that your irrational belief is wrong, more positive behaviors will be much easier to come by. Your self-esteem will improve, you'll be bolder, or you'll just feel a lot better overall.
- In most cases, REBT can be done without the aid of a therapist. This model can help anyone get to the root of their negative behavior and arm them with the tools they need to change. It motivates people to look deeply at how their thoughts are developed and how to apply rationale to their beliefs and replace negative thoughts with a more realistic view that will build them up rather than tearing them down.

Put your negative thoughts on trial: You may also find it useful to hold a trial for your anxious thoughts where you act as the judge, prosecutor, and defense attorney. To get started with this practice you are going to want to act as the defense attorney for the negative thought that you have had. You will want to make an argument as to why you believe that the negative thought is true and the right response to the current situation. While doing so it is important to make an effort to remove opinions, interpretations, and guesses from the argument you make and instead stick as close to the facts as possible.

With that done, you will then want to act as the prosecutor, making a case against the cognitive distortion and why it is not only inaccurate but potentially harmful in the current situation. Again, while doing so. it is important to make an effort to remove opinions, interpretations, and guesses from the argument you make and instead stick as close to the facts as possible.

Finally, you are going to want to act as the judge in this scenario and determine if the cognitive distortion represented an accurate view of the situation and the way you handled it was justified or if you should have taken an alternate approach instead. Ninety-nine times out of one hundred you will find that the more measured response is going to be the right one and the cognitive distortion only served to further exacerbate the situation.

Funeral exercise: When you're comfortable and ready to begin, start by imagining your own funeral. It's (hopefully!) a long way off, but it is inevitable. This is where privacy becomes really important. For some people, this and the following steps bring up a lot of emotions they weren't necessarily expecting. It helps if you express these things as they come, but it could be awkward to do so if there are people around, even those you are close to. Feel free to let it all out at any point in the process. With that said, you should also know your limits. If it becomes too difficult or painful, or if you sense you are moving towards a bad frame of mind while going through these steps, please stop. It is possible that if you aren't prepared, thinking about these things could worsen your anxiety or other mental health concerns.

With your funeral imagined, think about who you hope would attend. Keep this moment in the "now" by focusing on the people who are or who have been in your life and not those you have no real acquaintance with. It can take some time to determine which relationships you feel are the most important and those that you don't, so start making use of your paper here if need be. Most of us can rattle of a list of names without trouble—friends and family are always a good place to start—but take the time to really think about it as to not leave anyone out of the event.

With everyone named and imagined, give each one some time to speak. Here's where we get speculative: what would you want them to say if given the chance? How would you want to be remembered? What is the impact that you want to leave on each of these people?

People like to think that we have no control over how we're remembered, and there is an amount of truth to this in that we cannot control the thoughts of others. But our actions influence how we are seen just as they influence how we feel. So, if you want to be remembered fondly, it's entirely possible. Envision what that is like and write down what you would hope each person would say at your funeral and how to make it happen.

Learn to tolerate uncertainty: Having a plan to manage uncertainty is a part of CBT that assists people in replacing the worries they have about unpredictability using some coping mechanisms. These mechanisms allow a person to know what to do when experiencing the emotional stresses that occur when encountering a difficult situation.

A big part of anxiety is not being able to handle feelings of uncertainty and not knowing how to cope. Intolerance is an issue where a person is not willing to accept that a certain situation might or might not happen. An intolerant person is not ready to accept that some fear they have could be unlikely or unwarranted. Some of the things that an intolerant person might do include:

- Find ways to avoid situations
- Delay those situations so as not to have to deal with them
- Look for reassurance to see that their beliefs or thoughts are fine

Avoidance coping is a problem that often comes as a result of uncertainty intolerance. This is a situation where a person will try to avoid situations. That person will work very hard to avoid situations that they are unable to control or predict. This form of coping is often a threat that makes life restricted. The main reason a person engages in avoidance coping is that the person feels that something negative might happen. There might be some improper comparisons that the person is making. These include situations where a person assumes that one problem will come about following a certain action.

The best thing that a person can do is to be ready to handle the uncertainty in one's life. This can be accomplished by determining the specific behaviors one might engage in. Look at the situation that has been presented and think about the possible outcomes. People who are anxious often assume that very specific outcomes might occur. By considering at all the different outcomes, it becomes easier for someone to get find an answer about dealing with a certain situation. Look at the anxious thoughts and consider how realistic or outlandish some of the thoughts might be. Make a list of what can be controlled versus what cannot.

Decatastrophizing: When it comes to dealing with anxiety-based cognitive distortions you will then need to practice a process called decatastrophizing to make sure that you can deal with them and leave them properly stored. As they become easier to spot, you will often find that your cognitive distortions reflect reality more or less accurately, expect that one aspect is often extremely skewed.

For example, if you are someone who frequently has anxiety attacks, then prior to going on a date with someone new you may be stuck with crippling anxiety thinking about how the other person might not like you, how you will likely have nothing to talk about and all the ways you may potentially embarrass yourself. When scenarios like these are running through your head you will find that if you take the time to really think the situation through you will generally find that the potential consequences aren't nearly as dire as you may have thought from the start.

When you find your mental state slowly but surely spiraling out of control, all you need to do is stop and consider the absolute worst things that were to happen if the situation you were dwelling on came to pass, as these worse-case scenarios will rarely include death or dismemberment, then thinking through the worst outcome, as well as that which is most likely, will likely allow cooler heads to prevail.

Continuing with the dating scenario, if you thought it through to the conclusion of you making a fool of yourself, what is the worst thing that could happen? As you can't literally die from embarrassment, the worst thing that could happen is that the date could end early and you would never have to see the other person again, which as an added bonus means no one you know would ever need to hear about the way in which you made a fool of yourself. Finally, if you really think about it, then a person who would walk out on a date because of something embarrassing probably isn't a person you want to spend more time with anyway.

In general, when you use this technique you will often find that the things you were spending so much time and effort worrying about aren't really all that serious after all. This, in turn, will make it far easier for you to put aside your cognitive distortions in the short-term, while also making it much more likely that you will end up breaking through them in the long-term. Either way, it should help you stop spiraling out of control at the moment and also make it easier for you to avoid similar issues in the future.

Consider the accuracy of your thoughts: After you have come up with a list of the cognitive distortions that are causing you the most grief, the next thing you will need to do is test each of the distortions to ensure they are actually not reflecting reality in any meaningful way. These rules or assumptions can make it easier to stick to a moral code, but they can also limit or frustrate us for no good reason. In order to get started with this exercise, the first thing you are going to want to do is to think about all of your assumptions in an effort to determine if they are valid in an effort to determine which you are going to modify.

The second step is to determine how the assumption currently affects your daily life, in both positive and negative ways, if applicable. After you have determined the scope of its impact on you, you will then need to consider where it first came from. Don't worry if this is something you haven't thought about before, this is rarely the sort of thing that people question on their own. With this out of the way, you will then be able to compare its advantages and disadvantages, of which there may be more than one.

Learn to be soul-centered: When you are self-centered, you are consumed with the things that are happening in your life. Your mind is only filled with the negative emotions that you have towards a certain situation and you are not focused on finding a solution. You are too fixated on the problem that you have such that you are unable to see other things that revolve around you. However, when you are soul-centered you are filled with compassion towards other people and yourself. You are able to acknowledge that you have challenges that you are facing in your own life, and you know that there are certain steps that you can take towards achieving your goals.

You take the time to get out of your own self and dedicate some time to help other people. When you are soul-centered you are able to see beyond your own mind and understand that other people have problems as well. Seeing things as they are, spares you a lot of time and emotional baggage. Your mind is not clouded by any false judgment. A person suffering from stress or who has a lot of underlying issues may not be able to think in the right way that they should, their mind is clouded by the wrong judgment. You can learn to take control of your thought life and come up with better ways of processing the negative thoughts in your head.

Acceptance and Commitment Therapy (ACT): This exercise is considered a third generation CBT method. It uses the fundamentals of CBT except with the ACT; it explores in more detail the role of acceptance in an individual's cognitive and emotional conundrum. ACT emphasizes the body knowledge as a method of learning what illogically happens when we try extremely hard to control our inner emotions and our thoughts. Mindfulness exercises are also used to re-experience the acceptance of our inner states.

The use of mindfulness exercises is increased in ACT because many emotional disorders have the possibility of becoming worse when attempts of over control, compulsiveness, and compensation are used. Apart from mindfulness exercises, ACT also incorporates present orientation, values exploration, the non-literal experience of our thoughts as well as the expanded definition and experience of our self. Created by Steven Hates, ACT ensures that acceptance and mindfulness are integrated scientifically to psychotherapy theory.

If you want to begin implementing ACT into your own life today, you are going to need to implement the same five-step approach that therapists use when they are helping their clients integrate ACT into their own lives. These five steps include: facing your current situation, acceptance, cognitive diffusion deliteralization, valuing as a choice, and self as context. Each of these steps it outlined in greater detail below so that you can effectively move through the therapy process on your own and experience a greater sense of acceptance in your own life towards the things that you cannot actively control.

Facing the current situation, or "creative hopelessness" as ACT therapists call it, is an imperative step in healing from any problematic emotions that you may be experiencing. In this step, your goal is to start focusing on what you have honestly tried in order to improve your experience, how much effort you have honestly exerted into this practice, and whether or not you were truly holding space for growth to happen.

The next step in effectively integrating ACT is developing acceptance skills so that you can begin to reduce your inner motivation to avoid the things that are bringing you pain in your life, such as memories associated with upsetting experiences. In this particular stage, ACT therapists will place a heavy emphasis on a practice that is known as "unhooking" which essentially means that you will be removing the belief that thoughts and emotions require follow up actions.

The next step in ACT is called cognitive diffusion deliteralization, which essentially means that you start viewing your thoughts and experiences as an ongoing process rather than as being things that are attached to any particular outcome. In other words, you need to start realizing that thoughts do not have to create your reality and that you can change your thought processes and start experiencing something more positive.

The next step in ACT is valuing as a choice, which means that you need to start identifying what you value and what gives your life meaning. When you can understand the distinction between what you value in life and what your goals are in life, it becomes easier for you to declare your values and set goals that are related to your values.

The final stage required in order to implement ACT into your life successfully is coming to understand that you are ultimately separate from your experiences which means that the things you have been through do not need to define who you are as a person. While they can certainly give you new and unique ways of looking at the world, if you don't like their outcomes there is no reason you have to keep them around. This step is all about realizing that you can successfully cast them off and never look back.

10

STICKING WITH IT

Improve your self-discipline

At this very moment, you have a big decision to make. You have the choice of staying in your comfort zone, with all your old patterns and habits, living in a way that feels as though you're always missing out. Or you can decide right now that you will use this book as the motivation you've been needing to become your greatest self. This could really be the turning point where you start to develop self-discipline and amazing willpower. This is your choice, and only you can make it. So, what do you need to do in order to improve your willpower and self-discipline?

When it comes to achieving the goals and happiness that you want out of life, there is one simple thing you can do that will increase your chances of success 10 fold: improve your self-discipline. While the requirements to achieve your goals will vary based on the specifics, they will all have one thing in common, dedication and hard work will get you there, and self-discipline will make it possible.

Studies show that the more self-discipline and self-control a person has, the happier that person is as they tend to feel as though they are generally more prepared for anything that life can throw at them. This is because, while those without self-discipline spend time motivating themselves to do things, those with self-discipline simply did them which makes them more productive overall.

While those who lack self-discipline likely think that it is an innate behavior, in all actuality it is a skill which means that like any skill it can be improved with practice over time. There are a number of ways that you can strengthen your resolve and improve your ability to maintain your self-discipline even when it may seem difficult or impossible to do so; first, however, you must understand that it is up to you, and no one else, to make better choices in the first place. Your future self is directly influenced by what you choose to do in the present, do yourself a favor and choose wisely.

The human mind is designed to enjoy cause and effect, and indeed, often goes too far and finds patterns where there are none. When it comes to improving your self-discipline, you can use this too your advantage as after the first few instances of persevering and achieving your goals, thus releasing serotonin, the chemical which causes pleasure, your mind will link self-discipline with achieving goals and be anxious to do so more often in an effort to repeat the process. As such, while it will be difficult to power through and ignore all possible distractions at first, it will be easier than that the second time, even easier the third time and will eventually feel like the easiest thing in the world.

This idea exemplifies the *paradox principle* which states that it is better to do the difficult thing in the present as that will make it easier to do in the future. Inversely this means that if you had started something the first time you thought about it you would be an expert at it by now.

Another way to ensure that you will fully commit to something even if you have not yet mastered the art of self-discipline is to apply the *buy-in principle.* The buy-in principle states that the greater the personal stake in a project, the harder you will try to ensure that the project doesn't fail. When attempting to break into new fields it is best to take on a single new project at a time as over committing to several projects, even if you have the self-discipline to finish what you start, will only lead to several subpar projects and no outstanding ones.

This is an example of the *magnification principle* which states that if you dilute your focus you dilute your results. In this ever-connected world, it can be extremely difficult to take the time to focus on a single task at a time. What separates the truly successful from the pretenders is their ability to focus all of their concentration on the right task at the right time. You must learn to have the self-discipline to avoid the temptations of social media and the vast wonders of the internet and do what you need to do.

If you find this difficult, focus on the *creation principle* which provides a simple four-step process to ensure you finish what you start. First you think it then you speak it, then you act it and finally, you do it. Thinking a thing is easy but you must ensure you have the self-discipline to see ventures through. This is why speaking it can help as by putting the thoughts into words you are making yourself accountable in ensuring the task is completed.

By directing your self-discipline completely towards the concepts of creation you help to implement the *harvest principle* which elaborates on the idea that success is simply effort magnified by proper timing and bolster by a regular routine.

Practice gratitude: When we are grateful for things we have, we are less likely to satisfy that urge for instant gratification. It takes us a step away from always wanting more of what we don't have. Take the time to appreciate all those around you and even the little things that they do.

The benefits of gratitude are probably more than you might imagine. It has not only been able to boost your mental health, but it also encourages you to be more balanced emotionally, and spiritually. Gratitude, over time, helps to make you feel like you have an abundance even when you are living with limitations.

To practice gratitude, start by taking at least 10 minutes every day noting down all the things you are thankful for. This doesn't have to be limited to physical things, but it could also be abstract things as well. Are you thankful for your family, the sunrise, your health, friends, even the food on your plate? If you can't think of anything to be thankful for, then take a closer look inside of you, there is always something, you just have to dig a little deeper to find it.

Be forgiving: Being forgiving clears the mind. Think about the last time you were angry with someone, what were you thinking about? Likely your thoughts got stuck in an endless repetition of the offence and you could think of nothing else. This doesn't mean that you have to approve of the wrong done to you, but you no longer allow that offense to take control over your mind because when it controls your mind, it will affect the whole body.

Forgiving means letting go of the negativity that zaps our strength. It is also an excellent exercise in self-discipline because usually in the beginning it is painful to let something hurtful go. We all innately want to be right and we want justice, but most of the time, the things we want are completely out of our control. So, we find ourselves spending endless days, weeks, months, and even years waiting for an opportunity to set things right for us. Look at how much of that time is wasted when we could be focusing on more important factors in our lives.

Set the right goals

Once you have lain the ground work to ensure that the change you do decide to enact is going to stick, it will be time to consider the goals that you can set to ensure you take advantage of your new mentality as effectively as possible. The best way to go about doing so is through what are known as SMART goals. Simply put, the SMART system posits that all goals should be achievable, specific, measurable, relevant and have a stiff timeline that by and large cannot be changed in order to ensure that the goals you undertake are going to be legitimately worth your time and all of the effort that you plan on exerting making them a reality.

The first SMART goal that you set should be one that is at the same time straightforward enough to more or less ensure your success while at the same time being relevant enough to your day to day life that actually succeeding will be a moment that you can easily recall in the future when success on a future goal is not nearly so assured. This way you will start forming the right type of neural pathways as soon as possible, which will then form into patterns which will eventually become habits. With this in mind, you want to start off with a goal that is, at least tangentially connected to the negative pattern that you are the most anxious to start to change. You don't need to have an exact goal in mind at this point, just the start of an idea that you can build into something larger later on. Consider the following to ensure that you are on the right track.

S: SMART goals are specific. Good goals are specific which means you should be able to concisely express them in just a few sentences. They should provide you with a clear idea of the requirements for reaching your goals along with any constraints that may prevent you from reaching them successfully. You will also want to make sure that they have a clear timeline and will want to be aware of any outside help you may need to reach them successfully.

M: SMART goals are measurable. When the goals you choose are measurable it will be clear to you how you will be able to tell if your email marketing campaign has either been a resounding success or an absolute failure. Furthermore, you should be able to split your goals into more manageable pieces and then be able to clearly measure each piece as well. Doing so will make it easier for you to remain on the path to success.

A: SMART goals are attainable: A good goal is one that is realistically attainable which means that you understand any potential roadblocks that may stand between you and the goal in question and that they will be ultimately surmountable. This means you are going to want to take a good hard look at your goal from all sides and be realistic with yourself about your chances for success. While looking at your goal through rose colored glasses might make you feel better, it is truly in your best interest to be as critical during this step as possible.

R: SMART goals are relevant. When it comes to setting financial goals for the future, it is important that you choose those that have the most relevant sub-goals when it comes to getting your financial situation as it currently stands as much in order as possible. This, in turn, will allow you to focus on aspects of the broader goal which will improve your current station in life most thoroughly. Improving your current situation will then make it easier for you to focus on larger aspects of the goal and so on and so forth until you have managed to successfully conquer your goal once and for all.

What's more, starting with the issues that are going to have the most immediate impact on your life will help your mind to more naturally associate the hard work and dedication that you are putting in now, with greater rewards further down the line, improving your dedication and determination naturally in the process. This improved mindset will them make it easier for you to commit to tasks that are even more complicated further down the line.

T: SMART goals are timely. Studies show that you are statistically more likely to continue to works towards the completion of a complicated or difficult task if it has a deadline associated with it. What this means is that you will want to determine what your ultimate goal will be, determine a timeline for completion, and then do the same for each of the sub-goals you set as well. When it comes to setting a due date for your goals, you will want to consider periods of time that are long enough to allow you to realistically experience a few setbacks along the way, without being so lax that you never actually get around to accomplishing anything. What you are shooting for is something that will force you to stop dreaming about financial freedom and start working towards it, not something so strict that you have no realistic chance of success.

Be confident enough to burn your ship: If the time of your first goal's completion is at hand and you aren't quite sure if you will have the guts to go through with it, just remember Cortez and what he did to his ships in the 1500s on the shores of South America. Cortez and his men had just made landfall after months at sea, and instead of finding a land free of inhabitants, or at least inhabitants willing to accept Spanish rule, they found a land full of those willing to fight to keep what belonged to them. Cortez knew that his men were not looking forward to the coming conflict, so he did the only thing he could do to get their morale to where it needed to be. He burned their only way home.

Cortez ordered all of his men ashore before lighting their ships on fire and swimming to meet his men while they watched the show. Now understanding that they had no choice but to succeed, his men fought as hard as they could to subjugate the locals. Despite his extreme methods, Cortez had one thing right; if you take the time to put yourself into a situation where you have no choice but to make your goal a reality, then you will have no choice but to be successful. Take a chance on yourself, burn your ships.

Keep it up

Remember not to get discouraged. Remember that you do no need to be perfect all the time and don't ignore your feelings too much. Cut yourself some slack. Do not be so hard on yourself. You want to form new habits, new coping skills. You do not want to be that person in the room that is so focused on themselves it makes people want to lie to you for fear of breaking you.

There's no way to find out more about yourself if you do not put in the hard work. Try to sweat it out and try some of the ideas here that require you to leave a seated position. A runner may stumble in the field sometimes, but he gets up and continues to run until he reaches the finish line. The true winner is not who reached the finish line first, but those that didn't give up. At times you may still have difficulty managing your emotions and holding back your inner demons, but that's normal and understandable. We're not perfect and may go the different way sometimes. But always remember what your goal is and how much improvement you've made so far.

CONCLUSION

Thanks for making it through to the end of *Cognitive Behavioral Therapy: Rewire Your Brain by Overcoming Anxiety, Depression, Phobias, and Eliminating Negative Thoughts*, let's hope it was informative and able to provide you with all of the tools you need to achieve your goals, whatever it is that they may be. Just because you've finished this book doesn't mean there is nothing left to learn on the topic, and expanding your horizons is the only way to find the mastery you seek.

Now that you have made it to the end of this book, you hopefully have an understanding of how to get started down the path to a healthier mental state using cognitive behavioral therapy, as well as a strategy or two, or three, that you are anxious to try for the first time. Before you go ahead and start giving it your all, however, it is important that you have realistic expectations as to the level of success you should expect in the near future.

While it is perfectly true that some people experience serious success right out of the gate, it is an unfortunate fact of life that they are the exception rather than the rule. What this means is that you should expect to experience something of a learning curve, especially when you are first figuring out what works for you. This is perfectly normal, however, and if you persevere you will come out the other side better because of it. Instead of getting your hopes up to an unrealistic degree, you should think of your time spent improving your mental state as a marathon rather than a sprint which means that slow and steady will win the race every single time.

Finally, if you found this book useful in anyway, a review on Amazon is always appreciated!

DESCRIPTION

The bad news is that approximately 40 million people between the ages of 18 and 54 are currently dealing with some form of anxiety that is more intense than that which is experienced by their peers. The good news is that this issue is manageable without the use of pharmaceuticals and one of the most effective ways of taking control of your mental state is through the use of cognitive behavioral therapy. If you are looking for a way to control your crippling anxiety once and for all, then *Cognitive Behavioral Therapy: Rewire Your Brain by Overcoming Anxiety, Depression, Phobias, and Eliminating Negative Thoughts* is the book that you have been waiting for.

Cognitive Behavioral Therapy (CBT) is a form of psychotherapy that seeks to analyze why you feel certain ways and how you see certain situations. Because anxiety is a reaction to these things, and because it results in distorted thinking and perceptions of reality, CBT shows patients a healthy, more realistic way to think.

First, you will learn all about cognitive behavioral therapy and the many ways it can benefit those who are in your situation. With the basics out of the way, you will learn more about the issues that cognitive behavioral therapy deals with most effectively so that you can be prepared to get started putting them behind you once and for all.

From there, you will find a wide variety of starter exercises to help you start dealing with you issues in the moment, as well as a detailed look at mindfulness meditation, what it 's good for and why you should already be practicing it. Next, you will find a discussion of the bad habits in your life and why getting rid of them will likely do your mental state a world of good along with specific chapters focusing on exercises devoted to cleansing the mind of negative thoughts, depression, phobias, and anxiety. Finally, you will find tips for sticking with it in the long-term and ensuring you remain successful throughout.

So, what are you waiting for? Take control of your mental health issues like never before and buy this book today!

Inside you will find

- The differences between the brains of those with severe mental health issues and those who don't have to deal with those issues.
- The ways in which your habits are contributing to your mental health issues and how to change them for the better.
- How fear and anxiety are connected and ways to break this connection for good
- A wide variety of exercises designed to help you start controlling your issues ASAP.

- Thought exercises which will make it easier to break free from negative thought patterns once and for all.
- ***And more…***

SELF DISCIPLINE

Develop Daily Habits to Program Your Mind, Build Mental Toughness, Self-Confidence and Willpower

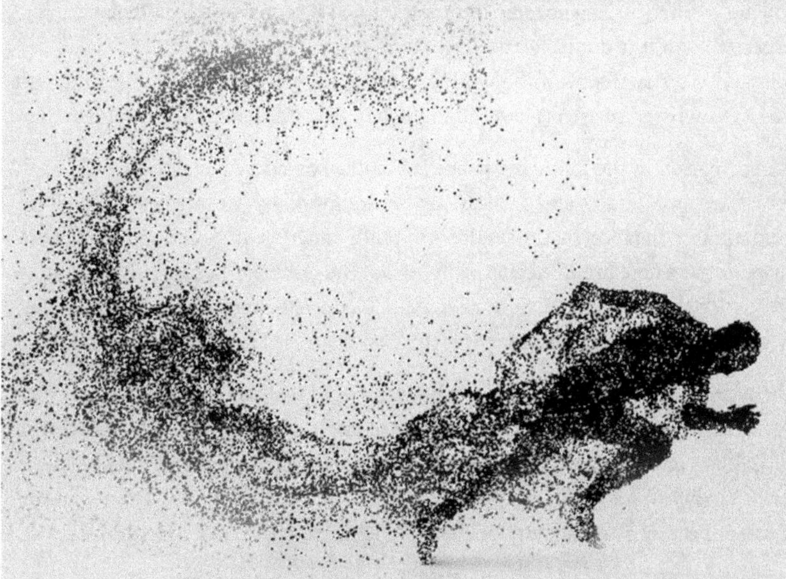

RAY VADEN

Additionally, the information in the following pages is intended only for informational purposes and should thus be thought of as universal. As befitting its nature, it is presented without assurance regarding its prolonged validity or interim quality. Trademarks that are mentioned are done without written consent and can in no way be considered an endorsement from the trademark holder.

Created with Vellum

INTRODUCTION

In *Self-Discipline: Develop Daily Habits to Program Your Mind and Build Mental Toughness, Self-Confidence, and Willpower,* Ray Vaden will show how it is possible to develop a workable plan to reach the ultimate goal of self-discipline. Self-discipline goes by many names—self-control, sense of self-worth, and self-drive. They all point to the same fact: this person is in charge of themselves and knows how to utilize their inner strengths to get what they want out of life.

Many people wonder why self-discipline is so important. They wonder why they cannot just go on as they have been going on all this time, whirling around in their merry little unorganized lives. They can—if they so choose. Self-discipline is not mandatory. It is not something that is graded and measured such as the mortgage paid and what score was achieved on the driving test. Self-discipline is a purely internal force, and whether people have it and use it or not is a purely personal decision.

However, take a moment to consider a world without personal self-discipline. Think about what that might look like. In this world, no one has self-discipline. No one worries about getting anything finished in a timely manner. There are no priorities. There are no goals. Everyone just wanders through life happy and ignorant, choosing to ignore the fact that a better world might exist somewhere. This happy life is all well and good until the lights go out because the power was shut off because someone did not pay the power bill.

Now, imagine the same world where everyone has a sense of self-discipline. Of course, some people will be more highly developed than others—and that is okay—because everyone develops self-discipline at their own personal rate. Now, in this world, order and organization reign supreme. Bad habits are at a minimum. Good habits abound like happy little snowflakes floating everywhere. People are successful. Work gets done. The power bill gets paid, so no one is eating dinner in the dark.

Maybe that was embellished a bit, but it does paint a compelling picture. Life is so much better when the people running it possess a good sense of self-discipline. Self-control and self-discipline give humans the power to do anything they want to do. People with self-discipline are more successful at work because they are able to do more work in less time and really impress their bosses. Self-employed people with good self-discipline are able to take regular days off work to enjoy life because they, too, get more work done in less time. Now, they are impressing their families. In life, people with self-discipline are generally healthier because they know what needs to be done in order to replace bad habits with good ones. They also know ways to avoid starting a bad habit in the first place. Moreover, in relationships, people with self-discipline usually enjoy a deeper, more rewarding companionship because they know how to take care of themselves and others and how not to fall into petty little relationship-breaking traps.

By showing us ways to develop useful daily habits, this book will teach us that the goal of self-discipline is not only reachable but desirable as well. From learning to create a plan to acknowledging reality in our lives—all the way though enjoying the rewards that come with self-discipline—every necessary step will be outlined in easy-to-follow details. Mr. Vaden's hope is that everyone will learn the joys and rewards of self-discipline and how it can be used to make every area of life more satisfactory and fulfilling.

I

THE POWER OF SELF-DISCIPLINE

SELF-DISCIPLINE IS EXACTLY WHAT IT SAYS—THE ABILITY to discipline oneself. It is the ability to know what to do in situations and the fortitude to actually do what is correct in the situation. It is a habit that is vital to daily success. Truly successful people are usually highly disciplined people.

No one is born with the ability to *truly* self-discipline. Babies only care about being taken care of and having their needs met. As children grow older, their parents are in charge of their discipline—at least in the beginning. Parents make the rules, and children follow them because small children lack the thought processes needed to make good decisions on a regular basis. Small children only see the here-and-now, the immediate gratification. They do not know and do not care that a bigger, better reward might be in store for them if they wait patiently. They lack foresight. As children grow older, they begin to see the reasoning behind their parent's rules. They begin to make choices that mirror the choices their parents have made for them in the past. They show that they are learning to discipline themselves. At this point, the parents may begin to step back a little and to loosen the reins. They may allow the child a bit more freedom in making decisions, with the understanding that the parent is available if the choice turns out to be unfavorable. In this way, the child learns in the safety of the home and with the protection of the parents to make good choices and formulate good decisions. The child learns to self-discipline.

In a perfect world, this is the way children would be raised. Unfortunately, this is the real world and not a perfect one. The problem is not that parents do not care about their children—it is that many parents do not *know* how to teach the art of self-discipline to their children. Maybe the parents are not self-disciplined, maybe the parents feel the child will learn it eventually, or maybe the parents simply do not want to let go complete control over the child. For whatever reason, most children are not taught self-discipline as a way of life and reach adulthood with no clue of how to be in charge of themselves.

However, the good news is that self-discipline can be learned. While best learned while growing up, as a part of learning to be an adult, it is possible to learn as an adult and begin to practice self-discipline skills immediately. Moreover, by learning self-discipline in adulthood, the person has a total by-in to the idea. This is a personal choice. This is something that needs to be done in order to enjoy a better life. This does not mean that learning self-discipline as an adult will be easier or faster, but at least, the adult who makes the conscious choice to become more self-disciplined has a personal stake in its success.

Self-discipline is nothing more than managing one's own personal affairs. It is a way of behaving where people automatically choose to do what should be done, as opposed to what would more preferably be done. It is studying for a test instead of going to a party. It is washing dirty laundry on a regular basis so that clean clothes are always available. It is following a budget so that future financial goals can be realized. Self-discipline is that inner voice controlling outward actions. It is using willpower to become mentally tough enough to control one's actions by oneself.

Almost anything that a person does to focus on an end goal rather than immediate satisfaction is self-discipline. The underlying problem is that it is always much easier to follow the path of impulse. Impulse is fun. Impulse is now. Impulse allows for joining the group and having a fun night on the town instead of studying and doing laundry. Impulse is the exact opposite of self-discipline.

Granted impulse is much more fun than discipline. Impulse gives the opportunity to have fun and be with friends. Impulse means staying up late and sleeping in tomorrow. Impulse means spending the extra money on the desirable frivolous toy and not saving anything this week. But impulse will not finish homework, wash clothes, follow a schedule, or save money. Self-discipline is needed for those things. Does this mean that impulse has no place in a life ruled by self-discipline? Absolutely not! Impulsive action is an almost automatic action. A cake is meant to be eaten. Self-discipline should never be so rigid that people go through life acting like little robots with no feelings and no desires. Everyone wants a cake. Having self-discipline just means eating one slice of cake and not the whole cake.

Practicing self-discipline requires great self-knowledge. Think about that for a minute. How can anything be changed if all the facts are not known? Imagine walking into a kitchen and seeing a small child and a puddle of water. The first instinct would be to believe the child spilled something. But what if someone else spilled something and then left the puddle on the floor? What if the pipe under the sink is leaking? Without knowing all the facts there is no way to come to the correct conclusion. The path to self-discipline begins with knowing, and admitting the existence of, personal weaknesses. Everyone has those things they would rather not do. People would rather not admit to being imperfect, but all are and must be prepared to admit to imperfections to be able to begin the journey to self-discipline. The next step is to be prepared to move everyday temptations out of the way. This is usually easier said than done, but it must be done to properly begin along the path toward self-discipline. Once ready to begin, make sure to set clear, realistic goal and make a plan to achieve them. Do not be afraid to set several smaller goals as opposed to one large ultimate goal. Nothing worthwhile is ever reached in one straight path. There will be roadblocks and pitfalls along the way that will necessitate reworking the plan. So it may be better to start with smaller goals that will give a sense of accomplishment that will help ease travelling this path.

Keep the plan simple. Self-discipline does not need to be complicated. The idea of self-discipline itself is actually a very simple concept. The plan to get to self-discipline should not be overly complicated. The plan to reach self-discipline should be as simple as possible while encompassing all aspects needed to reach the goal. A complicated plan may be impossible to achieve and will probably lead to defeat—and giving up is not an option on the road to self-discipline.

Self-discipline is a powerful tool to possess. Self-discipline is a positive force in life. It does not mean giving up those things that make life satisfying; but rather using innate strength and creativity to achieve desired goals. With self-discipline, life is more enjoyable, and the little cheats that help make life enjoyable when people have the self-discipline to learn to enjoy these little cheats only occasionally. Again, it is not necessary to completely give up cake; just do not eat the whole thing!

Self-disciplined people do not deprive themselves, but they use focus to stay on track when goals conflict with one another. Let us imagine that friends want to have fun tonight with a pub crawl. Let us also imagine there is a huge chemistry test tomorrow. The self-disciplined person would stay home and study chemistry, thus giving better odds to getting a good grade and not worrying about the risk of oversleeping and missing the test altogether. The bars will still be there another time.

People who have a high level of self-discipline are more satisfied with themselves and how their life is going. Self-discipline allows for a better sense of self and a higher level of self-esteem. Life is not out of control. Life has meaning beyond today. Worthwhile goals are in sight in the future—and this works in a cycle. Creating goals and making a plan to achieve them leads to a higher sense of self-control. A higher sense of self control leads to more goal setting and plan making. The cycle just keeps going around.

Self-discipline allows for more time being able to do the things that will bring satisfaction and less of the things that provide no growth or satisfaction. Self-disciplined people set a goal and work toward it. Self-disciplined people are proactive, not reactive. This means they anticipate problems and work to prevent them, rather than trying to solve a problem when it occurs. Proactive people spend time every day wondering 'what if?'. *What if the car does not start tomorrow? What if the washing machine breaks down? What if the tree in the backyard falls into the house?* Proactive people imagine scenarios and decide on a plan of action before it is needed. If the plan is never needed then at least there is a plan in place. Reactive people, on the other hand, spend a lot of time doing things that are not producing a future goal. Reactive people react when the problem occurs. They have no preset plan in place. If the car does not start one morning then they scramble to find an alternate means of transportation for the day. The proactive person might give up eating lunch out every day in favor of brown-bagging lunch then saving that money for a down payment on a house. That is self-discipline. The reactive person will suddenly start scrambling trying to dig up down payment money for a house when the monthly rent increases yet again.

While missing restaurant lunches in order to save money for that future house might seem negative at the moment, it is positive in the long run. With a bit of sacrificing a future goal is achieved. Focusing on daily choices makes living more at the moment than looking toward the future. So while planning a daily brown-bag lunch might seem like an in-the-moment choice, it is really a part of a long term goal. Deciding on a different restaurant each day is truly in the moment—and when the goal is achieved, a tremendous sense of satisfaction replaces any feelings of deprivation that may have been lingering.

Boundaries are not scary things, but rather necessary limits to achieving a future goal. Boundaries are needed to achieve the level of self-control needed to become fully self-disciplined. Setting boundaries requires knowing exactly what the future goals are and how to follow a path to achieve them. This allows the self-disciplined person to understand themselves better than most people, to be much more comfortable in their own skin than most people. This also allows the self-disciplined person to know exactly what lengths they are capable of achieving in order to reach a goal.

Moreover, becoming self-disciplined will showcase who is a friend and who is not. True friends will assist in achieving goals. True friends will not try to block the hard work needed to become self-disciplined. By making the conscious decision to become self-disciplined, the sad truth of reality means that not everyone can stay around. But the self-disciplined person has the power to create the world as they want it to be.

Self-discipline takes an extreme amount of energy to achieve. It is not just choosing to be self-disciplined—it must be constantly worked at, and that takes energy. This will require good lifestyle practices. Eat healthily, sleep regularly, exercise when possible—all these activities will energize the body and mind and make working toward the goal of self-discipline more easily attainable.

2

HOW TO USE THIS BOOK

THIS BOOK IS INTENDED TO BE AN IN-DEPTH GUIDE TO developing self-discipline. It is not just a pleasant read to be read once and set on the coffee table to use for looks. This book is meant to be an in-depth guide toward knowing and implementing all the steps needed to achieve self-discipline.

READ THROUGH THE BOOK ONCE, AND THEN READ through it again. The first read is merely to become familiar with what self-discipline really is. The second read should be slower and more in-depth to allow the reader time to process the tips and tricks included here and to imagine how these changes will fit into their current lifestyle. More importantly, this will allow time to begin to visualize these changes as a part of the everyday lifestyle and how the changes will fit.

SOME OF THE IDEAS CONTAINED IN THIS BOOK WILL make more sense when they are actually used. Let's say that one goal is to save more money. Work out a plan to save—a personal plan. If cash is still the basis of most daily transactions, then put a dollar a day into a jar on the dresser. Take the spare pocket change and dump it in the jar every night. Many financial institutions offer ways to take money from the checking account, based on transactions, and transfer it to the savings account. A payroll deduction to a savings account might work. Whatever the method, the first most important step is to set the goal and the method that will be used to achieve the goal. Now, sit back and watch that money grow. Watch that jar on the dresser get a bit fuller every week. Watch how the amount in the savings account keeps increasing. This is how goals are achieved. It is not enough to want to save money. It is necessary to make the goal to save money as well as the plan to save money and then watch it grow.

Do not be afraid to try and fail. No one succeeds completely with the first attempt. Actually, that is a good thing. If self-discipline were that easy to achieve, then everyone would have it and possessing it would no longer be so special. Besides, trial and error is an important part of personal growth. The important thing is to begin, to try. Talking about beginning will not work. It is a good thing to spend some time considering this new journey, but the person who waits for some far off ideal moment will never begin. "Tomorrow," "someday," and "eventually" no longer have a spot in the vocabulary of the person who desires self-discipline. The time is *now*.

Use the ideas contained in this book and choose a goal. It does not—and should not—be a huge one. Start small. Smaller goals are much more manageable than large goals, and completing them is more certain. Completing a goal gives a marvelous sense of self satisfaction and helps drive one to further goal achievement. Make a plan to reach that goal. Start doing the tasks necessary to achieve that goal. Make the little sacrifices that have been identified as necessary to reach that goal. Give up the bad habits that need to go away. Embrace the new good habits that will lead to a better lifestyle and an increased ability to resist temptation. Trip and fall. Fail miserably. It will happen. However, do not give up when it does. Get up, dust off the dirt, and start over. It may be necessary to rework the path to success at this point. Maybe the failure was due in part to a faulty plan. This also happens. No plan is inherently perfect. Every plan can and should be adjusted as needed.

Keep sight of the ultimate goal. Do whatever is needed to keep that goal fresh in the mind. Draw a picture and hang it on the refrigerator. Keep a detailed journal of daily events that will lead to the achievement of the goal. Tell family and friends about the goal. The more it is out front and visible, the harder it is to ignore—and by not keeping it a secret, the chances of failure are decreased. No one wants to fail in public!

By using the ideas contained in this book and really putting effort into it, anyone can become more self-disciplined. It will not happen overnight—but with hard work and concentration, it will happen.

3

SELF-DISCIPLINE HABITS

SELF-DISCIPLINE IS A WORK-IN-PROGRESS AND A GOAL. The goal is to become more self-disciplined. However, being self-disciplined is not something one achieves once and considers it done. Once self-discipline is achieved, it must be considered a lifestyle—it must be nurtured daily and constantly refreshed to stay relevant and useful. Self-discipline is a habit—a good habit to have to make life more worthwhile.

Self-discipline is the backbone of a successful person. Whether a person desires personal success, professional success, or both, self-discipline will lead them to their goal. It begins with a strong ability to control oneself with strict discipline. Thoughts are under control. Emotions are under control. Behavior is under control. This does not mean that thoughts never run wild and emotions never flow to the surface. It just means that they are never allowed to control the person. One might get a little misty eyed at the birthday card with the cute kittens on it, but one would not let this feeling take over the entire day. This is self-discipline. The person controls thoughts and emotions. Self-control becomes a habit—a new personal best friend.

A burning desire to achieve these goals will not be enough to achieve these goals. Strong knowledge of personal strengths and weaknesses combined with a good understanding of how to discipline oneself is the key to being successful. Good habits make the difference between failure and success.

Successful people know that discipline is the key that unlocks the door to future goal achievement. They use discipline daily to enable themselves to be able to achieve their dreams. They know how to use a strong foundation built on strong habits to enable them to be successful. They are fully aware that self-discipline will allow them to accomplish more in less time—making them a more valuable member of the team.

But where does this discipline come from? How does one person seem so at-ease with controlling their actions and behaviors while other people fail on a daily basis? How do some people live lives of total self-control, while other people never seem to know where their shoes are, much less where they are going? The answer is habit. Behavior is mostly driven by habit. If someone can control their habits, they can have strict control over their personal habits.

Moreover, developing good habits really is as simple as knowing where the shoes are. A self-disciplined person would have a dedicated space for shoes. When the shoes are removed from the feet they are placed in this dedicated space. The self-disciplined person is never almost late to work because they cannot find their shoes. If this sounds familiar, then try this little exercise. Pick a dedicated place for the shoes. It does not matter where; the closet, tucked under the bed, next to the night stand, wherever. The dedicated spot is a personal choice. Now, every night, make a conscious effort to put the shoes in the dedicated spot every time they are removed from the feet. One day, it will be apparent that this has become a habit—a good habit to have—because now, there is no more searching for the shoes on cold, dark mornings. While this exercise may seem quite simple, it is a prime example of setting a goal, making a plan to achieve that goal, and achieving that goal.

Good habits will allow a person to create a good plan for achieving future goals. Without good habits, self-discipline will never become a reality. But how are these habits developed? Why is it so difficult to overcome bad habits?

The problem is the pathways in our brains. Whenever a habit is begun, whether it is a good habit or a bad habit, the brain creates pathways that tell the body to act a certain way when certain things happen. A cigarette smoker will want to light up a cigarette when someone else does. Seeing the cigarette, smelling the cigarette, triggers the nerve pathways in the brain of a smoker to have their own cigarette. This is why cigarette smokers who are trying to quit are often encouraged to change some of their daily habits. Smoking is often tied to other activities. Beer drinkers who smoke will smoke more when drinking. Coffee drinkers who smoke will automatically light up while pouring that first morning cup. People who smoke on long car trips may be encouraged to chew gum instead. People who drink may need to stop frequenting the local bar. Coffee drinkers will need to find something to do with their hands instead of lighting a cigarette. The nerve pathways that the bad habit created can be broken. It will take time and hard work. But then NOT smoking becomes the new good habit.

Creating good habits from bad requires effort but it can be done. Good habits take time to build and bad habits take time to break. Start small, work hard and consider a few simple tricks that might help ease into the habit of fostering good habits.

Start by taking the time to be thankful for what is already present in life. Humans spend much more time than needed wanting bigger, better things. Once people learn to be happy with the things they already have and not waste time wanting things they do not have, they can begin to see what is really important in life and begin to make a plan to add to those things that are really meaningful.

Humans spend far too much time feeling useless emotions like guilt or anger. Negative emotions use way too much energy that is needed to focus on the good things in life. Letting go of negative emotions frees the mind, the heart, and the soul to be able to focus on the positive effects that building new habits will create. Learning how to let go of negative emotions is actually an excellent way to build self-discipline. It is a way of letting the world see the strength inside.

Daily meditation has a wonderful effect on the ability to become more self-disciplined. Meditation leads to a clear mind, a relaxed heart. It improves physical and mental health. A few minutes of meditation daily leads the body to sync up better with the mind. It is much easier to create good habits that will lead to self-discipline if the mind is relaxed and ready to receive good thoughts.

It is important to set specific goals by writing them down. Once a goal is committed to paper it becomes an active thing, something that can be seen. Goals that are kept in the mind do not have the same strength as goals that are written down. Goals in the mind can be forgotten or pushed aside. Goals written on paper are seen every time the paper is seen—and when they are written down, it is impossible to ignore them. They want attention. They want direction and planning. They want to be considered, cared for and loved. They want attention. Start small and work on them daily.

Remember to eat healthily and sleep well and regularly. The body cannot process new habits if it is undernourished. Good healthy food is crucial to giving the body enough energy to work on new and better habits. This is especially necessary when trying to break bad habits. Bad habits require extra energy to put aside. Sleep is especially important too. Most adults need between seven and nine hours of sleep every night. Play around with these numbers until the correct amount is determined, and then stick to that number. Make every attempt to go to bed at the same time each night and wake up at the same time each day. This is a good habit that will lead to self-discipline of personal habits. Of course, things happen, and sometime people fall off the schedule. But get back on it as soon as possible and do not regret one or two small slips. They happen.

Exercise is another good habit that must be settled into the daily routine. Regular exercise is important in keeping the body healthy. Usually, the word 'exercise' gives bad connotations to many people. But exercise does not need to be a negative thing. It does not mean running out to join the neighborhood gym or begin training for a marathon. Anything that gets the body moving is exercise. Go for a walk, jump rope, play with the kids in the front yard—anything, just get moving. Join a sports team. Remember how much fun baseball used to be. Rake leaves, clean out the garage, push the lawn mower around the yard. Regular movement releases stress and tensions and is another way to create a good habit.

Practice organization. Some people are naturally organized, and some people need to work very hard to be organized. If the latter group seems more familiar, do not try to become completely organized overnight. The organization will not happen but failure definitely will. Being well organized is a habit—and like any other good habit, it will take work to achieve. Begin by organizing one thing. Begin with a drawer. It is small and easy to organize. Have some boxes ready. When removing things from the drawer look at them closely and try to recall the last time they were used. If it has been more than six months then the item is not needed. Have some boxes ready while doing this. If the item is still in good condition it goes in the box to be donated. If the item is beyond usefulness then it goes into the box to go to the trash. Be firm! Do not hold onto something because it might get used. If it's a family heirloom and impossible to give up, put it in a box in the attic. When one drawer is clean, go to the next one. When all the drawers are organized move to the cabinets. As long as unnecessary items are not brought back into the house, then the house will remain clean and well-organized. Cleanliness will become a habit.

Time management is another goal that is necessary to embrace to build good habits and become self-disciplined. If there is no time management then time is the manager, and time is a very bad manager. Unmanaged time will slip away rapidly, leaving no time left in the day to do all the things that need to be done. Time management is nothing more than a plan to reach a goal of order and organization. An important part of time management is cleaning out the activities. Just like cleaning drawers of unused items, there are many unnecessary activities clogging up daily life. After the drawers and cabinets are cleaned and the house stays organized, one unneeded activity (constantly straightening the house) will be eliminated. It really is that simple.

Think of all the time that is actually wasted throughout the day engaging in unnecessary activities. How much time is wasted digging through a laundry basket looking for socks, when it would be so much quicker if the socks were in the drawer. How much time is wasted deciding what to cook for dinner when there is no set menu plan available to consult. How much time is wasted trying to find lost shoes? It all adds up.

No level of discipline will be successful without persistence.

Temporary failure is not a reason to give up. Persistence is what keeps people going even through times of extreme failure. As far as progress goes, failure is an important part of life. Think of it not so much as doing something the wrong way but in finding yet another way that just did not work. In that instance, it is a learning opportunity and not a failure. This will also help lead toward greater self-discipline, by refusing to quit.

Habit and discipline go together hand-in-hand. Building a new habit is difficult in the very beginning because the body and the mind need to be taught a new way of thinking and working. But chasing good habits with persistence leads to greater self-discipline. The longer a habit is practiced, the more it becomes a part of the routine. It becomes easier. It becomes a habit, and no longer need to be practiced daily. It just naturally gets done—and once one new habit is set, it becomes much easier to add each successive one. If someone makes the decision to quit smoking, then not smoking is the new habit that will be cultivated. Once it has been persistently practiced long enough so that it is not so difficult anymore, then it is much easier to add healthy eating. After all one good habit deserves another, right? With two new good habits in place, it just makes sense to add the habit of regular exercising. This is how new and better habits are formed and how habits build upon each other to create a lifestyle of self-discipline.

Self-discipline is nothing more than practicing a series of good habits until they become ingrained in the daily routine to the point where they are a part of life. As more bad habits are replaced with good habits, then the good ones take over and lead to a more orderly and organized life. As life becomes more organized, it becomes easier to manage—and now, it has become a life of self-discipline.

4

SELF-DISCIPLINE STRATEGIES PART 1 – CREATING A PLAN AND ACCEPTING REALITY

To be successful at developing self-discipline, one needs to make a plan. This plan will be different for everyone. No two plans will be alike. Each plan will be specific to the person who is making the plan. Everyone needs to develop a personal plan to be able to develop more self-control and, ultimately, more self-discipline.

Before creating a plan for self-discipline, it is necessary to accept life as it is now. Acceptance is the first most important step toward self-discipline. Acceptance means that life and reality as it exists now is truly accurate. Admit to what is. Acknowledge what is there. It is impossible to create change without knowing the full extent of the reality of now. Hence admit to the bad habits, the half-done items, and the failures left behind. Embrace them. Do this as kindly as possible. Do not use labels; they are self-defeating. A person is not fat; they need to lose weight. A person is not a slob; they need to get better at keeping the house clean. A person is not lazy; they need to become more organized at work using time-management strategies.

While this might seem like a simple thing to do, it is really very difficult. Anyone who regularly has problems in one area of life probably has a serious flaw in that area. Continuous problems in one area point to the reality that all problems may be rooted in that area. It is not always an easy, obvious thing to see. It is usually an inability to see the true reality and accept it for what it really is.

Many people wonder why self-discipline is so dependent on acceptance of life as it really is now. This fact has its basis in the reality that makes the current situation one that needs change. Failing to correctly see the current situation means that honesty does not exist in this reality. Failing to fully see the current situation means that it cannot be fully accepted. Fully accepting the current situation is necessary for being able to create a plan for change. In anything that needs a plan, the first step is knowledge and acceptance of the current situation. If someone wanted to lose weight, for example, it would be necessary to know exactly what the current weight was, and to be able to accept that number as fact, before being able to make a weight loss goal and to create a plan to lose that weight.

Failing to accept the current reality means that improvement in this area is not really possible. Just like in the previous example, it is vital to know the current weight before the current weight can be changed—and that number must be accepted as it is. The number the scale gives is just the beginning. If it is more than expected then acknowledge it. The reality of now must be accepted before it can be changed. Now that it has been accepted and acknowledged, a plan for weight loss can be implemented. A goal can be set and hopefully achieved.

Working to increase self-discipline works the exact same way. It is vital to know where the level of self-discipline is now. Is it high and strong, or low and weak? What goals seem to be too difficult?

Are any goals currently impossible to reach? When considering daily challenges, do not leave anything out. Think of all the things that cause struggles throughout the day.

Does the house need organizing? Is weight a problem? What addictions need to be faced and conquered? Are promises regularly kept? Is bathing a part of the regular daily routine? Is a regular sleep schedule observed seven days a week? Is regular exercise a priority? Are work hours focused or haphazard? Leave nothing out. No complaint is too small or insignificant, and that is just what these are—complaints of an unhappy life. When life lacks organization it cannot hope to be truly happy. When life lacks organization it lacks self-discipline.

It is common knowledge that muscles fall into separate groups and are best trained using different exercises. Just like muscles, the areas of self-discipline are very different and require alternate types of exercise to develop discipline. The best starting point is to identify an area where discipline is seriously lacking and develop a plan to train in this area first. Start slowly at first, building up to progressively harder goals as the training progresses.

Just as when building muscle, training self-discipline with ever increasing steps works well. Just remember to start with small goals and work up to large ones. Suppose the scale gave a number that was fifty pounds over what had been expected. After accepting that number as reality, a plan is made to lose those fifty pounds. It is not reasonable to expect those fifty extra pounds to be gone in a week or even a month, but it is not unreasonable to lose two pounds in a week. This would mean a weight loss of eight pounds in a typical four-week month. In six months and two weeks, the fifty pounds will be gone. This might sound like an extremely long time, but those pounds were not put on overnight and will not be lost overnight. Also, slow and steady progress is what makes habits. Good habits make self-discipline.

If it seems to be impossible to accept life as it is now, then the only things left are denial and ignorance. If the problem is ignorance then it will be impossible to ever know exactly how much discipline is lacking in everyday life. Unfortunately what is not known can hurt. There can be no hope of improvement without knowing exactly how much work needs to be done. If improvement is attempted without knowledge of reality then any failures will be blamed on the actual thing that needed change. If the problem is denial, then there is an incorrect view of reality—and just like being unable to accept the actual number on the scale, there will never be any progress toward goal completion because there is no discernable starting point.

Following the path to self-discipline will bring numerous rewards and benefits. Goals must be intentional. No one ever lost weight, found a better job, or organized the house without a plan to reach a goal. Progress does not just happen. It must be intentional. It must be reached on purpose. There must be a conscious effort to progress toward a given goal. No one accidentally became more self-disciplined. Goals must be reached progressively. This means that once a goal is successfully reached, work on the next goal is begun. Failure to continuously challenge the status of life will not gain self-discipline.

However, it is equally bad to try to push too hard when beginning this new journey. It is impossible to transform an entire way of life in one day. It just will not happen. Deciding to correct all bad habits at once in an attempt to develop instant self-control and instant self-discipline is a recipe for disaster—and failure just breeds more failure. If the goal is impossible to reach, and it is not reached, then it is taken as a sign that this whole process is impossible. Trying to set several new goals and expecting immediate perfection is a definite recipe for failure. Use whatever tiny bit of self-discipline already exists to build upon. The more self-discipline is practiced, the easier it becomes to build more. In the beginning, everything seems like an insurmountable challenge. As self-discipline grows the challenges become easier.

Never use other people's progress as a yardstick. Everyone develops at a unique pace. This is quite normal. This is not a race. This is a new lifestyle that requires hard work and dedication. No two people will face the same challenges, and no two people will develop at the same rate. Comparing the progress of two different people will only highlight deficiencies.

Building self-discipline requires creating good habits that will create pathways in the brain that will make the mind automatically default to good activity. Think of a little baby. Babies are not born knowing how to walk. Their little leg muscles just cannot hold them up. But babies are quite determined to be mobile. They see everyone around them standing on two feet and they know that they must also stand on two feet. So they find a piece of furniture, grab on, and try to pull themselves into a standing position. On the first tries, the baby falls back to the ground because its little legs are still not strong enough to support the body. But the baby is determined. So the baby keeps pulling on the chair until one day the baby is standing on wobbly legs while everyone rejoices. The baby's brain has created a pathway in the brain to that exact spot that controls standing in the baby's legs. Now that the baby has stood, that pathway is complete. It needs only to be used over and over so that the pathway, like the legs, will become stronger in time. A new habit is formed.

Once a habit is formed it must be built upon to create another habit. This is how the path to self-discipline is laid. Think again of the baby. Now that the baby is standing, the baby must learn to walk. It is not enough for the baby to just stand there because then the baby would not grow and develop properly and would never get across the room where the toys are kept. So something in the baby's mind tells it to put one little foot out in a step. The baby does that and falls down. There is no pathway in the brain for the act of walking—not yet, anyway. The baby will build one. This is using one habit to build upon to create another.

Never fall into the trap of looking at other people in a more favorable light. The misguided thinking that all other people are so much stronger is self-defeating. This exercise has no sense behind it. The only person whose progress is important is the person making the progress. Even identical twins do not develop at exactly the same rate. If they do not, then there is no sense expecting that everyone's progress will be exactly identical. Admit that this is where the starting point is, and this is a personal path to reach a personal goal.

Once reality has been accepted, once the starting point has been acknowledged, it is time to create the plan; the plan that will lead down the path to self-discipline. Begin with a clear vision of the goal. Decide on the first thing that needs changing; set the first goal. An entire life of laziness and failure to succeed will not be corrected overnight. One goal must be achieved so that it can be used as a successful model and a building block for subsequent goals. Set the goal and formulate a plan for achieving the goal. Write it down on paper and look at it several times a day. Goals written down are more concrete than goals floating around in the mind.

Remove any temptations that will get in the way of achieving the goal. If weight loss is the ultimate goal, then clear the house of unhealthy foods. If stopping smoking is the ultimate goal, then toss the cigarettes in the trash. It may also be necessary to change parts of the daily routine. For example, if weight loss is the goal and the daily commute to work goes right past the best donut shop in town, a new way to work might be needed.

Keep the goal simple. Simple goals are easier to achieve than complicated ones. The goal 'to quit smoking' might be too difficult for someone who has smoked for decades and really depends on cigarettes in the daily routine. So a small goal would be best, to begin with. Begin by only smoking outside, never in the house. Even if it is in the middle of a blizzard or a monsoon, no smoking will be done in the house. Sometimes it just is not worth it to get up and go outside for a smoke. Then the first goal is achieved. There is no more smoking in the house. The next goal might be no more smoking in the car.

Smoking is a physical habit as well as a mental one. If quitting smoking is the goal then it will require getting past the physical cravings as well as creating a new pathway in the brain that leads to the idea of not smoking. Positive goals might include a fresher smell in the car or house, no more lingering smoke odor on the clothes. Perhaps when the urge to smoke hits it is replaced by a quick walk down the street or scrubbing the kitchen counter. This is how bad habits are replaced by good habits, and good habits build self-discipline.

Do not overlook willpower. Everyone knows that a stubborn person who just will not change their ways for anyone. That stubborn person possesses willpower. Willpower is just a nice word for stubborn. So be stubborn. Decide early what their goal will be and do not let anything get in the way of achieving that goal. Be stubborn about goal achievement. Do not take no for an answer. Do not change the goal no matter what happens. Being stubborn creates willpower that is vitally important to reach desired goals.

Create a plan, and then create a secondary plan. All good plans have a backup waiting in the wings for those awkward moments. If the ultimate goal is weight loss, then eating healthier will help achieve that goal. That is very easy to do at home where ultimate control over the menu exists. But since no one wants to be a hermit, what happens when the party invitation arrives? No happy human can resist a good party with friends and loved ones. But what about all that food? This is when the backup plan comes into effect. The plan to eat less is already in place. Now, the plan at the party might be to try one bite of everything offered and then to spend the remainder of the evening engaging in sparkling conversation with the other guests. This is the secondary plan. This will assist in keeping the original plan in place and allow the path to the goal to remain unbroken.

When setting the goal originally remember to allow for a treat when the goal is achieved. Humans work well on a system of rewards for good behavior. So chose a reward that fits the achievement of the goal. If smoking is no longer done in the house then buy some paint and refresh the walls. The house will look so much better and will smell marvelous. If the car is no longer smoked in then get it detailed; a fresh car smells amazing. If a weight loss goal is achieved, buy a new outfit, or at least one new wardrobe piece.

Moreover, accept that failure will happen occasionally. This does not mean to seek out failure. This means to accept failure when it happens—and it will. Humans are, well, human. They *will* fail. They will try hard, and they will sometimes fail. When failure happens, acknowledge its existence. Embrace the failure. Do not feel guilty or angry. These emotions, while quite normal, only succeed in stalling any future progress that can occur once the path to the goal has been restored. Learn from failure. What happened? Why did it happen? How can this be avoided in the future? Once the failure is accepted and analyzed, it can be worked past. The path to the goal is still there. Maybe it needs a bit of reworking. Maybe a slight bend in the path is necessary. No matter what happens, getting back on the path is the first step in continuing on toward the achievement of the goal—and *that* is the first step toward self-discipline.

5

SELF-DISCIPLINE STRATEGIES PART 2 – REMOVE ROADBLOCKS AND PRACTICE PAIN

THE MOST BASIC COMMON TRAIT AMONG TRULY successful people is self-discipline. People who have a high level of self-discipline are traditionally more successful than people who are not self-disciplined simply because they have the inner strength to set a goal and do all that is needed to achieve it.

Think of a professional athlete. No good professional athlete allows themselves to get out of shape in the off season—or even in an off-week. Muscles must be constantly worked in order to keep up a certain level of strength and function. This means that pro athletes must have the self-discipline to commit to a training schedule of regular exercise even during the off season.

Self-discipline is a powerful personality trait to possess. It allows for a stronger sense of purpose and self-esteem. Self-discipline gives a feeling of accomplishment that may be otherwise lacking. The self-disciplined person is generally more open and honest with themselves because they know what they want out of life and have a plan in mind to achieve that goal. Self-discipline is the key to personal freedom.

But just as self-discipline can be nurtured and grown, it can also be destroyed quite easily. All paths lead somewhere. Once goals are set a path is created to enable access to that goal. But that path can be obliterated by debris. Life will set up roadblocks on a clear road whenever possible. Humans will also derail themselves by seeing a clear road and inventing roadblocks. Knowing what to look for will save time and trouble during the journey. Life happens. People get sick or injured. People get new jobs. People have new babies or move to a new house. Sometimes humans are their own worst enemy. They wonder what will happen if this, or that, or the other. They put road blocks in their own clear roads.

Remember willpower? Willpower is a vital tool in building self-discipline, but willpower can be overcome. Humans are weak, and donuts taste good. When people rely solely on willpower to reach goals, failure is surely following. Instead of planning to muscle the way through with sheer stubbornness, smart goal setters realize that temptation will happen and will likely not fall in the face of willpower alone. Instead, smart goal setters make a plan for the appearance of temptation and devise a way to stop it. The temptation is a roadblock that will hinder or completely stall progress if allowed.

This goes back to the idea of the party treats. The plan to avoid temptation is to sample one piece of each goodie and then spend the remainder of the night mixing and mingling. This is a plan to avoid temptation. The buffet at the party is a roadblock on the road to successful weight loss. A secondary plan for sampling the buffet and then walking away is a way of facing temptation head on—in essence, it is putting a roadblock in temptation's path instead of the other way around.

Another common roadblock—and one that many people fall prey to—is setting up hopes that are not realistic in everyday situations.

People expect that once something is decided as a lifestyle change, then it becomes fact, and the world just does not work that way. A bad habit is a habit—and like any habit, it requires work to change to a better habit. People fail because the goals set are impossible to achieve in the way they were set. They may be too large, too soon, or too hard. Remember the pathways in the brain. A new habit must make a new pathway. Let's say the goal is to lose weight. Setting a goal of losing fifty pounds by next month is an impossible goal to achieve. It is too large, the deadline is too soon, and it would be too hard if not nearly impossible to lose that much weight in a few short weeks. It is far better to break the goal down into smaller, more easily attainable goals and not risk setting up false hopes that will never come true.

Self-discipline itself will not help anyone achieve an impossible goal. Neither will sheer willpower. There is a path to the goal. It is important to follow the path—one step at a time—until the goal is reached. It is vital to be aware that impossible goals are doomed to failure and not risk setting up impossible goals in the first place.

Another common roadblock in the path to the goal is stress. When people are experiencing extreme amounts of stress, the temptation is to ignore the path to the goal in favor of taking the easy path to self-indulgence. People who are under stress usually eat poorly or not at all, neglect exercise routines, and smoke like chimneys. They often become angry for no apparent reason and may stop taking care of cleaning their houses or persons. Attention to commitments often suffers as well, particularly the commitments made to reach specific goals.

Stress affects self-control. Self-discipline will not grow and develop if self-control does not exist. During times of stress, it is quite common to forget good intentions and revert back to bad habits. When this happens self-discipline will begin to deteriorate. This can be easily prevented by acknowledging the possibility that it might happen and preparing an alternate plan. Just as an alternate plan was made to avoid temptation at the party, have an alternate plan prepared to avoid falling victim to stress. Make an alternate plan to incorporate some sort of relaxation method into daily activity. Meditating, walking, listening to music, reading, enjoying a hot bath; the list is endless. The important thing is that this is used as a stress relieving activity to combat a rise in stress and it is seen as an enjoyable activity. It is usually not a good idea to try to beat stress by cleaning out the garage. Some activities will just bring their own level of stress. Look for the relaxing activities.

Self-discipline as a long-term goal depends on long-term work. A common problem people face when attempting to build good habits to develop self-discipline is not realizing how much work each goal will need. People want instant results. Someday is too far away. People tend to try to revamp their lives all at once. They will set several goals at the same time and expect them all to be easily attainable and to last forever and ever. The real truth is that even the people who are already highly self-disciplined need to work on new goals in small steps. It is even a good idea to take small, planned breaks periodically. A weight loss goal is a good thing. But it will be more easily attainable and seem less like a punishment if regular meals or even days are built in for a bit of cheating. People are human. Only the very strongest can resist temptation forever. With adding a meal to cheat periodically in a diet plan, it becomes less of a temptation and more of a secondary plan to avoid a roadblock, much like the party plan. It will be easier to stick to the diet plan knowing a treat is coming at the end of the week.

There are other ways to build in secondary plans to allow a bit of 'cheating' to avoid falling prey to large roadblocks. Work hard at work, but take regular time off to recharge and relax. Exercise well and often, but take days off to allow the body time to recover.

Study hard, but allow for the occasional night out or spent relaxing in front of the television. Humans are not machines and cannot continue running indefinitely without either taking a break or breaking down—and without taking periodic breaks, the goal suddenly becomes a thing to be despised.

Time is another massive roadblock that can prevent the goal from ever being reached by preventing the path from ever being started. This is the type of time that is referred to in "I will begin working on my goal....." Once a goal is determined, then the start time must be determined. It should be as immediate as possible. Anytime someone says that goal achievement begins next week, at the beginning of the year, when things are going better, just understand that time will never come. Tomorrow never comes. So never intend to begin a new plan tomorrow unless it is named, as in a day of the week, such as "Tomorrow, Monday morning, I will....." Giving it a specific name gives it a specific start point. Not beginning immediately is just another way of saying goals do not matter.

Always keep in mind that self-discipline comes with pain. All humans feel pain at one time or another. Pain is a part of life. But choosing to feel pain in order to develop self-discipline may not seem like a very good idea. But it, too, is a necessary part of life. Remember that self-discipline involves doing what needs to be done as opposed to what would be more fun to do—and that in itself is painful. Achieving self-discipline means making sacrifices.

Remember that discipline is often used as a synonym for punishment. In a way it is true. Building self-discipline is painful and will often feel more like self-punishment. The self-discipline to follow a healthy eating plan may feel like punishment when there are fresh donuts in the break room at work. The self-discipline to stop smoking will seem like a punishment when everyone else is lighting up. The self-discipline to exercise regularly will definitely feel like punishment during the workout! The goal is easily visualized. Following the path to the goal is the hard part.

When working on self-discipline people must act as both the student and the teacher. Humans on a quest for greater self-discipline must be prepared to teach themselves the way to follow the path to the goal that will eventually lead to self-discipline—and that is where the underlying problem begins. While people usually love sharing knowledge and usually love teaching others what they know, they are often reluctant to learn from the very lessons they teach. Think of an overweight doctor. Common sense says that the doctor should be the first one with an acute awareness of the dangers of obesity. It is even reasonable to believe that the doctor is well equipped to teach patients how to monitor their own weight and adjust down as needed. Why, then, does the doctor not follow this same advice? Because it is much easier to tell someone else what to do than to do the same thing. Think of the teacher self as the adult and the pupil self as the child. It is not uncommon to hear adults tell children "Well, I'm an adult, so I can……." Simply being a grown up is not a free rein to do whatever seems like a good idea. But that is where a lack of self-discipline comes from.

The underlying problem here is that it is very difficult to teach oneself something one lacks knowledge of or the ability to perform. People can know what to do to become more self-disciplined, but the actual process of doing it may be difficult—and when humans fail at achieving self-discipline, are they to blame? No, it is usually some nameless outside force that caused the failure.

Think of the goal to lose weight. The outside forces that might cause a person to fail at this goal include holidays, getting morning coffee at the donut shop, snacks in the breakroom, and a marvelous sale on cookies at the grocery store. Any old excuse will do. If these outside forces did not exist then it would be easier to lose weight. But all of these things, and other excuses like them, are nothing more than the roadblocks that crop up in the path to self-discipline. They need acceptance, acknowledgement, and an alternate plan to avoid them. Yes, this will cause pain. It is much easier to eat the donut than to ignore it. It might also be necessary to seek morning coffee at a place that does not sell wonderful tasting food. Perhaps morning coffee could be made at home.

When discipline causes pain it merely means the person is doing something they really do not want to do—but know they must do in order to achieve a greater goal. Staying true to a goal means giving up something pleasurable. Pleasure is not something given up lightly. But to hopefully avoid the future pain of failure the current pain of sacrifice is necessary, even desirable. After all, pain can be a great motivator. The pain of giving up cookies in order to lose weight might be enough incentive to prevent future late-night cookie binges. So suffering pain now prevents greater pain later.

Discipline pain is not necessarily a physical pain but more of a commitment to a problem or issue. A commitment to lose weight will bring moments of pain. There will be a pain every time your favorite food is bypassed to allow consumption of something healthier. There will be a pain every time the scale does not show as much progress as was desired. There will be a pain, over and over, every time the goal is revisited and the realization dawns that the goal has not yet been reached.

People who are unwilling to suffer through the pain that comes with building self-discipline will later face the pain that comes from regretting the loss of a goal. Regret remains in the soul for a long time. It hangs over the heart, making life more difficult than necessary. The biggest difference between the pain brought by discipline and the pain caused by feelings of regret is that discipline pain will eventually end, while regret hangs around forever. There are ways to avoid the pain that comes with a lifetime of regret and leads to self-discipline through short-term suffering.

Find something to do that creates a great sense of passion within. Anything that creates internal passion means that it is something desirable, something wanted. It is so much easier to commit to feeling pain for a short time in order to reach a goal of something that is desired. This makes it much easier to stay on track with daily discipline. The goal must be believable and achievable.

Set priorities that are clearly defined. A goal can be interesting or it can be a commitment. It can be a noose around the neck or it can be a shining light at the end of the tunnel. Know when to commit to something and when to turn it away. Having a clearly defined plan to achieve a future goal is a constant reminder of the importance of sticking with the plan.

Once a goal has been chosen, feel free to share. Write it down on paper and tape it to the refrigerator. Tell the work buddy what is going on. Sharing the existence of a goal will often remove some of the pain associated with achieving the goal. When the path gets rough and starts climbing uphill it is wonderful if someone else knows the goal and can provide encouragement. This will help to remove a lot of the pain and replace it with encouragement and determination.

Make a mental picture of the goal. Do not spend too much time worrying about what it will take to achieve the goal. This is just a painful reminder of the pain that is waiting just around the next bend in the path. Instead, keep all focus on the goal. "I would love to eat a donut today, but I would be even happier fitting into a new swimsuit." Use what works. Even if the ultimate goal of weight loss is to be healthier, a little vanity never hurt anyone.

Choose a system of rewards and consequences. When goal setting for self-discipline, there is no outside force to put blame on if the plan fails. People choose to fall off the path, either intentionally or unintentionally. Since consequences are not pleasant, it is much better to set up a small series of rewards than to suffer future consequences that come with failure.

The pain that is naturally experienced while working toward a goal of self-discipline is a great strength builder. Self-discipline is wonderful for building muscles in the mind. Eventually, the mind will grow stronger and more resilient, and self-discipline will become much easier to maintain.

6

SELF-DISCIPLINE STRATEGIES PART 3 – ACCEPT MISTAKES AND REAP REWARDS

When working toward self-discipline, goals are made, and the path is determined. Resolutions are made and the journey begins. The way is not too difficult—progress is noticeable, and reaching the goal is becoming more of a reality every day. Then one day, it happens: a mistake. The pathway became momentarily too difficult to walk and falling off was the only option. The mighty has fallen—and now, lying beside the path and looking up at the goal that once seemed so close but is now even further away, the normal human might ask themselves, "What's next?"

People make mistakes. Things happen. Maybe the good intention of only eating one piece of cake at the birthday party was overridden by the fact that it was the best cake ever. Maybe the weeks of faithfully not smoking were ruined by one night at the bar. Maybe the weeks of running daily were interrupted by a major snow storm. Whatever happened, happened—and now, there is a mistake to deal with.

It is normal in life to make mistakes. The hard part is learning from the mistake. The person who can look at a mistake, accept it for what it is, and go on from there is probably someone who already has a great deal of self-discipline. The average person will look at a mistake, fall apart, and suffer regret. However, it is important to use the mistake as a learning experience in order to avoid repeating the mistake later.

There are steps anyone can take in order to recover from a mistake and get back on track. These are things anyone can do with any mistake, no matter how large or small it might be.

The first thing to do is to admit the mistake happened. Accept that people are human and flawed and mistakes will happen. Realize that it is not the end of the world, but a learning opportunity. This is often hard to do because humans do not like to admit to being less than perfect. Future progress will be delayed by failing to accept and own the mistake.

Next, realizing the difference between making a mistake and being a mistake is important. People are not mistakes. People do make mistakes. This distinction is crucial because making a mistake does not mean being worthless or meaningless. Making a mistake means being human.

Admitting to the mistake is important in another way. It is necessary to be able to understand exactly what went wrong. The why of the situation is very important. Things do not just happen, they happen for a reason. If the mistake in question involves losing sight of a goal and failing to follow the prescribed path to success, then why did this happen? What exactly caused it to happen? Was it one event or the accumulation of many small events?

Consider the goal to lose weight. The ultimate goal was set. The overall amount of weight to lose was decided. The smaller more manageable goals were decided upon. A system of periodic rewards was put into place. Then one day, a mistake was made. Was it the three pieces of birthday cake eaten at the party? Or did a disgruntled customer lead to a longer than normal workday that made the commute home later and longer in the pouring rain that led to the consumption of half a chocolate pie? Whether the mistake was caused by an isolated event or a series of events is important to know because it will assist in making a plan to avoid such mistakes in the future. If the event that caused the mistake was an isolated event, then a secondary plan should have already been in place to avoid such pitfalls. If one did not already exist, then now is the time to make one. The secondary plan can be as simple as eating something healthy before the party in order to avoid overeating, or by just deciding to exercise self-control and not eat more than one piece of cake.

If the mistake was caused by a series of events that led up to a minor catastrophe, then the secondary plan will be quite different. This plan would involve finding ways to avert disaster before one bad event piled up on top of another, then another, and so on. In the second scenario, it might have been a good idea to take a break after the disgruntled customer. Taking a moment to silently meditate, clear the mind and slow the breathing, might have prevented the series of disasters that followed and led to a binge eating event. It is important to know exactly what went wrong so it is not repeated.

Moreover, never forget there is something good in every mistake. Making a mistake allows a person to realize they are human. Making a mistake allows a new choice to be made—if needed. Perhaps the current path was not right in some way. Examine the path and decide if changes need to be made. Maybe the mistake happened because the path was not going in just the right way.

Sometimes life consists of one mistake after another. When this happens it is a definite sign that the path has too many flaws to be properly navigated for the time it will take to achieve the goal. This mistake might be the best thing ever—if used in the correct way.

So if the goals are wrong in some way, either too loose or too rigid, now is the time to restructure them. The path to the goal is never straight. It winds around obstacles, uphill, and downhill—until the goal is achieved. Perhaps this mistake happened because the goals were wrong in some way. Only the person who made the goals can determine that. Mistakes can be used as leverage to help renew a goal or change it as needed. A situation that is difficult, such as making a mistake, can help with future growth and goal setting—and the benefits that come from learning from a mistake are totally personally. They will always belong solely to the person who made the mistake.

Do not be afraid to use a mistake to its best advantage. This does not mean to constantly dwell on the mistake. Review the mistake as needed to get all possible learning from it. Then move on. Never let the mistake define the future. It was an event; do not make it a way of life. Learning from the mistake and moving on paves the way toward goal achievement. When that happens, it is time to reap the rewards of success.

Developing self-discipline often involves feeling pain for a short time in order to achieve a long term gain. This is sometimes difficult to do in a society where gratification is expected to be instant and satisfying. No matter what the goal is, finding the self-control from deep inside is often very difficult. But one of the main traits found with self-discipline is the strength to do without an instant pleasure in order to achieve a long term goal. This is especially true where the goal requires much effort.

Now that the first goals have been reached and the road to self-discipline is a familiar place, it is time to begin realizing the rewards—and the rewards of self-discipline are many.

The first reward of learning self-discipline is the fact that goals are now easier to set and to work toward. Personal priorities are more in line with the future desired goals. Having set priorities also leads to a better ability to focus on future goals. Decisions are easier to make without having to wade through bouts of confusion and uncertain ideas. Life is much more structured that it ever was before—and personal outlook on life improves drastically with every goal gained.

Developing self-control and self-discipline means that a person is well on the way to mastering control over themselves and their habits. It is easier to develop good habits to use to replace the former bad habits—not to mention all the rewards that cultivating those good habits brings—and addictions and failures are less likely to take over because personal self-control has been mastered.

Emotions can bring a person down, both in mind and in the body—but having stronger self-control means fewer feelings of guilt over mistakes that have been made because fewer mistakes are being made. This is the joy of self-control. A person with self-control is able to resist the temptations that lead people into making mistakes that bring deep feelings of guilt and regret. Having the self-control to resist the temptation that would eventually lead to negative emotions is a reward in itself.

Living a life filled with self-control automatically leads to an elevated standard of life, at least emotionally. People with self-control and self-discipline know what they are worth and are not afraid to demand more of themselves in order to achieve ever increasing goals. The idea of receiving gratification immediately is no longer a viable option. Working toward a goal becomes a way of life.

Fulfillment comes to people with high self-discipline. These people have the ability to see a goal and develop a plan to work toward it, never wavering even in the face of adversity.

The biggest roadblock standing in the way of success has now been removed. The person creating the goals is usually the person's own worst enemy. But with experience in how to create the goals, stick to them, and reap the benefits of those goals—then the person has learned to correct flaws within themselves.

The level of self-sufficiency increases enormously. People who have demonstrated the ability to set goals and achieve them are much better at taking care of themselves. They have a vision of how life should be lived, driven by the goals they have already achieved and those they wish to achieve for themselves in the future. They are also much better at defining future goals and implementing a plan to reach those goals. These people have a clear view of their ultimate potential.

Moreover, having better self-control makes relationships with others even better. People with good self-control are seen as being more reliable and trustworthy. When people learn to work toward goals and learn to keep promises with themselves they are much better at meaning and keeping those promises made to others.

Self-discipline is a great time saver. People with self-discipline have control over their daily activities. Having discipline allows people to do things when they should be done, without procrastination. This in itself will save people a lot of time and energy. There is no longer a need to panic at the last minute, worrying over what will and will not get done. This allows for a calmer and collected lifestyle.

Now that life is well on the road to one filled with self-control and self-discipline, it is time to relax a bit before beginning work on the next goal.

7

FINAL THOUGHTS ON DEVELOPING SELF DISCIPLINE

SELF-DISCIPLINE IS THE ABILITY TO DEVELOP SELF-control over ones wants and desires and use them to develop a better person. As children, self-discipline is usually driven down our throats by parents and teachers alike. There is no way to escape the constant onslaught of being told that self-discipline will be needed to achieve any kind of success in life. Unfortunately, children usually just make faces and run away laughing.

As an adult, self-discipline and self-control is much more important than it was as a child. However, if this skill was not developed as a child, then it must be developed as an adult if any level of success in life is ever to be hoped for. It is quite true what all the parents and teachers said once upon a time. Self-discipline is the truth and the way.

So now comes the time for developing self-discipline by making small goals, achieving them, and working toward larger goals. Self-discipline is finding an important reason to achieve a goal and then making a serious commitment to work hard to achieve that goal. This may require completing a task or taking part in an activity that is not necessarily fun or pleasant at the time but that will bring future gains and rewards.

Developing self-discipline and self-control makes demands on a person. It is necessary to have a serious desire to do something better and to become a better person. It creates an internal drive inside a person to be a better person—and it helps create the motivation needed to work toward the desired goal.

Self-discipline gives people the ability to control inner desires in order to strengthen the resolve needed to achieve a goal. It is a way to keep impulses in check in order to allow time to focus on the achievement of a goal. If excess energy is not being used to chase desires that are not helpful in reaching any kind of meaningful goal, then that energy can be used for something more useful. Keeping impulses in line is another way to save excess energy and put that energy to good use—because achieving the desired goal requires focus and hard work.

Developing self-control and self-discipline depends on a constant daily focus on the methods required to consistently build everyday habits that will develop into the desired goal. Given enough time and energy, the outcome will be that the ideal goal is reached. This consists of taking baby steps. It will be necessary to practice consistent everyday actions that will form the basis of the path that will eventually lead to the desired goal.

Having self-discipline is not merely doing an activity regularly. It requires regulating daily habits to systematically remove the bad ones. It involves correcting the events that lead to the practice of bad habits, and it will mean regularly changing and adapting to changing events and conditions that may mean revamping life's circumstances and the pursuit of goals.

The key to growing a sense of self-discipline lies in being proactive about losing bad habits and not starting new bad habits. People are forced to train the mind to follow a new group of rules and to create new pathways to learn to follow these rules. More focus will be needed for daily tasks to ensure they align with the practice of new good habits and the loss of old bad habits.

There is great value in growing a good sense of self-control and, with it, self-discipline. Productivity in work, school, and life will be greatly improved. Self-confidence will soar with every passing day. A new level of self-discipline allows for a better sense of self-worth. It gives a greater feeling of control and a greater sense of being able to complete the necessary tasks at work and at home. It is easier to focus on tasks for longer periods of time. With this comes an elevated level of tolerance for other people and events in life. It will seem to take much less effort to be able to get more work finished in a shorter amount of time.

Self-discipline is a hard thing to master, but it gives its own set of rewards in a greater sense of self-worth and a greater ability to accomplish tasks—and achieving the desired goal can be its own best reward.

CONCLUSION

Thank you for making it through to the end of *Self-Discipline: Develop Daily Habits to Program Your Mind and Build Mental Toughness, Self-Confidence, and Willpower*! Let's hope it was informative and able to provide you with all of the tools you need to achieve your goals —whatever they may be.

The next step is to begin to use the steps contained in this book to revolutionize your life. Use these ideas to learn how to set goals, eliminate bad habits, get rid of negative thoughts and emotions, and just overall build a better lifestyle. People who have a higher level of self-control and self-confidence automatically perform better in school, at work, and just in life, in general. It is your time to shine.

Thus, use this book for what it was meant for—a self-help manual for developing a greater sense of self-control and self-confidence. Gaining a better level of self-confidence will require hard work and dedication. It will mean deciding what is important in life—what can stay and what must go. It may mean giving up some events that are fun—things that were once considered a vitally important part of life. It will certainly involve making great changes and experiencing many new things in life.

Building mental toughness is not as difficult as it sounds. It merely means using the growth of good habits to retrain the pathways in the brain to eliminate bad habits—and in the world of self-discipline, the word "willpower," also known as personal stubbornness, is a good thing.

So please, use this book and the tips and trick contained inside to better your own life. Read the examples so that you will fully understand the point that is being made. Make notes if you find that helps you to better understand and remember. Read the book, and then read it again more slowly. Study it closely. The advice in this book is meant to give you a chance to make your life much more fulfilling by increasing your personal level of self-control and self-confidence.

Realize that these changes will not happen overnight. Change for the better always takes time. It is necessary to eliminate the bad habits while working to cultivate the good habits one wants to pursue. This might mean changing such habits as for where you drive, where you eat, and when and where you decide to go out for a fun evening—but know that at the end, when self-confidence is at an all-time high, that the journey was well worth it.

Finally, if you found this book useful in any way, a review on Amazon is always appreciated!

MANIPULATION

Techniques in Dark Psychology, Influencing People with Persuasion, NLP, and Mind Control

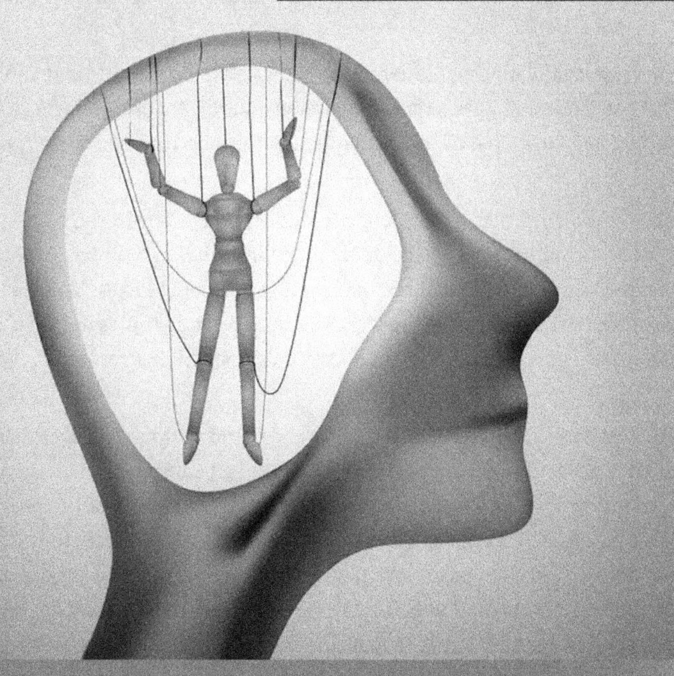

EDWARD BENEDICT

INTRODUCTION

Manipulation is the conscious act of causing someone to do a certain thing or act in a certain way. Manipulation is clever, skillful, and sometimes unscrupulous. Manipulation is not always a bad thing. The clay bowl created in an art class was made from clay that was manipulated by someone's hands. The doctor put the broken bone back into place by using manipulation. The snowman was built by the hands of children who manipulated the snow into place.

Sometimes, manipulation is a bad thing. People can be manipulated to do things they would not usually do. Spouses manipulate each other. Parents manipulate children. And supervisors manipulate employees. People who manipulate others often act as though they have only the best interests in mind for the other person. They use caring as a disguise in getting what they really want, no matter what the other person wants. People who manipulate others in a negative way are usually known by an uncomplimentary term, such as sociopath or narcissist.

Knowing that manipulation is happening is the first step towards ending it. By knowing the signs of manipulation, people can often stop it before it becomes a bad habit or a detrimental way of life. Understanding how manipulation works is the key to controlling it and eliminating it.

1

MANIPULATING THE MIND THROUGH NLP

MANIPULATION HAS COME TO CARRY A NEGATIVE meaning but that is not necessarily true in all cases. Manipulation merely means to shape or mold something to a new, more desirable shape. Snow can be manipulated into the shape of a snowman. Clay can be manipulated into almost any shape. Small children being taught to take turns when playing and to use their manners are, in a sense, being manipulated by their parents. So manipulation is not always a negative event.

USING MANIPULATION TO CONTROL THE MIND OF another person is powerful and fascinating. Since the mind is the key to everything a human being does, the ability to control that mind gives multitudes of power and ability. Techniques used to control the mind work because they take control of the thoughts a person has. These techniques are based primarily on the method of Neuro-Linguistic Programming (NLP). Using NLP makes it possible to control other people's minds using specific patterns and strategies.

. . .

THE HUMAN MIND WORKS IN A SPECIFIC WAY. IT LOOKS for cause and effect. The mind creates an event in response to a stimulus it has received. Sometimes doctors use a test called an electroencephalogram to measure the actual physical working of the brain in order to look for patterns of activity that are associated with certain diseases and conditions, such as epilepsy. The two brain states most often studied are the alpha state and the beta state. The beta state is a high-function, active state. The alpha state has much lower frequencies than the beta state. It is the place where the mind experiences calmness and peacefulness. This state is very important because it is the state psychologists and hypnotists use for programming the mind, simply because this state carries fewer thought patterns than any other state in the brain.

THE TECHNIQUES USED IN NLP ENABLE THE PERSON doing the programming to introduce thoughts into another person's mind when it is unconscious that the person will not necessarily be aware of when conscious. The power of persuasion in NLP makes it a strong technique that is often used in fields such as marketing, politics, and the business world. Signals are used to convey thoughts into the unconscious mind that will influence the mind when the person is conscious.

SKILLED PROFESSIONALS WHO REGULARLY USE NLP TO control other people know that the mind can be programmed to do amazing things if the person will allow it to happen. Often, people are resistant to this type of control because they are afraid of what might happen. There are countless jokes about a hypnotist making someone bark like a dog at a certain stimulus when they are awake. That is possible. But NLP has many good, positive uses.

THE MAIN OBJECTIVE OF NLP IS TO BRING ABOUT INNER changes in the way people see the world. It creates mental changes in the way events are perceived and teaches ways to engage in communication that is more responsible. It helps people make choices for more effectively responding or communicating in a given situation. It does not matter if the situation is of a professional or personal nature. These techniques enable the person to make better choices and also to feel empowered to carry out the choices.

SOMEONE TAKING ADVANTAGE OF THE POWER OF NLP will experience techniques similar to those used in hypnosis. During a therapy session, the person will be placed into a deep state of relaxation so that they are able to access the deepest section of their mind where unconscious thought is formed. They are then led on a mental quest through years of accumulated thoughts and beliefs. The ultimate goal is to access the experience from childhood that caused a particular pattern of behavior. The theory behind NLP is that all people carry all the resources needed to make positive life changes in their own minds. NLP merely gives them access to this information and gives them the techniques to use to make needed changes.

THE THERAPIST DOES NOT EVEN NEED TO KNOW ABOUT the problem that the person wishes to address. Techniques can be taught that will enable the person to make the necessary corrections without the therapist ever knowing what the actual problem is.

THE THERAPY TECHNIQUES IN NLP ACT ON THE THEORY that all humans are perfect creations of nature. NLP therapists use this belief to teach people how to access their own sensory abilities and how to use these abilities to act on a particular stimulus or event. NLP practitioners also believe it is possible to teach the mind how to control the body to eliminate certain diseases.

The techniques used in NLP are not invasive and do not involve the use of medication. NLP can help with ways to increase self-esteem, correct destructive patterns and behaviors in personal relationships, improve the personal level of self-confidence, and are better able to cope with events that cause anxiety. There are many different techniques that NLP practitioners use to enable people to use these methods effectively.

NLP CAN BE USED TO TREAT SIMPLE CASES OF POST-Traumatic Stress Disorder (PTSD). With PTSD, the person has experienced a traumatic event and that they experience stressful reactions when they encounter an event similar to the original traumatic event. This technique involves taking the person mentally through the event from beginning to end, reliving it in the mind as closely as possible. Then the therapist takes the patient through the event again, but this time from the end to the beginning. The idea is to take the person back to a safe place from the traumatic event so that when recurring events happen the mind automatically goes to the safe place and not the reaction place.

. . .

A METHOD FOR TREATING ANXIETY IS A PROCESS THAT teaches the person to mentally track the physical path of the symptoms the feeling causes in the body. The patient is taught to think of an event that would cause feelings of anxiety. Then the patient is told to mentally follow the track of the physical response. For example, the physical response might begin in the stomach, travel to the chest, and then go down through the arms. Once the path is traced, the patient then turns their attention to the actual shape the feeling takes as it travels through the body. What size is the shape? Does it have a particular color? By totally understanding what the feeling looks like, the patient is able to reduce some of the power the shape holds. Then the patient is instructed to feel which way the feeling turns as it comes up through the body. Does it turn clockwise or counterclockwise? By determining the direction of the spiral the patient is then taught to turn the feeling in the other direction, effectively unwinding it and removing its source of power. The patient is also instructed to change the shape and color of the feeling, changing it to something more pleasant.

NLP CAN BE USED TO EFFECTIVELY TO CHANGE PROBLEM behaviors or emotions into positive ones. One process used provides a transformation process for the very core of the person. This process is highly client involved because the client personally addresses the problem mentally. The first step is for the person to ask the negative feeling what its intention is, and what it hopes to gain if it gets what it wants. Then the patient asks the feeling what its secondary desire is to achieve, once it gains its first desire. The patient continues in this vein until it reaches an answer that is based on emotion, such as happiness or peace, instead of a behavior or a thing. Once the end result is revealed, the patient then instructs the problem to automatically look for the pleasant emotion first, bypassing all other steps. Then the event that triggered the negative reaction originally will now cause a positive reaction.

ANOTHER POPULAR NLP PROCESS IS FEEDBACK. Sometimes, this is referred to as biofeedback, especially when it is used in a medical setting. The basis of this technique lies in the idea that there will not be a failure but that the feedback will be successful. The idea is that a successful outcome will not be instantaneous but will be the result of a constantly repeating loop from the feedback. The lack of immediate success is viewed as a flaw in the feedback and not an immediate failure. This requires a feeling of ultimate faith in the process which is sometimes difficult, but it is necessary for success.

THIS METHOD WAS CREATED TO CHANGE THE BELIEFS that cause humans to see limits to their personal capabilities. This method runs under the assumption that multiple sensory experiences gather together to form a body of experience much like an emotional molecule. Revisiting the experience usually gives the person a mental picture of the event in great detail, feelings and emotions that were mentally gathered during the event, and messages gathered from others. Anything that has formed an attachment to the memory is examined in great detail. Then these attachments are examined, one by one, taken separately from one another. This removes the power from the memory group as a whole because each individual part of the memory has no power on its own. Then the mind is taught to use individual parts to create a new memory molecule that is made up of the remembrances the person chooses.

. . .

Another popularly used method is anchoring. This method employs the use of different colored paper circles that the patient uses to move from one event to another. The first circle is used to recall the unwanted stimulus and the particular event that leads to it. The other colored circles are used to represent a different, happier feeling. Thus the patient is taught to stand on the original circle to recall the unwanted emotion, and then move to another circle in order to replace the negative emotion with positive emotion. Once the emotion is changed to a positive one, the patient then returns to the original circle. The idea is to replace the negative emotions the event evokes with a new, more positive emotion.

One method that has shown success in relieving the physical effects of anxiety and insomnia is to follow the feeling. Using this technique the patient begins by relaxing deeply. Then the patient is instructed to name where the feeling is placed in the body. This will be uncomfortable but it is necessary for the patient to know exactly where the feeling is and to acknowledge its presence. The patient is told to just feel it but not interact with it. Then the patient is told to ask questions of the feeling. Ask the feeling what it needs to help it leave the body. Take note of the first thought that comes into the mind. Check to see if the feeling is still present. If it is, then ask the feeling the question again. Keep accepting the feeling while questioning it. Keep asking the same question until no more answers come and the feeling is gone.

NLP may seem to have its basis in something dark and mysterious, but it really does not. NLP is nothing more than a method to use to teach the mind how to release the control that negative events have on the physical well-being and emotional state of the person. Think of the mind as a series of pathways. Every habit a person indulges in has its own pathway in the brain. When a stimulus occurs—something seen, heard, smelled, or remembered—a message is sent to a particular spot in the brain along a particular pathway. This is the spot that holds the memory for the reaction the mind has decided is appropriate for this stimulus. If a person sees their favorite cake they experience hunger. This is the mind's response to the stimulus the body received. So pathways can be created from good and bad experiences. The purpose of NLP is to reroute the pathways of negative stimuli and change the reaction to something pleasant and not something harmful or negative. In this way, NLP can be used for great benefits to people.

2
THE POWER OF PERSUASION

THE POWER OF PERSUASION MEANS NOTHING MORE than using mental abilities to form words and feelings used to convince other people to do things they may or may not want to do. Some people are better able to persuade than other people. And some people are easier to persuade then other people.

The ease of persuading other people is directly tied to their current mental or emotional state. Someone who is lonely or tired is easier to persuade, simply because their defenses are lowered. Someone who is momentarily needy may be easier to persuade than someone who has a strong sense of self-worth. People who are at a low point in their lives are easy prey for others who might try to persuade them to do something they might not usually do.

Think of the publicity surrounding religious cults in the past. Everyone wanted to know how someone could fall prey to the teachings and ideals of the cult. The answer is simple: the victim was seeking something the cult offered. Whether the dangling carrot was food and shelter or love or religious freedom, the cult offers something tangible to the person who feels their life is lacking something important. And the person who joins the cult does not see themselves as a victim, but a participant. Think back further to the flower children of the sixties and seventies. These people lived in communes where everyone had a particular role to play. Some people would grow gardens to feed the members of the commune while others might wash laundry or clean houses. Everyone helped everyone else. The idea behind living in a commune was to leave behind the trappings that 'society' deemed as markers of success, such as fat paychecks and huge houses. These people wanted to live simply and enjoy what love and Mother Nature had to offer.

For every good group that assembles for the good of the people and works to help its members, there are countless groups that are brought together by forces that have no desire other than controlling other people for their own good. These leaders are very charismatic and very dangerous, because a person who is temporarily weak in mind or in the soul may not be able to resist their promises. It is important for everyone to understand how persuasion works in order to be able to resist it when needed.

The first step in persuasion involves the idea of reciprocating. If a person does something nice for someone else, then the receiving person usually feels the need to do something good in return. If someone helps their elderly neighbor carry in groceries from the car, that neighbor might feel obligated to bake homemade cookies for that person. A coworker who helps complete a project is more likely to receive assistance when it is needed. Many people do nice things for others all the time without expecting anything in return. The person who does nice things for people and then mentions some little favor that can be done in return may be someone to watch closely.

Nonprofit organizations use this tactic to gain more contributions to their causes. They will often send some little trinket or gift to prompt people to donate larger sums of money, or even just to donate where they might not have originally. The idea behind this is that the person opening the letter has received a little gift for no reason, so they might feel obligated to give something in return.

The consistency of self is the next step. People who commit to something, through verbal or written methods, are more likely to follow through on the idea that someone who makes no promises, Even if the original motivation is gone or the original incentive was taken away, people see this promise as being part of their image. They made a promise. This is often why counselors tell people to write their goals down. People are more likely to follow a written list they can refer to daily.

It is easy enough to change someone's image of themselves, especially if that person is needy or mentally weak. During times of war, it is customary to get prisoners to denounce their own country in order to hopefully turn others against that country. This is easy enough to do when starved prisoners are also mentally weak and have few defenses to use to deflect their captors. By constantly repeating statements that denounce the home country the captive begins to believe what they are saying because it must be true because they are saying it.

Another thing to be careful of is what is known as the herd mentality. Humans live in groups. Most of us want to belong to the herd and want to enjoy the safety being in a herd brings. Monkey see, monkey do. People tend to mirror the behavior seen around them. Think of the story of the emperor that runs around with no clothes on. His tailors had him convinced he was wearing fine garments, so he convinced all the people of his kingdom. And because they could not question the king, they had to believe what he was saying. This can also work in seriously negative ways.

Think of the mob mentality. This is just another way to follow the herd, but it usually involves illegal or dangerous activities engaged in only because someone else was doing the same thing.

Some people are automatically tempted to follow authority. People in positions of authority can command blind respect to their authority simply by acting a certain way or putting on a uniform. The problem with this is that authority figures or those that look like authority figures, can cause some people to do extraordinary things they would not normally do had a person in a position of authority not been the one asking. And it is not simply held to people in uniform. People who carry themselves a certain way or speak a certain way can give the impression that they are something they are not.

For someone or something to be considered a credible authority, it must be familiar and people must have trust in the person or organization. Someone who knows all there is to know about a subject is considered an expert and is more likely to be trusted than someone who has limited knowledge of the subject. But the information must also make sense to the people hearing it. If there is not some semblance of accuracy and intelligence then the authority figure loses credibility. Even the person who is acknowledged as an expert will lack persuasive abilities if they are seen as not being trustworthy.

People want to be liked. People want to like other people. The problem is when some people use this fact to cause other people to do things they might not ordinarily do. People who are easy to like usually come across as very persuasive. People want to believe them. Con artists are extremely likeable people. The problem is that even likeable people may not have your personal best interests at heart. In fact, they probably only have their own interest in mind. Even someone who is totally legitimate, like a salesperson, is really most interested in their own interests. They may want their customer to be perfectly happy with their purchase so they will recommend that salesperson to their friends, but their ultimate concern is with themselves and their sales goals.

The worst part of the power that goes along with persuasion is that things that are scarce or hard to get are seen as much more valuable. People value diamonds because they are expensive and beautiful. If they were merely pretty stones, they would not be as interesting. Inconsistent rewards are a lot more interesting than consistent rewards. If a cookie falls every time a person rings a bell, then they are less likely to spend a lot of time ringing the bell because they know the cookie reward will always appear. If, however, the cookie only appears sometimes, people will spend much more time ringing the bell just in case this is the time the cookie will fall.

There are ways to improve the power of persuasion. Just like any other trait, it can be made stronger by following a few strategies and by regular practice.

Never hesitate to ask others what they think. Usually, those in a position of authority will not look for advice from other people. This is an opportunity many leaders neglect to take advantage of. Instead of asking others for their opinion and ideas, they miss the chance to make everyone feel like part of the group with an equal role to play. Besides, leaders who are not afraid to ask for input from others might learn something they did not know before.

Always remember to ask for advice, not feedback. People love being asked to give advice. Asking for feedback means that an opinion has already been given and the speaker wants to know what everyone else thinks of their own opinion. In many situations, there will be no responses because no one wants to disagree or be seen as argumentative, particularly with an authority figure.

But asking for advice gives people a chance to voice their own opinions.

Before asking for any type of assistance, set the stage. People do not like being put on the spot. Walking up to someone and immediately asking for a favor sends two messages. The first one is that the favor is more important than the person. In this case, the favor needed is the focus of the conversation. Say that Bob walks into the room, goes straight up to Bill and asks Bill to assist at a fundraiser that weekend. Bill is caught off guard and must make an immediate decision. Does he say no, in front of others, and look like a mean-spirited person for not helping at the fundraiser? Or does he answer with yes without really knowing if he wants to do it or not? Whichever way the conversation goes, when Bill looks back on it later he may wonder if Bill even considers him a friend or if he just comes around when he wants help with something.

Now if Bob had bothered to set the stage for asking for the favor, he would have approached the conversation in a totally different manner. First, he would have approached Bill with a friendly greeting and cheerful smile. He would take a few minutes to make small talk with Bill, perhaps asking about his work life or his family life. After chatting cheerfully for a few minutes Bob would approach the idea of the fundraiser in a casual manner. "Hey, Bill, by the way…." He would explain what he needed Bill to do, explain how much he would really enjoy having Bill's presence at the fundraiser, then asking Bill to get back with him as soon as possible with an answer. He would assure Bill that whatever decision he made would be fine, although he really hoped Bill would be able to join him.

What is the difference between the two situations? In the second situation, Bill feels wanted. He feels needed. He feels as though his presence, or the lack of it, is important to Bob. In the second situation, Bob is most likely to get an honest answer. And what if Bill is not able to help Bob at the fundraiser? Bill will be more likely to help Bob in the future because he not only feels valued but he feels like he owes Bob something, Bill would probably be thinking that he owed Bob one in the future.

Persuasion is a powerful tool in the game of life. Persuasive people know that they have an amazing power, and they know how to use it correctly. They know how to listen and really hear what other people have to say. They are very good at making a connection with other people, and this makes them seem even more honest and friendly. They make others feel that they are knowledgeable and can offer a certain sense of satisfaction. They also know when to momentarily retreat and regroup. They are not pushy. They are persuasive.

3
DEFINING DESIRED OUTCOMES

The idea behind being a persuasive person, the main objective of persuasion, is to get something in return. There is no sense in practicing the art of persuasion if there is nothing desired in return. Persuasion means to cause someone to do something specific. Therefore, some sort of gain is desired, some sort of end result.

In order to know the intended end result of the persuasive effort, there must be a defined desired outcome. The person doing the persuading wants something tangible, something definable. But what do they want? Well, that is completely up to them to decide. But they must decide, before engaging in any form of persuasion, exactly what they hope to achieve at the end of the conversation.

This is what is meant as defining desired outcomes. The thing that is desired must be decided before any kind of persuasive tactics begin so that the person doing the persuading understands the desired outcome.

Pretend the office is holding a meeting to decide the location of a new office. The old office is small and cramped. The business is growing and needs more room to be able to continue to grow. So an office meeting will take place where, hopefully, the new location will be decided upon. This is the first step in defining the desired outcome, knowing what the proposed outcome is. In this case, it is the location of the new office.

So the meeting has been set for a particular time and place. Finished, right? Wrong. Without some sort of order and organization, the meeting will be unproductive and the desired outcome probably will not happen. The meeting is crucial to the desired outcome. Without some sort of specific plan then the meeting is nothing more than people in an office meeting in one room to make conversation.

So now it is necessary to set up the meeting; to have a plan as to how the meeting will proceed. Since this is a meeting of the entire office, there is no need to decide who to invite since everyone will be in attendance. So the next step is to create the agenda for the meeting. Will there be time for questions? Will certain people be invited to participate by offering specific recommendations for the new location? How will the ultimate decision be reached? All these factors need to be decided before the meeting begins.

When beginning the meeting be sure to mention the desired outcome. Let everyone know exactly what they are there to discuss. Make sure everyone involved knows and understand the desired outcome. Set a specific time for discussion and a time when the decision will be made. Then when the meeting is reaching the end of its prescribed time restate the objective and determine if a decision can be made or if more research is needed.

An outcome is nothing more than an end result that can be seen and measures. It is the consequence of the action. It is the conclusion that comes from persuading someone to do something. In any desired outcome there are four things that will need to be decided before the desired outcome can be decided upon. Those four things are: is something specific desired, is something already owned needing to be kept, who should be connected with and how, and what skills are needed to achieve the desired outcome.

It is important to decide these things because the underlying objectives will definitely affect the way the outcome is to be gained. It is similar to a football game where there is a defensive team and an offensive team. One group attacks the opposing team and one group defends against the attacks from the opposing teams. Each team will have a different set of priorities and procedures. Their desired outcomes will be quite different from one another. Each team will need to decide what it is they want to learn, defend, or acquire. The goal will determine the game plan.

The goal is the desired outcome. Behind any goal and its desired outcome is the need for change. Some sort of change needed has been identified and will be achieved. The path to achievement begins with setting a goal. The end of this journey is the desired outcome. It is necessary to understand that these are two separate entities that work together to achieve a result.

A goal is a destination. An outcome is a specific thing; it can be seen and measured. While setting the goal is vital to receiving the outcome, they are two quite different things and should be treated as such.

Goals always have reasons behind them. Something that is thought of as being necessary to happiness, to wealth, to health, or just because it is truly desired, is just not there. Whatever the reason is, it is that exact reason that drives forward progress toward the desired outcome. In order to be able to progress, to go forward to the goal, that goal and the idea of achieving it must be firmly entrenched in your mind. Without a steady focus on the goal, there is no possibility that the goal will ever be reached.

Imagine going to work every day for fifteen years, doing the same job every day. Imagine this is a job that needed college courses, so it was a chosen job. During the past fifteen years, doing the same job every day has been rewarding and profitable. There have been several promotions, the last of which came with a private secretary and a lovely large office. Several other people, who have not been working here quite as long, are now the team that directly reports every Monday in this large new office.

But going to work has become somewhat boring. The job just does not bring the amount of satisfaction it once did. The problem is not in the job itself but in the person doing the job. What seemed so right all those years ago now feels so wrong. What is really desired is more interaction with people. In managing other people, a new skill has emerged: the ability to take raw recruits and mold them into productive team members with a bright future. That is the job that brings happiness and satisfaction.

But while this thought has been firmly entrenched in the mind for months now, no changes have been made to get closer to the goal of that type of occupation. And so every Monday morning is filled with team meetings, every day is filled with spreadsheets, and every Friday is filled with boundless joy that another work week has passed. Why?

The answer to *Why?* Is procrastination. Whether intentional or unintentional, procrastination has ruined many good intentions. Unintentional procrastination does happen sometimes. Everyone has that moment of "oops, I meant to take care of that today I'll get to it first thing in the morning." That is unintentional; something was forgotten. Intentional procrastination means knowing something needs to be done but putting it off until whenever. Many people do this with dreams and desires, especially those that will require extra work to accomplish or simply just a big leap of faith. Changing careers when one is firmly established is a scary thing. But what someone wants at twenty is not necessarily what they want at forty. People change. Their hearts change. They must be willing to follow their dreams and make them a reality. But people procrastinate out of fear.

So ask these three questions:

1. What exactly am I afraid of? Do I fear to lose a great job that will pay for my kid's college and not being able to find one that pays as well? What if I have to take a pay cut and can no longer pay the mortgage? What happens if I lose my health insurance? These are all valid question that must be addressed when considering a large change in employment.
2. What will I gain if I am able to conquer this fear? What great gain will be realized? Will it be a new job, a new career that is more in line with current life goals? Maybe the real dream is the chance to help other people.
3. What do I do to fight this fear? Accept the fear as real. Acknowledge its existence. Then make a plan to reach the new goal and proceed without waiting. Go forward without procrastination.

Now, it is time to set a goal to make this dream a reality. Identify the goal as specifically as possible. The more specific the goal, the better the chance is to realize that goal. Vague goals are nothing more than wishes. It is as simple as the difference between "I want to lose weight" and "I want to lose twenty pounds." The second statement is a specific goal that can be measured as work toward it progresses.

Know exactly what is desired as a reward when the goal is

achieved. If the goal is weight loss, perhaps the reward is being able to wear that dress featured in the store window. If the goal is learning how to swim, then maybe the goal is to swim in the ocean for the first time ever. Plan how this goal will be achieved. Think about the senses that will be used along the way and how they will make this progress easier or more difficult.

Visualize the plan and try to imagine any possible obstacles. That does not mean putting the obstacles in the path, but in being aware of the possibility that they might crop up and having a plan to defeat them. If the intended goal involves weight loss, what will be the plan for coping with the buffet during the holiday season? If the goal is to complete classes online then what happens if the internet goes out or the computer crashes? It is necessary to have a back-up plan to deal with life's little emergencies.

What will be used for markers along the way to track progress toward the goal? If the goal is weight loss, then perhaps a wall chart with every five pounds lost marked in red. Perhaps a drawing of a thermometer, with the goal being the mercury bulb at the top, and the thermometer is filled in gradually with every pound lost. Have a system in place to track these milestones.

Be aware that working toward any goal might come with negatives attached. Changing careers will most certainly mean a change in income. What if the career change means moving to another state? Is that a viable option? An extreme amount of weight loss will mean constantly refreshing the wardrobe. It is important to be aware of anything that might be seen as a negative effect of reaching the goal. These must be acceptable or the goal will need to be changed.

And when little distractions occur along the way, do not let them cancel out any progress that has already been made. Life happens. All roads have bumps in them. Even Shakespeare knew that no matter how good the plan was, it might not work. So acknowledge the fact that little bumps in the road will happen and have a plan to overcome them. Maybe it was a temporary lapse in judgement. Maybe it is a sign that the current path needs to take a bit of a different direction. The choice is solely up to the person who set the goal and created the path. And when the goal is reached, so will be the desired outcome.

4
MIND CONTROL TECHNIQUES

MIND CONTROL INVOLVES USING INFLUENCE AND persuasion to change the behaviors and beliefs in someone. That someone might be the person themselves or it might be someone else. Mind control has also been referred to as brainwashing, thought reform, coercive persuasion, mental control, and manipulation, just to name a few. Some people feel that everything is done by manipulation. But if that is true to be believed, then important points about manipulation will be lost. Influence is much better thought of as a mental continuum with two extremes. One side has influences that are respectful and ethical and work to improve the individual while showing respect for them and their basic human rights. The other side contains influences that are dark and destructive that work to remove basic human rights from a person, such as independence, the ability for rational thought, and sometimes their total identity.

When thinking of mind control, it is better to see it as a way to use influence on other people that will disrupt something in them, like their way of thinking or living. Influence works on the very basis of what makes people human, such as their behaviors, beliefs, and values. It can disrupt the very way they chose personal preferences or make critical decisions. Mind control is nothing more than using words and ideas to convince someone to say or do something they might never have thought of saying or doing on their own.

There are scientifically proven methods that can be used to influence other people. Mind control has nothing to do with fakery, ancient arts, or even magical powers. Real mind control really is the basis of a word that many people hate to hear. That word is marketing. Many people hate to hear that word because of the negative connotations associated with it. When people hear "marketing," they automatically assume that it refers to those ideas taught in business school. But the basis of marketing is not about deciding which part of the market to target or deciding which customers will likely buy this product. The basis of marketing is one very simple word. That word is "YES."

If a salesperson asks a regular customer to write a brief endorsement of the product they buy, hopefully, they will say yes. If someone asks their significant other to take some of the business cards to pass out at work, hopefully, they will say yes. If you write any kind of blog and ask another blogger to provide a link to yours on their blog, hopefully, they will say yes. When enough people say yes, the business or blog will begin to grow. With even more yesses, it will continue to grow and thrive. This is the very simple basis of marketing. Marketing is nothing more than using mind control to get other people to buy something or to do something beneficial for someone else. And the techniques can easily be learned.

The first technique in mind control is to tell people what you want them to want. Never tell people to think it over or take some time. That is a definite mind control killer. People already have too much going on in their minds. When they are told to think something over they will not. It will be forgotten, and then it will never happen. This has nothing to do with being stupid or lazy and everything to do with just being way too busy.

So the best strategy is to take the offensive and think for them. Everything must be explained in the beginning. Never assume that the other blogger will automatically understand the benefits of adding a link will be for them. Do not expect anyone to give a demonstration blindly. And merely asking for a testimonial, while it might garner an appositive response, probably will not garner a well-formed testimonial to the product. Instead, be prepared to explain the blog, show examples, and offer compelling reasons why this merger will be a benefit to both parties. Have the demonstration laid out in great detail with notes on what to say when and visuals to go along with the notes, so all the other person has to do is present the information. Offer the customer a few variations of testimonials that have already been received and ask them to choose one and personalize it a bit. Always be specific in explaining what is desired. Explain why it is desired. Show how this will work. Tell the person how to do it and why they should do it. If done correctly it will feel exactly like one friend advising another friend on which is the best path to take. And the answer will be yes simply because saying yes makes so much sense.

Think of the avalanche. Think of climbing all the way to the top of the highest mountain ever. Now, at the top, think of searching for the biggest heaviest boulder that exists on the mountain. Now, picture summoning up superhuman strength to push this boulder, dislodging it from the place it has rested for years and years. Once this boulder is loosened, it rolls easily over the edge of the cliff, crashing into thousands of other boulders on its way down the mountain, taking half of the mountain with it in a beautiful cascade of rocks and dirt. Imagine sitting there smiling cheerfully at the avalanche that was just created.

Marketing and mind control are very like creating an avalanche. Getting the first person to answer yes might be difficult. But each subsequent yes will be easier and easier. And always start at the top, never the bottom. Starting at the top is definitely more difficult, and it is more likely to come with more negative responses than positive responses in the beginning. But starting at the top also yields a much greater reward when the avalanche does begin. And the results will be far greater than beginning at the bottom of the mountain. Yes, the small rock is easier to push over. Then it can be built upon by pushing over another small rock, then another. This way can work, but it will take much longer than being successful at the top. No one ever went fishing for the smallest fish in the pond or auditioned for the secondary role just to be safe. Everyone wants that top prize. Do not be afraid to go for it.

On the other hand, never ask for the whole boulder the first time. Ask for part of it. This may seem directly contradictory but it is not. Always start with a small piece. Make the beginning easier for everyone to see. Let other people use their own insight to see the end result. When the first bit goes well, then gradually ask for more and more and more.

Think of writing a guest spot for someone else who has their own blog. By sending in the entire manuscript first, there is a greater risk of rejection. Begin small. Send them a paragraph or two discussing them the idea. Then make an outline of the idea and send that in an email. Then write the complete draft you would like them too use and send it along. When asking a customer for a testimonial, start by asking for a few lines in an email. Then ask the customer to expand those few lines into a testimonial that covers at least half a typed page. Soon the customer will be ready for an hour-long webcast extolling the virtues of the product and your great customer service skills.

Everything must have a deadline that really exists. The important word here is the word 'real'. Everyone has heard the salesperson who said to decide quickly because the deal might not be available later or another customer was coming in and they might get it. That is a total fabrication and everyone knows it to be true. There are no impending other customers and the deal is not going to disappear. There is no real sense of urgency involved. But everyone does it. There are too many situations where people are given a totally fake deadline by someone who thinks it will instill a great sense of urgency for completion of the task. It is not only totally not effective but completely unneeded. It is a simple matter to create true urgency. Only leave free things available for a finite amount of time. When asking customers for testimonials be certain to mention the last possible day for it to be received to be able to be used. Some people will be unable to assist, but having people unable to participate is better than never being able to begin.

Always give before you receive. And do not ever think that giving is fifty-fifty. Always give much more than is expected in return. Before asking for a testimonial from a satisfied customer, be sure to make numerous acts of exceptional customer service. Before asking a blog writer for a link, link theirs to yours many times. This is not about helping someone out so they will help you. This is all about being so totally generous that the person who is asked for the favor cannot possibly say no. It might mean extra work, but that is how to influence other people.

Always stand up for something that is much bigger than average. Do not just write another blog on how to do something. Use an important issue to take a stand and defend the stance with unbeatable logic and fervent passion. Do not just write a how-to manual. Choose a particular idea and sell people on it, using examples of other people with the same idea living the philosophy.

Never feel shame. This does not mean being extremely extroverted to the point of silliness or having a total lack of conscience in business dealings. In the case of mind control shamelessness refers to a total complete belief that this course of action is the best possible course and everyone will benefit greatly from it. This is about writing the best possible blog ever and believing that everyone needs to read it to be able to improve their lives. It is about believing in a particular product so deeply that the feeling is that everyone will benefit from using it. It is knowing deep inside that this belief is the most correct belief ever and everyone should believe it.

Mind control uses the idea that someone's decisions and emotions can be controlled using psychological means. It is using powers of negotiation or mental influence to ensure the outcome of the interaction is more favorable to one person over the other. This is basically what marketing is: convincing someone to do something particular or buy something in particular. Being able to control someone else's mind merely means understanding the power of human emotion and being able to play upon those emotions. It is easier to have a mental impact on people if there is a basic understanding of human emotions. Angry people will back down when the subject of their anger is not afraid. Angry people feed upon the fear of others. Guilt is another great motivator. Making someone feel guilty for not thinking or feeling, in the same manner, is a wonderful way to get them to give in. Another way to use mind control over someone is to point out how valuable they are to the situation. Controlling the mind of another does not mean depriving them of free will and conscious thought. It means knowing what to say to impact the other person so profoundly they cannot see any other way to go but the one proposed.

5

MIND CONTROL WITH NLP FOR LOVE AND RELATIONSHIPS

PEOPLE ARE OFTEN A PRODUCT OF THEIR ENVIRONMENT, whether they want to be or not. The way people are raised directly affects the way they act in later life. Someone who is raised by alcoholics has a greater chance of becoming alcoholics in adult life, or they may choose never to drink at all. People who are raised in a house where everything is forbidden may cut loose and go a bit crazy when they are finally out on their own. People who are raised in total disorganization may grow up to be totally obsessive about household cleanliness.

Nurture affects people in other, less severe ways, too. Many people believe that Mom's meatloaf is the absolute best and no other recipe exists. People come from different religious and economic backgrounds. People have different beliefs about what is good and bad, what is acceptable and unacceptable. The problem comes when two people are trying to have a relationship, but neither wants to change their way of thinking. When that happens there is no relationship. There are just two people living together under the same roof.

Achieving success in love is just like achieving success in anything else. It is mostly a function of developing good relationships with other people in order to be better able to influence them. Those people who are successful in creating and keeping good, mutually satisfactory relationships with others usually enjoy much more success than people who do not do this. The ability to grow and maintain satisfactory relationships is a trait that is easier for some people. But even if the ability does not come naturally it is easy enough to learn. And Neuro-Linguistic Programming (NLP) makes this skill easier to learn by offering tools and ideas to enable almost anyone to learn the ability to develop great relationships.

People never stop communicating with each other. Any type of social contact is done with some form of communication. Even if there is no actual speaking, there is communicating. If a couple has an argument and stops talking to one another, they are now using frustration and anger to communicate in silence. Teenagers who close themselves off in their rooms and refuse to speak to the remainder of the family are silently communicating their desire to be left alone. Even in situations that are more neutral people continue to communicate with looks, sighs, and body language.

Becoming more aware of this will bring a hugely different perspective on personal relationships. A great deal of the actual communication between two people is unconscious and not verbal. People send out unconscious signals all the time to other people without even realizing they are doing it. The first most important step in improving relationships with others is to understand the ways people communicate without speaking and to become aware of these habits when they happen. Becoming better aware of these habits is a total life changer. Even if no other changes are made. Becoming better aware of the proper way to interact with others in life will make a huge impact on the quality of personal relationships.

People usually think their own opinion is right, that their own opinion is the best one there is in existence. NLP teaches us that humans see all experiences from behind a group of filters such as things that are expected and values that have been learned. These filters have been developed over a lifetime of learning. Once this is understood and accepted, it is infinitely easier to form an understanding of what drives the behavior of other people. Other people act in ways that may be quite different. People look at the world through lenses that see things differently. Other people have a different mental model of the world or they may travel on a different internal path.

In NLP, people are reminded that traveling the map is not the exact territory. Everyone has their own map. A normal course of action highly defends the home map. Instead, NLP guides people to try to understand the maps other people use on their travels through the world, and to make every attempt to learn from the differences in travel maps.

People who truly want to control a situation will learn to behave with the most flexibility. Think of the situations seen in nature. Plants and animals that are most likely to survive are those that are able to quickly adapt to the situation. Plants grow in the desert because they have adapted to the lack of water and are able to survive on very little. Small rodents survive a harsh winter by storing food to eat when there is not readily available food. Animals in the Arctic Circle will fatten up during the fall in order to have fat stores to feed them during the lean months of hibernation. This line of thought is also applicable to humans.

Using the map of the personal world analogy, think of it this way: people who can easily switch their thoughts among different world maps will easily be able to communicate with many different groups of people. These people will be much more effective at creating and maintaining meaningful relationships with others. Those people who only see and understand one method of behavior or one distinct way of viewing the world will eventually be left behind. They will become isolated as situations in the world change until they are no longer relevant in the real world.

When others do not understand the message, it is automatically seen to be their own fault. A person gives a message and expects that it will be easily understood by everyone else. This is often not the way things work. Using NLP gives a new perspective on this understanding. NLP teaches that it is the responsibility of the person sending the message to communicate in a way that the message can be easily understood. If it is not easily understood, the fault lies with the sender, not with the receiver. This all goes back to the idea of flexibility. If a person wants someone else to get the message, that person needs to speak in the other person's language. It is necessary to know exactly what the other person feels, what their concerns are, and what they are driven by. A person needs to set aside their own view of the world as much as possible. Communication is the responsibility of the communicator; if the message is not received, then it probably needs to be communicated in a different manner.

When babies are learning to walk and they fall over they usually cry. This is how they communicate with the people around them. Experience has taught them that if they cry someone will come to help them. Adults behave in much the same way but they do not indulge in kicking and screaming—usually. Adults learn more complex ways to behaving, hopefully, more sophisticated ways of getting their point across. But the underlying principle is still the same. People will believe in a way they feel will bring about the best results. But when using NLP, the goal is to make all behaviors have an intention that is positive.

It is much easier to develop meaningful relationships if time is taken to understand exactly why people act the way they do. People should not use their own point of view when doing this. People must look at the point of view of other people and try to see things the way they do. Then it will be possible to offer other people new ideas in order to help them develop a behavior that is more productive. People make the best possible choices they can, based on the information they already possess. Sometimes the best alternative someone can offer another person is a new way of looking at a situation. It is never helpful to constantly solve someone else's problems for them. This practice does not work forever. The best method is to give people the tools they need to be able to solve their own problems. Doing this will also help to strengthen relationships between people.

The real idea behind NLP is taking responsibility for personal actions. NLP tells us that people see life as being a function of either cause or effect. People operate from one perspective or the other. If people see themselves operating from a cause position, they see themselves as totally in control of a situation and able to manipulate the situation to control the outcome. When people operate from the idea of the effect, they easily blame other people or life circumstances for their problems. There is always a valid reason to justify why they are not happy or healthy or successful. The real truth is that no matter what opinion people operate from they are always in control of the situation and the choice of which point of view to operate from.

When a relationship is not going well, for whatever reason, the best choice is always to consider personal behavior and how it can be changed. If operating from the position of the cause, then the person has the ability to make improvements in the situation. This is done by understanding the other person's point of view by hearing what they are really saying and learning to communicate with others on a level they can communicate easily on.

Remember that people will do the best they know how to do with the tools they have to work with. Personal resources determine personal behavior. If people had different tools or a different point of view they might act in a different way. People should never be labeled based on their behavior. This perspective will never help with the development of great relationships. Behavior can change as people learn new skills and grow and develop. Sometimes relationships are labeled as stagnant or bad. Sometimes relationships are unproductive and unfulfilling. But these relationships can be turned around and saved by both parties learning to take responsibility for the situation and learning to be proactive in their behavior. Everyone is capable of accomplishing wonderful things. Everyone is able to enjoy a world full of fulfilment and success. The fact that everyone is responsible for their own destiny is often a frightening thought.

Another tactic that can be effectively used to improve interpersonal relationships is to work to find some form of common ground. The first step is to ask questions about general topics that the other person seems to have an interest in. This will provide a basis for understanding the other person. Then more in-depth topics can be discussed. This is a good method for learning about common values and principles that can be used as the basis for a meaningful relationship. It is also a good idea to ask questions that will give more information into the thought processes of the other person. Stay away from specific ideas. Instead, talk in generalities that will give more of the big picture.

Once there is a common ground to work on, then the other tactics of the NLP method will be able to be used to intensify the feelings between the two people in the relationship, including the feelings of love that pass between them. Love is nothing more than an intense reaction of fondness for a particular person. Love is impossible to define because everyone has a different view of what makes a person loveable.

All the methods of NLP can be used to strengthen the love between two people. The first thing to do is to admit that everyone has a different idea of love and what it means, based on how they were raised and what they saw growing up. Differences will not matter as long as two people truly love one another and want to make the relationship work. Understand the different maps people travel on. Remember that the way people behave will often depend on the path they travel in life. Also, remember that people look at the world differently. Everyone's life experiences will cause them to look at life differently. Everyone's reaction to love and affection will be clouded by the filters they are looking through. By understanding this, it is easier to communicate with loved ones.

Also, keep in mind that the way a relationship is approached will greatly determine how the relationship will turn out. People who can approach a relationship with caring and thoughtfulness will end up with a much better relationship than people who demand their own way in the relationship.

6

THE MOST POWERFUL MIND-POWER TOOL

HUMANS SPEND COUNTLESS HOURS SEEKING NEW WAYS to work just about anything. Through endless hours of research, they pour over books and journals looking for the message that will tell them the secret to harnessing mind power. Many never realize that the most powerful mind power tool is already on board and just aching to be used. It is the human brain, the mind itself.

Every time a person practices a new habit or thinks a new thought, they make a new pathway in the brain. Every time the habit is used, or the idea is thought, the nerve pathway becomes even stronger. The human brain is wired at birth to be an efficient machine and it is ready, from birth, to make an ever increasing amount of nerve pathways and to strengthen the pathways that are used the most.

Sometimes thoughts and habits need to be changed for the improvement of the person. When people decide that they would like to make a change in their lives, there will be a period of adjustment. This is true whether the change is mental, emotional, or physical. During this period of adjustment, there will be some level of discomfort. When a habit or a thought is already formed, it has made its own path in the brain. When a stimulus is seen or heard, the message travels along the preset nerve pathway to the spot in the brain that controls that thought or habit. In order to change a thought or a habit, it is necessary for the nerve path to be changed. Until the nerve path is changed, the old nerve path will remain in the brain. The discomfort comes from the brain trying to automatically access the old pathway and the new pathway at the same time. This is painful for the brain to do.

It is easy to become frustrated when the brain goes back to its old patterns of thought and habit. Never fall into the habit of placing blame on a lack of willpower. Willpower has nothing to do with it. It is a very difficult thing to override preset pathways in the brain. The brain is a very powerful tool. When will power fails and mistakes happen, remember to use kindness and compassion in dealing with the failure. The brain is very efficient at doing what it does. The only way to change the pathways in the brain is to keep working on new pathways that will eventually obliterate the old, undesirable ones.

The brain needs a clear understanding that changes are about to take place and new pathways are about to be laid down. Remind the brain that new habits and new thoughts will be replacing the old ones. Blaming failure on a lack of will power is a self-defeating statement. The process of making new nerve paths in the brain takes hard work and time. It will help to keep reminding oneself of the impending change. By doing this over and over, it makes the process no longer about possible character flaws. The focus is now put on the habit of thought that is being built.

Is it possible to build new nerve pathways in the brain? Yes, it is possible, and it can be done. If more proof is needed, just compare the adult brain to the baby's brain. Every current habit and thought a person has is the direct result of having spent time practicing them over and over until they created a pathway in the brain. New pathways can be created. Think of it this way: they already have. The baby's brain has no idea of anything. It has no thoughts or habits. Every nerve path currently in the brain was practiced until it became a part of the brain. Think of the baby. The baby lies around day after day and does baby things. Then one day the baby notices the shiny rattle that mommy is waving in front of its little face. The baby wants the rattle. As the baby is waving its tiny arms around, the mommy puts the rattle close enough so the baby can touch it with its wavering hand. After a few of these sessions, the baby gets the idea that if the arm is in the air it can touch the rattle. A nerve pathway is beginning to grow. So the baby decides to lift its arm to actively reach for the rattle. The baby will be unsuccessful at first because the arms will wave wildly and will not connect with the rattle. One day, the baby will actually grab the rattle, and the nerve pathway is then complete.

While this may seem like a very simple example, it is exactly how nerve pathways are created in the brain. Every action, thought, or habit has its own nerve pathway. All pathways must be created. No one was born knowing to sit in front of the television and mindlessly eat dip with chips. No one was born lamenting the excess pounds they carry in strange places. No one was born hating their body. All behaviors are learned, good and bad. And the bad ones can be replaced with good ones.

So if the ability to program negative thoughts into the brain exists, then the ability to disrupt those negative thoughts with positive thoughts also exists. The brain can be reprogrammed. It is a powerful tool, and its main function is to turn thoughts into reality. The brain is always working, so why not use the power of the brain to benefit rather than harm? Just because a particular habit or thought has been around all forever does not mean it needs to stay. Use the power of the brain to choose new habits and thoughts to focus on and replace the old, negative thought pathways in the brain.

The new thought needs to be believable; the new habit needs to be doable. It does not real good to try to stick to a habit that is impossible to accomplish or to try to believe a thought that is unbelievable. After years of seeing the reality of an obese body, it would be nearly impossible to suddenly believe that the image in the mirror is that of a skinny person. But the brain will likely accept something that mentions learning to take care of the body or learning to accept the body in order to correct its flaws. The brain will turn a belief in reality. Believing a positive thought will lead to quite a different result than the ending where only negative thoughts are present.

Be prepared to repeat and repeat some more. The primary key to being able to make a new habit stay is repeating it constantly. The more a new, desirable habit is practiced, the more the brain begins to accept it. The nerve path becomes stronger every day. With constant practice, this new nerve path will become the path the brain will prefer to use, and the old one will cease to exist.

In any case, be sure to allow enough time to effectively create a change. Accept the starting point and constantly visualize the ending point. Accept the fact that the path to the goal of a new habit or thought will not be easy or perfect. The path will almost never travel in a straight line. Sometimes people fall completely off the path, and that is okay too. Just get back up and get back on. Do not get sidetracked by the idea that this journey will be easy and carefree because it will not be. Just keep thinking of the new nerve pathway that will be created by the new thought or habit and it will eventually become a reality.

Most of the pathways in the brain are stored in the subconscious mind. This is the part of the mind that is always working without always being thought of. Think of learned skills like tying shoes, zipping a coat, and pouring milk into a glass. These were all learned behavior whose nerve pathways are firmly set in the subconscious part of the mind. This part of the brain is the bank of data for all life functions.

The communication between the conscious mind and the unconscious mind works in both directions. Whenever a person has a memory, and emotion, or an idea, it is rooted in the subconscious mind and translated to the conscious mind through mind power. The subconscious has the power to control just about anything a human does regularly.

For example, during meditation steady, deep breathing is usually practiced. The control of the breath is brought from the subconscious mind and given to the conscious mind to tell it to control the breathing. Once a pattern of deep steady breathing is begun by the conscious mind, the subconscious mind takes over and keeps the set rhythm going until it is told to stop. This is done by a conscious end to the deep breathing or an encounter with an outside stimulus like stress. The subconscious mind also processes the great wealth of information received daily and only passes along to the conscious mind those things that are necessary for the brain to remember.

When sending thoughts from the conscious mind to the subconscious mind, the brain will only send those thoughts that are attached to great emotion. The only thoughts that remain in the subconscious are those that are kept there with strong emotions. Unfortunately, the brain does not know the difference between positive emotions and negative emotions. Any strong emotion will work. Both negative emotions and positive emotions can be quite strong. Also, unfortunately, negative emotions tend to be stronger than positive emotions.

Step one in learning to use the power of the subconscious part of the mind will be to eliminate any thoughts that come with negative emotions. Also, negative mental comments will also need to cease. Fears will usually come true, specifically because they are drowning in negative emotion. This is why negative ideas need to be eliminated because they can be very harmful roadblocks on the road to harnessing brain power.

One best practice to use to get rid of negative thoughts is to counter them with positive thoughts. This will take time and practice, but it is a very powerful and useful technique. Whenever a negative thought pops in the conscious mind, immediately counter it with a positive thought that is dripping with strong emotion. The actual truth will come out somewhere in between the two thoughts.

Another way to counter negative emotions is to delete them, just like using a remote control. When a negative thought comes into the conscious mind, imagine destroying it. Imagine writing that thought on paper and burning it. Imagine pointing a remote control at the thought and pressing a huge delete button. Whatever form used to imagine deleting the thought, the important thing is to get rid of it before it can take hold in the subconscious mind.

Find something energizing and use it to reach a goal. Those things that are found to be energizing bring boundless energy to positive thoughts. It is often necessary to invent motivation, at least in the beginning, to learn to create new habits and thoughts. But with a bit of practice and a lot of positive thought, new positive habits will soon be burned into the subconscious mind and the old negative thoughts and habit will fade away.

⁂ 7 ⁂
ASSUMING SUCCESS

SUCCESS AND FAILURE ARE BOTH NORMAL PARTS OF LIFE. Unfortunately, fearing failure is a huge cloud that hangs over good judgement and can lead to extremely flawed thought patterns. When failure is seen as a possible outcome, then people automatically set their expectations lower. Working with lowered expectations means that there is not as far to fall when failure does happen. There are moments in life when it makes sense to intentionally set sights lower in order to minimize risks. But these moments are few and far between. People who doubt the possibility of success will automatically increase the possibility of less personal growth or eventual failure. Really the only way to guarantee future growth is to look at all the options with the idea of eventual success in mind, not in an arrogant manner but with quiet confidence in a successful outcome.

Keeping this attitude will be especially difficult in the beginning of this process when no positive outcomes have been proven. It is far too easy to just talk about success when failure is the only outcome known. The key is to practice positive thinking. The next time it is time to make an important decision to try to imagine a positive outcome. Try to imagine that failure is not an option or even something to worry about.

Assuming success means making good choices that will point toward success. Spend time on those things that matter and leave the unimportant things behind. The focus should always be on the big picture and never on moments where gratification is instant. Assuming success will also mean being ready to accept the responsibility for success and being accountable to use it correctly. It involves doing what is right and not just taking the easiest path to completion. Always be prepared to follow the path to the decided goal.

People who assume success are willing to give up the idea of staying within the zone of comfort. Dark fears must be faced in order to be conquered. Be prepared to put safety and security on the line in a quest for success that might mean taking huge personal risks. Safety nets are always nice to have but they are so *safe*. Safety does not often lead to success. The path to success is filled with great risks. Be prepared to have the courage to create a personal path and be prepared to walk it no matter what happens.

All things take courage when the ultimate quest is success. Achieving success takes hard work, perseverance, and great discipline. Persuasion is important too. It will often be necessary to engage others to assist with the travels on the way to the goal of success. Do not be afraid to use the powers of persuasion when needed to achieve these goals. And use mind control to enable the making of good choices. Luck will not enable anyone to achieve success; only hard work with good choices will take the path to success.

Each day is full of decisions that might affect the future of life as it is known now. Every day people must choose what to do and what things to say. Choices must be made to either be well behaved or to misbehave. Every day of every life is potentially filled with choices to be made that might actually affect the very outcome of life in the future. The burning question is whether the choices made today will lead toward future success. The answer should be a completely honest one because it is vital to the success of future decisions.

Making good choices is never easy. Good choices are difficult ones. But it is the good choices that will eventually lead to success. The first good choices are the hardest ones, especially if making good choices has not been a regular habit in the past. But each subsequent good choice will cause making good choices to become easier.

Some people will spend the whole of their lives trying to figure out how to be successful. Personal success is an achievable goal for anyone who truly wants to achieve success. Most people do want to be independent financially, to enjoy a wonderful career, and to have a strong and satisfying home life. People want to know they are important, that they matter to someone else, at least one someone else. Almost everyone wants to do at least one wonderful thing in their life. This is how most people measure the extent of success.

And achieving success is not dependent on built-in ability, intelligence, or background. Success does not care who a person knows. Everyone has the ability to do wonderful things in life and to achieve success. The key is to assume that success is the ultimate goal and no other potential outcome will be acceptable.

Do not be afraid to question the path of life if it is not leading toward success. It is quite alright to ask questions of other people if it is necessary to learn how to reach success. Just never assume that someone else's path will be the only one that exists. Everyone must choose a personal path to success. Everyone must define the idea of success for themselves. Take in advice from others and use the tips and tricks that make sense. Discard the rest. Only do what feels tight and acceptable.

The first goal achieved is perhaps the most important goal on the road to success. The first goal proves that goals can be achieved. The first goal will begin to program the brain to accept the idea of success and to develop new pathways that will facilitate becoming successful. People will only learn to succeed by achieving success. The more goals that are achieved, the more goals people want to achieve. Success builds confidence that leads to more goal achievement that leads to more success that leads to more confidence. It grows in an ever-widening circle.

The only real limit on success is a personal limit. With the true success, the sky is the limit. Once the decision to push aside limits of the mind has been made, then anything can be achieved. If goal accomplishment is approached with a completely open heart and mind then anything can be achieved. Once the habit of achieving goals is begun, there really is no limit on personal success. As long as progress is not halted, then success is practically guaranteed.

Be prepared to chase success mercilessly. Success is a goal and a way of life. Once success is first achieved, it creates a burning desire for more success. Never be content to stop with just one success. Always strive for more success.

Realize that sometimes life flows a certain direction and that direction cannot be changed. There are times that life will get in the way of the pursuit of success. Recognize these moments for temporary distractions and not permanent set-in-stone ways of life. All life choices will go off the rails at times. The path to achieving a goal can be disrupted by unexpected roadblocks. Life happens. Never lose sight of success or allow these interruptions to permanently derail the success train.

Always try to set goals that are realistic and achievable. No one can possibly hope to lose one hundred pounds overnight, or even in one month. That is not a realistic goal. Instead, be prepared to set many small goals that will lead to the achievement of the ultimate goal. There is no miracle transformation in sight. But, through hard work and attention to detail goal will be achieved and success will be assured.

Remember to stay positive. Positive feelings will enable the mind to create greater thought patterns that will lead to the brain making more connections between thoughts and ideas. Connections that are new and fresh to the mind can easily lead to a rush of creative thoughts. These creative thoughts can easily ferment in the mind and lead to wonderful new thoughts in the future. Learn to relax. Anger and stress are definite creativity killers. Using relaxation techniques will recharge the brain and relax the nerves to allow positive thoughts to flow through more freely. Before pondering any problem, take a few minutes to breathe deeply and relax.

Do not make the mistake of being too nice when traveling the path to success. Of course, everyone wants to treat themselves nicely, even if it is only occasionally, but do not make the mistake of being too nice to the mind. Pamper the body and work the mind. Of course, making extremely negative personal comments is never a good idea. The comments like "You are so fat" and "You will never amount to anything" are definitely self-defeating. But do not be too easy on that person inside who craves success. Being too nice can have negative consequences. Being too nice usually means not pushing oneself to one's ultimate potential. Failure is okay because it is expected. Thoughts like these will never lead to ultimate success. It is okay to be a little tough every now and then. No great goal was ever reached without a lot of sweat and agony. Be prepared to suffer. Suffering now just makes success all that much sweeter when it does arrive.

Success begins with a dream. Anything worth having is worth dreaming about. Open the heart and the mind to the possibility of success. Take the time to wonder how life will change when success is achieved. Think only positive thoughts. Negative thoughts are too discouraging. Dream of all the possibilities that come with real success. Keep the dream alive, fan its flames every time it seems to be growing cold. Never let the dream go away.

The dream of success needs to be big, huge, enormous. The dream of success needs to feel much bigger than anything that might be achieved in this life. In addition to feeling really intense, it also needs to be something that is believable. The dream must be seen as something that it is possible to achieve if everything falls into place correctly. If hard work if offered, if other people lend a hand, if certain life events happen at the right time, then the dream of success is one that can be achieved.

Everyone who is able to achieve great things is able to see those great things in their minds. They can picture themselves wallowing in success, whatever success means to them. Imagining a successful outcome makes achieving a successful outcome much more realistic. A basketball player will imagine the ball going through the net with every shot. A pageant queen will imagine the crown on her head. A jockey will imagine his horse crossing the finish line first. Imagining something to be a reality is the first step into making it a reality. And creating reality is the first step toward assuming success and all the perks that come with it.

Success depends greatly on mind control and assuming success is just another way to practice mind control to create a goal of success. Success itself is both a goal and a way of life. It is possible to program the mind to focus more completely on the idea of achieving success. Remember that every habit and every thought, both positive and negative, has its own pathway in the mind. All these pathways are created through repeated practice of these habits and thoughts. Negative thoughts will need to be replaced by positive thoughts. Negative habits will need to be replaced by positive habits. All negativity will create roadblocks to true success. The pathways of negative thoughts and habits will be eliminated by the practice of positive thoughts and habits. Success is one of these positive habits.

CONCLUSION

Thank you for making it through to the end of *Manipulation: Techniques in Dark Psychology, Influencing People with Persuasion, NLP, and Mind Control*. Let's hope it was informative and able to provide you with all of the tools you need to achieve your goals whatever they may be.

The next step is to make the conscious decision that success is the way of life you want to live. Read through this book carefully, making notes if needed. Take advantage of the information contained in this book. Pay careful attention to the sections on using mind control and developing new thought patterns in the mind. These sections will be especially helpful in learning to create a goal that will lead to the achievement of success, whatever success is in your life.

Finally, if you found this book useful in any way, a review on Amazon is always appreciated!

ANGER MANAGEMENT

12 Step Guide to Recognize and Control Anger, Develop Emotional Intelligence, and Self Discipline

RAY VADEN

ANGER MANAGEMENT

12 Step Guide to Recognize and Control Anger, Develop Emotional Intelligence, and Self-Discipline

❀ Created with Vellum

INTRODUCTION

Congratulations on downloading *Anger Management: 12 Step Guide to Recognize and Control Anger, Develop Emotional Intelligence, and Self-Discipline*, and thank you for doing so. Everyone gets angry from time to time, and we could all use some advice and reminders on how to deal with anger that flares up in our lives occasionally.

You already know that anger is not a bad emotion; it is quite useful. Not many things would have changed so far had someone not been unhappy and angry about a situation. If we were all grateful for what we have, we would never see the need to do better. Anger is only harmful and destructive when it is withheld and when it gains momentum before it finally erupts through physical violence, screaming, verbal outbursts, throwing things around, and other erratic behavior. However, we can all learn how to control anger in its infancy to keep it from wearing its ugly face and destroying our lives and our relationships.

To that end, the following chapters will teach you how to accept and understand your angry feelings. You will learn why it is necessary that you own up to what you are feeling before proceeding to deal with establishing controls. Examples of ways to control anger include pausing before you react or respond, expressing your anger calmly, and developing empathy towards the offenders so that you are able to understand their viewpoint which somehow decreases the intensity of the anger you have within you.

Besides control, you have the option of letting out the anger by redirecting your focus from the anger and onto more important things that will bring you happiness. Any pent-up anger needs to be released, ideally, in a creative manner. Instead, you ought to create room for mistakes so that you are not too hard on yourself and others around you. You will also learn how to let go of the anger and hurt by forgiving and letting go entirely in a way that takes the emotion out of the negative experiences, to allow you to move on completely, with no baggage from the past.

There are plenty of books on this subject on the market, thanks again for choosing this one! Every effort was made to ensure it is full of as much useful information as possible. Please enjoy!

I
ACCEPT YOUR ANGER

THE ADVANCEMENTS AND DEVELOPMENTS WE HAVE SEEN in our society have made us a comfort-seeking lot, and when things are not done our way, we flip out easily. We want the delivery guy to be on time, we want our partners to behave as though they were us, we get upset when the professor does not award us the grade we wanted, we want our children not to speak back at us, we get upset when our favorite show does not show – there are too many reasons.

No one likes the emotional burden that anger brings. We want to spring back to good emotions as soon as possible. In our strive for comfort, we do not want to experience painful emotions, and instead, we take up different coping habits, a majority of which are harmful, like shopping too much, gambling, overeating, and alcohol and drug abuse. These habits are meant to numb our feelings.

It must not be news to you to realize that avoiding emotions does not work. Whatever technique you take up to numb yourself, however, you are only likely to make your life more difficult. You also lose out on the important lessons that the negative emotions stand to teach you in regards to the decisions you have made, the manner in which you are living your life and the changes you ought to effect to improve your life. The problem with exposing your emotions is that society is likely to label or refer to you as someone with a problem. People assume that something is wrong with you if you express anger. They say you are having 'issues.' This is partly the reason why many people like to hide their anger or want to spring back to the good times quickly without processing the negative emotions they have had.

Researchers have studied the reason for taking the time to take in and process all kinds of emotions. They believe that having a jolly mood, optimism, or being happy all the time does not guarantee the stability of your emotional health. Instead, you ought to feel all your emotions in a balanced way, to achieve a sense of wholeness, and to learn how to manage life's twists and turns. It is said that learning how to tolerate distress and discomfort is even more important than the pursuit of happiness.

Many people fear expressing anger. They see it as a sign that they have lost control of life or failed in character, as though anger would drive them to anxiety thinking that the anger would force them into a rage. We are also conditioned, right from our childhood, that it is wrong to get angry. Whenever a child throws a temper tantrum, whether big or small, he or she gets punished for it. This teaches them that anger is bad and that they should refrain from expressing it. As an adult, whenever you display your anger, people avoid you and do not want to associate with you. Because of these negative reactions, we all want to remain jolly all day, refusing to acknowledge the negative feelings when they come up.

Nevertheless, researchers point to some benefits of feeling your anger emotions. Taking in your feelings of anger enables you to view the world more optimistically seeing that people who are able to accept their feelings of anger are more likely to take risks and plunge into unfamiliar situations.

People are provoked to take action and cause a change in the world only when they become angry because of what they can see. Altruism is likely to have developed from anger because it brings together different kinds of people and generates support for a particular cause. In some situations, anger can enhance performance and be a source of leverage in negotiations. Sometimes, it even raises the level of creativity.

Rarely does anger lead to violence. Instead, anger becomes a source of encouragement and it motivates you to defend yourself when your rights are threatened. When expressed properly, it can also be a way to ask the adversary to back off.

On the contrary, when you bury feelings of anger, you not only dampen the negative ones, you also do positive emotions like joy.

WHAT IT MEANS TO ACCEPT YOUR ANGER

Most people get angry and let everyone know their thoughts. Others say silly, stupid, and regretful things that they have to acknowledge and apologize for later shamefully. Getting angry, for us, is always about finding the external culprit and letting him or her know that they caused the anger and that you are not to blame.

However, accepting anger means taking an inward look at yourself. It requires you to spend time with your negative emotions so that you understand what is going on. Begin taking note of anger from its onset in the form of annoyances and irritations. Whenever you feel these emotions rising, take a moment to determine their triggers. Seek to know precisely what is causing you to feel as you are: there is always an underlying need that has not been met.

Once you follow through your anger, you will come to find out the things that are buried deep that you should have dealt with a long time ago. These things have been the reasons for the patterns in your life, which are likely to have limited your growth. Therefore, accepting your feelings will only improve you and help you overcome traumas from your past.

THE PROCESS OF ACCEPTING YOUR FEELINGS

This process is broken down into the following smaller steps:

1. Take note of the feelings you have and don't consider ignoring them.

Although this may be painful, you need to know how to confront your feelings and examine your situation realistically.

2. Take a break to boost your emotional health

Begin to think of how you can bring down the stress and emotional turmoil you are going through. You could use this time to do the things that you find fun. Physical exercise is a critical component of this downtime. It will help you work off your feelings.

3. Speak to your family

Share the opinions you have with your family. Let them know the progress you have made in dealing with the problem and with your emotions of anger. Talking provides you with an opportunity to express what you are feeling, to vent, and to accept better, the feelings you have been having. A family is a source of both reassurance and support to help you rebuild your self-esteem.

4. Speak to other people

Talking to other people, particularly those who have been in the situation you are before will provide you with the assistance you need. You also find that you are not struggling with the issue alone; many others are doing the same.

5. Maximize the use of your time

Some habits are detrimental to your time usage such as spending a lot of time watching television or drowning yourself on the internet. Think about the number of times you felt that you should have done some things better such as spending time with your children. Do some reading, go fishing, begin projects around the house, or take up that course you always wanted to.

At first, you may lack the drive or the will to try out these things. However, once your feelings have died down, take the opportunity, and put your time to good use. Working on the activities you do will bring you more satisfaction in life or bring you a new talent that will make you more productive.

EVALUATE THE SITUATION

If the situation you are in looks like it will be the same for a while, shift your focus and start thinking of alternatives. You may require help analyzing your skills to see what you are good at or to establish the need for additional training to help you pursue your desired goal, job, or career.

SEEK PROFESSIONAL HELP

The feelings brought by a loss of any kind are very strong and it may prove difficult for you to deal with them by yourself. However, discussing the issue with a professional will ease the process of working through your feelings, making recovery quicker.

2

UNDERSTAND YOUR ANGER

ANGER IS A NATURAL RESPONSE TRIGGERED BY THE fight-or-flight body physiology. Your body produces this emotional response against any perceived threats. While fear is the flight response, anger is the emotional energy that drives you to want to fight back. Surprisingly, your mind will create fear and anger responses even when the threat is not apparent when you imagine it.

IMAGINED V. REAL ANGER

Distinguishing between an imagined and a real threat can be difficult because, on many occasions, they happen at the same time. For example, suppose you are walking on the curb headed home and a rider on skates is swerving in your direction unable to control his speed. In a case like this, you will produce both a fight and a flight reaction driven by a combination of fear of the skater hitting you and the need to protect you and him from falling. The reality of the situation and the emotions pass very quickly, and so will your emotions.

Your mind, however, will not let you go. You will be left imagining the worst case scenarios. You start thinking about how you might have stretched a tendon while you were leaping out of his way. You begin to recall similar cases you heard about or videos you watched on the internet showing a similar situation and the dire consequences that followed. As you do this, you add more emotion to the situation and the response you give will be based on the imaginations that have been going through your mind.

You must be aware of the processes taking place in your mind, however. If you are unaware of the influence your imagination has and how it is leading you to project these scenarios in your head, you are likely to blame others for how you feel. Unfortunately, when anger is directed towards a false cause, it becomes a tool for destroying your life and your relationships rather than a tool that you use to protect yourself.

UNDERSTANDING YOUR ANGER

The truth is that anger is a natural response to have it just depends on how you perceive your emotions and different scenarios in the mind. It is okay to become angry, even if the situations are imagined because this is an indication that your body's emotional response system is working correctly. The issue remains to be the beliefs, thoughts, and scenarios that bring about the anger because most often, they are irrational.

Other problems come about when you are unable to refrain from anger outbursts. Reactions like these and their consequences often distract a person from the actual underlying problem. They make us believe that anger is the problem since it is what will take our attention first. However, your emotions and reactions are only an outward reaction indicating what has been going through the mind, whether real or imagined.

The way to overcome anger is to change the way your mind reacts or imagines stories. It is by controlling the extent to which these things influence your emotional wellness. For example, if the imagination of pain causes you to be frustrated and angry, the best way to eliminate the anger is to pull your thinking away from the painful memories. You also need to change or remove your assumptions, core beliefs, and mind interpretations.

MISPLACED ANGER

One of the most important things to note about anger is that it is motivated by the desire not to experience guilt. Blaming other people for how you feel creates a thrill, an excitement, and satisfaction because you do not have to take responsibility for how you are acting or the consequences of it.

We have agreed by now that anger is a primary emotion that comes when a person feels powerless, rejected, accused, unimportant, guilty, devalued, untrustworthy, unlovable, disregarded, and many other similar sentiments. These feelings bring considerable amounts of pain, which makes it understandable that people want to distance themselves from it. Therefore, the primary role for anyone who is not willing to face, accept, and understand his anger will be to create a cover-up to avoid vulnerability. The cover-up becomes an ideal vehicle for escaping the shame, upset, or anxiety a person feels, possibly because he has not developed the emotional resources he needs to cope with the issue at hand successfully.

Looking at an example, let's assume your partner has said something, intentionally or otherwise, that caused you to feel demeaned. Rather than becoming assertive and expressing your dissatisfaction with the statement your partner has made, which could reveal your vulnerability, you react, instead, by looking for something to use to get back at him or her. When you do this, you are, in effect, launching the tit for tat war. What happens is that as you engage in their retaliatory pursuits, your negative emotions will fade away. Worked? Well, yeah, but not quite. This only reinforces the childlike behavior of blaming each other endlessly, instead of each partner taking responsibility.

But looking at this example again, from your partner's perspective, what will happen to his or her temper? Your partner becomes the new bearer for the emotional baggage you have just successfully shed. Whatever feelings you had, you have transferred them to the partner. After this happens, your partner instinctively develops both hurt and fear. The fear comes about because he is now turned into an object of anger, and he subconsciously now thinks that you intend to harm him. Therefore, if you observe that taking out your frustrations on other people, it is not because they want to give you space to process your emotions, it is because they are instinctively led to keep a distance from anything that could harm them, psychologically, physically, and in any other way.

Some people are not as calm and will respond to your attack with an equal and opposite defensive attack. This is called counter-retaliation. The partner starts to blame you too, and this could result in a serious conflict, verbal or otherwise.

To change this uncomfortable cycle, you need to get a hold of what drives you into anger. You also need to study its effects. Surely, you cannot go about life retaliating towards every jab thrown at you. Instead, learn how to hold on to your most rational self and peacefully process whatever is happening.

3
PAUSE BEFORE YOU REACT

A LARGE PROPORTION OF YOUR LIFE HAS BEEN determined by the reactions you gave to things or people around you. Majority of these reactions are not the best courses of action, and because of this, we end up making ourselves or/and others unhappy. Some even make the situation worse.

We say the first thing that land in our mouths first without giving it a thought. We become defensive and are quick to talk back, which worsens the situation. In other areas of life, we are quick to put food in our mouths before thinking about how the foods would affect the body system. We make purchasing decisions in a split second, without even caring whether our finances can support the purchases. All these common scenarios indicate clearly how often we put action before thought, especially when driven by anger.

The reaction you present is driven by a gut emotion that has resulted from insecurities and fear. This is not often the most rational way to behave. The opposite of reacting is responding, and it involves taking in the situation and making a decision on the best course of action based on reason, cooperation, and compassion.

LEARN HOW TO RESPOND

It is often said that if you speak from your anger, you will make the speech you will regret forever. The seriousness of this statement is brought by the fact that once you utter some words, you can never take them back. Although sitting down with your sadness, frustration, disappointment, grief, and anger is quite uncomfortable, you will feel so much worse once you have poured out your vile on another's face. To do this, you need to learn how to pause between anger and reaction.

This internal pause is developed by becoming mindful and living more presently. It slows down the natural reaction because when you are mindful, you focus on living in the moment and this produces so much inner peace and tranquility such that when someone comes at you with an erratic rant, you will not fly off the handle either, you will be more accepting of people and their mistakes.

When you pause, you take your time to assimilate the information or the deed that has been done before you give a response to it. A voice inside your head tells you what you would typically have voiced out, but if you give yourself a few seconds, you will realize that the nasty statement you would have made was uncalled for and wouldn't make a difference anyway.

I hate to apologize. I hate having to lower myself to the ground asking for forgiveness. It feels as though I am worshipping the other person by swallowing my pride and begging them to forgive me. This attitude grew in me after messing up too many times. Whenever my anger flared out, I would spit any venom that came into my mouth, trying to make the other party feel as downgraded and looked-down-upon as I had been made to feel. I am a naturally calm and quiet person, and if someone hurt me, the natural way to fight back would be through words, even though they were said softly.

My conscience would not let me go after that. After lashing out, what would follow is an endless battle inside me, which would end with me crawling back to the person who offended me with my tail between my legs to say sorry. I grew to hate this so much until I devised a new strategy. I decided to put a pause between anger and reaction.

Today, whenever someone does something to hurt me and I want to lash out, I remember that I will have to go through the tedious process of asking for forgiveness and I stop in my tracks. I also take in the statements that have been said or the deed that has been done and considers what would happen. In those few seconds, I realize that I do not have to retaliate and that it is my opportunity to take the high road. Sometimes, you have to hate something bad enough to want to change how you behave or do things.

Here are a few steps you can take to initiate the internal pause

1. Take note of the triggers

Realize the sensations that build up in you to indicate that you are becoming irritated and angry. It could be an increase in body heat, your stomach knotting, pulsating in the head, and a tight chest. Once you recognize these as signs that your anger has been triggered, you need to activate your internal pause immediately.

When involved in an argument and you realize that your temper and ego are flaring, simple awareness and recognition of what is happening will send it back to where it came from.

2. Pause: This step requires you to press pause in your mind as you do it on your TV using the remote.

3. Breathe deeply: A significant amount of oxygen in your brain is useful for helping you gather your thoughts and makes you mindful of the moment.

4. Look around: When interacting with people, you need to hold off your thoughts and opinions and listen. It is not mandatory for you to give an immediate response to counter what you disagree with. Just take note of the ideas that are floating around in your mind and do not get attached to any of them. For example, if you are set on reducing your spending, take your mind back to a goal you set or a mantra you created regarding a situation like this one. Think, also, of the best possible results. How would you hope that the situation will turn out? Again, allow yourself to look keenly into all the thoughts that are passing through your mind.

5. Now 'Play': Now that you have examined all the good and bad ideas that your mind has run concerning this situation, it is now time to act. You need to do this mindfully. Think about what the most compassionate, respectful, and intelligent response could be. What could you possibly say to calm everyone down and resolve the situation in a better way?

You may not be very good at this process at first, but practicing will make you perfect at it. You will get better at pausing; don't worry if there is a miss or two. If you end up replying fast, take note of the emotion or thought that caused you to do so, and keep watch in the future to ensure that you are able to pause thoughts like that.

You must be thinking that this process looks too easy and good on paper, but that it would not work in real life. In the heat of the moment, no one would be able to grow through that long process.

However, this is not the case. This process has been tested and proven to be an ideal solution for people with reaction problems, which is practically the majority of the people.

Yes, the process may seem a bit too long, but if you have struggled with erratic responses, the process will help you to remember the importance of waiting before you respond. It makes a whole lot of difference because it grants you the chance to rewind, decide on a profitable course of action, and then continue your interaction in a way that makes you feel good about yourself and makes you a role model for persons with a hot temper over those that have difficulty controlling their responses.

4
EXPRESS YOUR ANGER CALMLY

MANY OF US HAVE TROUBLE MAINTAINING THEIR COOL and respect when dealing with some volatile situations, even when you intended to. You may have begun by pausing to think of your reply, but you are now unable to maintain your cool, especially if the other side is being disrespectful, lying, or starting to behave in angry ways. However, this entire process is not intended to make you a walkover such that other people can dump their frustrations on you and you only respond with happy, inspirational quotes: you are also allowed to express your negative feelings of anger, frustration, disappointment, and others, but just do it calmly.

Let's look at an example. Last year, my friend Jane found a suspicious text on her husband's cellphone and she suspected that he was having an affair. When she confronted him later in the day, the man reluctantly confessed to having sex with an old friend he had recently reconnected with. Jane was overcome with anger. She asked her husband to leave the house, but the man knelt, began to cry, and apologize, assuring her that he loved only her, not the other woman. Jane was overcome with emotion, and she allowed him to stay.

In the days that followed, anger was boiling inside of her. She felt that she couldn't express it, seeing that she had accepted his apology. So, whenever the negative feelings flared up, she bottled them and continued to treat him as though everything was okay between them. Part of her wanted to out her feelings of frustration and disappointment while the other felt that anger was unnecessary. She wanted to behave well, to prove to herself and the man that she was emotionally superior. However, in a couple of weeks, she became seriously sick, depressed, and she was experiencing mental and emotional fatigue.

Many of us have been like Jane because we have learned that expressing anger erratically, the only way we knew how to, is uncool. But, is it fair to keep these emotions bottled inside? We fear that if we express anger in our way, we will hurt those around us. If we keep it in, we beat ourselves. Science shows that when you get angry, the body secretes stress hormones, and if they are just circulating in the body, they will increase your propensity to cardiovascular disease and infections. So, what is the solution?

The most appropriate beneficial way to deal with anger is to express it in a healthy way so that you can turn this pent-up destructive energy into constructive action. Neuroscientists have confirmed that whenever we put the negative feelings we have into words, the activity of the amygdala (the emotions and decision-making part of the brain), decreases and this process enhances our physical and mental health. Evidence has also shown that people who openly express their emotions and feelings are naturally healthier than those who suppress them.

How should you go about expressing your anger in a calm way that will not hurt you or other people? Here are some positive, constructive ways that you can use to do it.

PUT WORDS TO YOUR ANGER USING THE GESTALT TECHNIQUE

The gestalt technique involves putting a chair across from where you are sitting, imagining that the person who made you angry is seated on that seat and telling the imaginary person everything that you have bottled up. Scream at the chair. Talk to it.

Another way to do it is to set a few plump pillows on your sofa. Pretend that they are the person that has made you angry. It is best to do this one when home alone. Now, hit those pillows, scream at them, picturing the person you are unhappy with.

In only a few minutes of doing these activities, your bottled up emotions will vent and you will relax.

- **Speak to the person you are angry with**

Sometimes, people do not realize the hurt and harm that they are causing you, or they could be doing it intentionally. However, whichever the case, they need to be called out on it. You need to sit down with the person and calmly air out your frustration about what the person did. When doing this, watch out for blaming and name calling. Before you do this, you may need to release your anger through two or three of the other methods described.

- **Write a letter**

This is a beneficial method. I have personally used it more than a dozen times. It involves getting all your angry feelings out onto the paper by writing exactly how you feel. Once the emotions are on the paper, they no longer have the freedom to roll around your body causing you physical and psychological harm.

Writing is also of benefit because once ideas start flowing one after the other, you will gain clarity which is another advantage. You are also able to get into it which is good for people who are unable to express themselves well through speech.

- **Vent to a friend**

Nothing beats a supportive friend when you are angry and ranting about something. It is therapeutic to talk to someone who will see things from your perspective, but in the end, give you an objective solution to your problem. Warn your friend that you are going to pour out all your frustrations, and when you get that opportunity, ensure that you exaggerate to get all the emotion out.

However, don't let the venting become a habit. If you are continually venting, particularly about the same issues, it ceases to be therapeutic and turns into recontamination. It will no longer be right for you.

- **Scream into a pillow**

THIS METHOD IS RELATIVELY COMMON. FROM experience, however, I have learned that you may want to announce the scream before you do it. You are likely to scare bloody Mary out of those around you. Now, go ahead and do it.

- **Sing your anger out**

Listen and sing along to music that carries the emotions away. If you are going through a breakup, for example, you could listen to "*Since You Been Gone*" by Kelly Clarkson or *Don't Come Back* by Tarrus Riley. You could also involve your creative faculties and come up with your own lyrics to express exactly how you feel. Once you do this, use your voice along with any musical instrument you play to sing away your feelings.

- **Paint or draw something**

In many art classes, students are asked to paint or draw what they feel. This is a technique used to channel the inner person so that you may bring out your innermost feelings. Go ahead and do it. Draw or paint whatever comes to mind, and as you take out that pent up energy, you will realize that the feelings of anger will fade away.

- **Dance your emotions out**

Dance until you feel free on the inside. You could try doing this at your home or at a dance studio, wherever you would be comfortable with.

5
PRACTICE EMPATHY

DEVELOPING EMPATHY IS A GREAT WAY TO KEEP YOU from developing anger. When I talk of empathy, I mean being simultaneously walking in the footsteps of your aggressor, thinking about how difficult it must be for him or her, picturing the aggressor's anguish, pain, and the ordeal he or she must have gone through. The more accurately you are able to reflect the intensity and tone of emotion, the more the other person will feel understood. Therefore, to give an appropriate response, you must listen to the person using both your heart and your head.

THE WORDS THAT YOU USE WILL SHOW THAT YOU understand. Below are some phrases you can include in your conversation to show empathy:

"HOW MAY I HELP?"

"I feel that you are hurting because..."

"I cannot imagine how it must feel to ..."

SOME OF THE WORDS YOU CAN USE TO INDICATE HOW the individual is feeling include frustrated, riled, angry, infuriated, betrayed, trapped, upset, furious, exasperated, and outraged.

THE MORE PRECISE YOUR IDENTIFICATION AND reflection of the emotions the person is feeling the better their release of the negative energy, which means that the person will not project his or her anger at you. When a person feels heard, he feels supported, he relaxes, and he begins the healing journey to regain his poise.

THE IMPORTANCE OF EMPATHY

Neuroscientists have found that a person is wired to take in empathy through the many mirror neurons located in the brain. These neurons reflect the actions we observe in other people, causing us to simulate these same actions in our brains. Whenever you see someone in pain, you are likely to feel that pain, to a similar extent as that person, and when you observe a happy person, you are likely to become happy to the same degree. The mirroring of these neurons is the basis for empathy because it creates a wave that connects our emotions to those people around us.

SOME PEOPLE ARE EMPATHETIC BY NATURE, WHILE others are not. The good thing is that empathy can be learned. Here are the five steps to getting over anger using empathy: (as you go through the stages below, picture yourself interacting with an angry person who is lashing out at you).

- **Stop, take a breather and set an agenda**

You need to pause and take a few deep breaths so that you are able to channel all your attention to the present moment. When you do this, you will also get the opportunity to use your imagination to come up with an intention or a goal for how you would want the situation to play in the end. At a minimum, the intention should be to listen, understand, and connect with the other party throughout your interaction. Let your agenda be that when the meeting ends, you will feel good about the composure you maintained and the fact that you took control of the situation with the ability to listen carefully and respond to the other party empathetically.

- **Observe the words you say to yourself**

The words you speak to yourself have immense power and they are of different kinds. Some are blaming thoughts. Some are judging thoughts, while others are discouraging thoughts among others. For example, after talking, you could find yourself saying, "How silly is he/she?" "What a jerk!" Take note of thoughts like those and be careful not to engage that line of thinking. Instead, refocus on to your initial agenda, which was to listen and connect with the person empathetically while retaining a calm presence. Remind yourself that what the other party said has more to do with him or her than with you. Therefore, whatever was said, choose to keep a distance and not take any of it personally.

- **Be in communication with your needs and feelings**

WHEN YOU ARE ABLE TO ESTABLISH A CONNECTION WITH your feelings and needs, you make the entire process real rather than just telling a person that you understand his or her perspective. Ask yourself what are you feeling exactly? From which part of your body are the feelings originating? What do you want to get out of a situation like this? Remember that if your inner self starts to judge, blame, and put negative labels on the other person, your anger will likely be triggered too.

INSTEAD, STRUCTURE YOUR THOUGHTS TO RESEMBLE the following statement: When my friend said that I am always late, I felt terrible because I only get late trying to get her favorite coffee at the store near my house, and there is always a long queue.

NOTICE THE STRUCTURE: WHEN ___ (OBSERVATION), I feel______ (feeling) because _______ (need).

- **Relate to other people's feelings and needs**

ONCE YOU HAVE CONNECTED WITH YOUR OWN NEEDS and feelings, you now have to connect with what the other needs and feels. Try to think of what they would need to feel safe. It is likely that the person could be feeling frustrated because he or she was not taken seriously when trying to deliver a point the person considered important. Hence, the person interpreted that you are not keen on his or her feelings.

ALTERNATIVELY, INSTEAD OF RELYING ON ASSUMPTIONS and basing your thoughts on unconfirmed possibilities, you should go ahead to seek clarification from the other party to know precisely what could have led him or her to feel as he or she does. You will not know the problem for sure until you are able to verbalize your thoughts and seek clarification.

- **Make your assumptions heard**

SEE HOW YOU UNDERSTAND AND INTERPRET THE feelings and emotional needs that the other person displayed. If you think someone is going through something, go ahead and ask, as the previous point suggests.

FOR EXAMPLE, ASK, "ARE YOU ANGRY WITH ME BECAUSE you wanted me to go get you the items from the store and I couldn't read into the urgency of your request?"

- **Beware Of the Limits**

SOME PEOPLE, HOWEVER, ARE SO EMPATHETIC THAT they forget about their own suffering and pain. Extreme empathy causes you to accommodate and understand disrespect and inappropriate behavior because you feel compelled to forgive and forget the disrespect to the point where you act as if nothing happened.

IT IS EASY TO FORGET YOURSELF WHEN YOU ARE focusing too much on how another person is feeling. Because you are suffering too much, you relate to the individual's pain and somehow become absorbed into their world. This can go to extremes where you begin to fantasize and create stories that would somehow excuse the person's behavior. You start to think about the possible bad upbringing the person had, how the individual must have been left to his own devices, you begin to imagine the insecurity issues the person could have or the undiagnosed psychological issues that the person might have. Extreme empathy gets you on a frantic search looking for reasons to excuse negative behavior at your expense.

EMPATHY EITHER EMPOWERS YOU EMOTIONALLY OR numbs you. It is admirable to be able to connect with other people's pain, emotions, pasts, and experiences, but there is a limit to it. As much as you are able to communicate with other people's pains, you need to stop for a minute and connect to yours too. You matter, you are of value, and you are responsible for nurturing your beautiful self, sometimes, even before you take care of other people.

. . .

In summary, developing empathy is the decision you make on whether to let your defense mechanisms take over or whether to shift your emotions and thoughts in your body and mind so that you and the agitated person who is around can calm down. It is not easy in any way, but when you realize the dynamics of empathy, you will want to adapt it as a useful tool to be used for the rest of your life.

6

REDIRECT YOUR FOCUS

ANGER IS ONE OF THE STRONGEST EMOTIONS A PERSON can feel because it provides them with push, power, drive, and motivation. However, research shows that 1 in every 5 Americans has an anger management problem, that 65% of the office employees have experienced office rage, and that 45% have lost their temper at work.

At worst, anger can be quite frustrating and it can be an obstacle to performance and success. At best, anger is the force that drives us to success, and ultimately, to happiness. The trick lies in the ability to convert the negative energy into a positive emotion that will inspire you to experience positive results or in redirecting your focus entirely to avoid its path completely. Here's how to do it:

CHECK YOURSELF

When under the leadership and control of a dominant negative emotion, it can be difficult to make smart decisions. Instead of having to talk yourself down from a cliff, how about not climbing the cliff in the first place? Take note of your anger triggers and the signs that will indicate to you that you are on the verge of getting angry. When you see these things coming up, walk away from that situation, and get yourself to relax and calm down to keep the irritation from escalating.

STOP DWELLING ON WHAT HAS HAPPENED

Some people have no problem rehashing an incident that happened and caused them to be angry. This is unproductive especially when the issue has already been resolved and the outcome of the situation already determined without a chance of revocation. You need to let go of what happened, and instead, focus on the things you appreciate about the case or the person that angered you. The change in focus is significant because it helps to take out the negative emotions and helps you to maintain your peace.

CHANGE YOUR COGNITION

Cognition refers to how you think. When you are angry, it is easy to imagine that things are even worse than they appear. You become overly dramatic and tend to exaggerate everything. However, you can turn back to rationality by replacing your negative thoughts to positive ones using a technique called cognitive restructuring. Instead of thinking, "my life is ruined, I have lost everything, everybody hates me, I am no good," tell yourself, "I am sad, but this is only a setback. It is understandable that I feel upset about it. It does not indicate the end of my world or my life. Getting angry will not fix my situation."

Avoid using words like 'always' and 'never' when you are upset and talking about yourself or about someone else. You cannot tell someone, "You always forget important things," or mutter, "This terrible washer never works." These statements are most likely false and are only meant to justify your anger, but they do not resolve the problem that you have. They also effectively alienate people you could otherwise be working with to come up with a solution.

Always keep in mind the fact that anger does not resolve anything and that reacting to it will not make you feel better either. You are even likely to feel worse.

Seek to lean towards logic always, rather than anger. Even when you are truly justified to be angry, you can easily switch and become irrational. Instead, even when you are mad, rely on cold facts to remind yourself that you are not just a victim and that there is more to life than what you are experiencing. The challenges you are facing are common to man, and that they are only the rough spots of daily living. Remind yourself of these facts whenever your anger flares up so that you achieve some objectivity in your perspective.

Another critical thing to help you avoid anger is to get rid of your sense of entitlement. You are likely to get angry when you demand things and they are not availed to you. For example, you may become angry because your secretary forgot to sort out your mail, possibly because she was too busy handling other tasks related to your office or just because she forgot. Getting angry because of this is irrational because if you were, to be honest, you also forget things sometimes or you may have too many responsibilities at a time and choose to prioritize the important ones. If you become angry, your secretary will start to think that her contribution does not matter much and that you do not trust his or her judgment to prioritize and make decisions in the office. Her motivation to work will reduce significantly and so could her productivity. Instead of getting angry and affecting the environment around you, voice your concern with kindness, and she will go out of her way next time to ensure that your mail is sorted.

Adopt better skills for communication. When people get angry, they are likely to mutter the meanest things that come to their minds, however unkind. Before you react, however, take a minute to stop and breathe. Give careful thought to what you intend to say, and if you feel the need to step aside from an angry conversation to calm down, do so, and then get back to the conversation.

RELAX

Simple breathing and relaxation techniques can effectively soothe angry feelings. Practice doing them in a normal situation and it will be easier to apply them in the heat of the moment. Some of these techniques include:

Attentive breathing: When you are angry, you tend to have shallow quick breaths. Therefore, to counter this, practice deep controlled slow breathing, ensuring that they rise from your belly rather than your chest.

Relax your muscles progressively: Progressive muscle relaxation involves tensing and then relaxing your muscle group one at a time. For example, if you begin working on your head muscles, proceed to your neck muscles, going downward up until you reach the muscles in your toes.

TAKE UP IMAGERY

Visualize what a relaxation experience would look like from your imagination. In the heat of an argument, visualize what the ideal situation would be, what it would look like without this conflict, and work towards achieving that.

BECOME ACTIVE

Physical exercise done in the regular is a perfect decompression tool. It burns off the excess energy, releases the extra tension, and it lowers stress levels. When your body is all relaxed and all energy resources are being used appropriately, you are less likely to have anger outbursts.

TAKE NOTE OF AND AVOID YOUR TRIGGERS

Think about the things that cause you to lose it. If you know that driving during the rush-hour gets you angry, take the train or the bus, or at least plan to make your trip at a different time of the day. If you often go to bed arguing with your spouse, avoid bringing up contentious issues in the evening. If seeing your child's messy room gets you angry, shut the door, and you won't have to see the mess.

7

CHANNEL YOUR ANGER CREATIVELY

When you are angry, you either express or repress your feelings. A repression is a form of denial of reality because it involves shoving down the powerful negative emotions by pretending that they do not exist. When you repress anything, it goes beneath and becomes a poisonous autocrat that lurks in the shadows, awaiting an opportune moment to break free.

Anger, when repressed, becomes explosive and uncontrollable. It becomes unpredictable and a force like no other. Many times, the inner feelings of restlessness become a volcano of emotions that are repressed. Once the pressure is released, the anger comes out in a rage and the person dumps all the bile on another person without any form of control. Self-expression of this kind is quite dangerous because it causes the end or death of many significant relationships and can be detrimental to the wellbeing and health of the people involved.

Accepting and acknowledging the fact that you are angry goes a long way towards defusing the energy and the power behind it. It involves willfully facing your subconscious mind and with compassion and empathy, meeting your emotional self in your darkest expression takes out the string out of the anger. Accepting anger also means that you acknowledge its intensity and are aware that it is only a messenger of an underlying bigger issue. What's more, the simple act of acceptance opens the doorway to creativity, vitality, and wisdom.

Once you give yourself the permission and the opportunity to express your anger in a masterful way, you unlock your inner power. You take control of the situation yourself, you come alive, and you begin to express yourself creatively and passionately. In this case, we can define anger as some hidden potential that flows through you guiding you towards unleashing your potential and towards taking the path that you should have taken all along.

Steve Jobs defined creativity as the ability to create connections. According to him, a person is creative when he or she can make connections between the experiences he or she has had to come up with new things. The reason the person will be able to make that connection is that he or she can think about experiences and deduce more substance from them better than other people can. In other words, creativity is born out of connecting your experiences with the circumstances in your present to generate new ideas that will become the solutions for the future.

Being angry makes you irrational and unpredictable. You start to imagine scenarios and events that did not even occur. You think about what would happen if the situation were to play in various ways. You begin to think of how you would react and behave in each situation. This sounds like potentially fertile ground to birth creativity. Your mind and emotions run beyond their usual thresholds, beyond the things that we consider possible.

Here's what to do to unlock your creativity when you are angry:

1. *Identify an activity that could take your mind and concentration away from the things that cause you to be angry but lets you release those emotions.* Exercise is a good example, but you have the liberty to choose from among valuable things that distract your mind, so long as they involve physical movement. It could be an interactive video game or a brisk walk in the park. Writing is also an ideal activity.

2. *Accept and embrace the negative emotions and use them to push yourself harder.* Do this for the next 10-20 minutes. During this time, avoid any positive thoughts, just let the negativity drive you to punch harder, run harder, or write better. Whatever you do, keep going. You will find that it is easier to 'get into the zone' driven by the negative emotions as opposed to the positive ones. Once the endorphins start running through your system, you will gradually begin to think clearer and feel better.

3. *Now that the negative pent up energy is used up, begin to think about the changes you want to effect in your life and the solutions you will be seeking.* During this time, your creativity starts to rise even higher. Allow your brain to do this process all by itself, do not be caught forcing anything. However, as you are doing your chosen physical activity, focus on the hindrances, the ambitions you have, and the obstacles you are facing. Think about these things in regards to the new personal boundaries you want to implement, a new project you want to initiate, changes you want to see a trip you plan on taking, a business idea you want to implement, or a career move you intend to make.

Be careful not to stretch yourself so much mentally while doing the same physically. Only allow ideas to flow freely as your mind clears. If nothing comes yet, do not despair, don't be stressed. The most important thing for you is that you get some experience connecting and synthesizing experiences over time so that when next something angers you, you will have the tools to work through it creatively.

The great people of our society like Nelson Mandela, Martin Luther King, Gandhi, and others like them simply tapped into their inner anger and used the energy they derived from it to bring transformation in their courses. They mastered anger and used it as an ally to guide them towards unleashing incredible creativity that led to the great mobilization of people and the fight towards making an incredible mark in society.

Just because you know that anger is beneficial does not mean that you should go around seeking for reasons to be angry. It doesn't mean that anger is useful in all situations and circumstances. There are situations in which expressing your anger will even lower the respect that others accord to you in society. The first thing you need to do as you learn about anger is to differentiate between reasonable and unreasonable anger.

Take note of the events and circumstances that you can change and those that you cannot. If you are walking in the park and a strong wind blows your hat off so that it falls into fountain water, there is nothing you can do about that, which means it will do you no good to express your negative emotions. However, if someone comes and snatches your hat, you have control over the situation: you can ask for your hat back or chase the person down if you can.

Whatever you do, ensure that your anger expression is justifiable.

8
RELEASE ANGER WITH EXERCISE

Physical exercise is rated among the most effective methods of taking down stress and anger. When exercising, you get the opportunity to let go of your emotions, especially when you feel the pressure building up fast and about to explode. Exercise lowers the stress levels, too, by causing the body to produce endorphins, the feel-good hormones that boost your mood. Exercising also gives you an opportunity to think about what prompted you to be angry in the first place and what you would want to do about it.

Here are some exercises you can engage in to release the anger:

Boxing

Boxing is one of the best ways to let out your aggression and rage while benefitting from the burning of calories. It can also be a great way to learn how to defend yourself. One of the famous gymnasts recommends hitting the heavy bag for 30- to 60-seconds intervals of all-effort before you take a 30-to 90-seconds rest. Do this repeatedly 6 to 10 times in a session. Be careful to keep your wrists straight when punching.

Medicine Ball Slams

Another therapeutic way to get rid of aggression is to slam stuff. Don't go throwing and breaking things in your house; you will have to pay for them later. Instead, do the work using a medicine ball. Here's how to do it.

Lift the medicine ball, and with a straight back and a tight core, press the ball above your head and driving strength from your core, slam the ball to the ground. The ball will bounce right back. Use this momentum to repeat the exercise without having to bend over.

Do 10- 20 slams per set, factoring in the weight of the ball. Complete 4 set.

You are cautioned that if the medicine ball you are using is made of rubber, be careful so that you do not get smacked in the face. Instead, lean over and pick it up.

Deadlifting

Deadlifting is simply lifting some weight and putting it back to the ground. Very simple. You will feel very capable once you can raise a weight and not get overwhelmed by it.

To do it, ensure that your back is straight and that your core is tight. Sit back on your heels and drive through them, pulling the bar right up to your standing position. Squeeze your glute muscles at the top, and then lower the weight just as you lifted it. To ensure that you are engaging the right muscles, ensure that the bar grazes your legs the entire time.

When working with a weight that challenges you, do 3 or 4 sets each made up of 6 to 8 reps. Your anger will go away and your muscles will become stronger.

Hill Sprints

No matter what drove you to anger, once you go up a hill running in a sprint at maximum speed, sometimes, you will have no choice but to relax at the end of it.

How to do it, pick a hill and mark a finish line for the distance that would take you 20 to 30 seconds to run at maximum speed. Run this distance the fastest you can up, walk back down as you catch your breath, and then run up the hill again. Your rests should take only between 60 and 90 seconds and you should be back in the ascent immediately that time is spent.

For maximum effect, do the exercise 6 to 10 times. If you do not live up a hill, choose to do it in a flight of stairs or set your treadmill to a steep incline. Now, go ahead and try it.

Sledgehammer Twists

This exercise is best performed using an old tractor tire lying on its side if you can find one. This exercise is a great way to build muscle strength, to burn calories, and of course, to let out the anger. Most people swear by it, saying it beats exercising on the treadmill tremendously.

If you cannot get your hands on the old tire, use a woodchopper. It uses the same motion, only that you do the exercise with a medicine ball and not a tractor tire.

To do this exercise effectively using a sledgehammer, swing it as you would a baseball bat, and you will feel the effects of the swing and a release of the built-in emotions.

Yoga

Yoga is an exercise that works to purify and enhance the wellness of the mind, the soul, and the body. It is a spiritual approach to anger that, depending on its intensity, can be quite an intense workout by stretching the body, focusing on your breathing, and increasing your flexibility. In the course of doing all that, the anger you have built in will just melt away. One particular pose, the warrior pose, is a powerful stance that could cause you to release all the sadness and anger within. It focuses on instilling courage and balance which you could particularly use now.

Aerobics

Aerobics are some of the most useful high-energy workouts. They get your heart pumping, reduce blood pressure, and ease your anxiety. You could try skipping rope, cycling, the treadmill or jogging at the park.

Walking Briskly

Whenever I feel like I need to clear my mind, I go for a walk. The primary reason I choose to walk is that I do not like to jog or run; aerobics are not my thing. Instead, I take a 30-minutes walk, which can be turned to an hour's walk, sometimes. Walking significantly lowers the level of your stress hormones, breaks down calories, and improves on your agility.

Walking is also one of the best activities to do if you need to spend some time alone for self-reflection. Because when you are alone with your thoughts, you are able to connect with yourself. You do not have to think about the problem you are dealing with during your walk, focus on you only, and when the internal systems are working well, you will make a sound decision about the issues once you get back.

Begin by taking a 20-minutes walk, at least thrice a week, and increase this time gradually.

9
GIVE YOURSELF A BREAK

Our society encourages us to be on the go all the time. Faster, higher, and better are used too often to indicate to us the pace of life we should maintain. If you are offended, it is best to get over your anger sooner. You are advised to become better at withstanding sad things like discouragement and heartbreak so that you can move forward faster. However, in our haste, we forget to give ourselves room to breathe and be.

Many of us will feel the pressure mounting, but we cannot stand to take a moment to slow down or rest because then, we won't be branded as successful, we won't be liked, our value will go down, and if you do not overcome your hurt fast enough, people will not talk about what an amazing heart you got. It would seem like the more you bear, the more relevant you become. However, what happened to resting for a while? How about if you would just take some time to be by yourself and process your emotions slowly?

. . .

For you to give yourself the break you desperately need, you need to have compassion on yourself. Having compassion means that you are aware of the suffering you are going through. You are aware of who you are and you are responding to the pain you are going through with kindness, love, and gentleness.

Psychologists have discovered self-compassion to be a performance enhancement tool in different settings, from the corporate field to athletics. It even has aging benefits. People with self-compassion also tend to have higher esteem although the sense of self-importance it brings is innate and is not dependent on a comparison between yourself and other people. People are now beginning to take care of themselves and their wellbeing genuinely, and eventually, they recover from their setback.

A person with a high level of self-compassion has three distinct characteristics. First, he is kind and not critical of himself. Second, he recognizes the fact that he is a human being, and human beings make mistakes from time to time. Third, he takes a balanced approach toward his negative emotions whenever he fails. He takes the time to feel bad about the mistakes but does not let the negative emotions take over his spirit.

A college professor carried out a study to asses these three elements of self-compassion. He found that among other things, people with self-compassion have an innate desire and motivation to improve themselves and are more likely to develop strong feelings of authenticity about themselves. (Authenticity, in this case, referred to the sense of being true to yourself).

Motivation and authenticity are both critical in the development of a successful career. The advantage is that both traits can be acquired, cultivated, and enhanced.

IN LIFE, ALMOST EVERYONE, INCLUDING YOURSELF, IS rooting for you to make continuous improvement. While we have already established that self-compassion is critical for this to happen, you need to do a realistic assessment of where you are and where you stand in terms of your strengths and limitations before you can move forward.

Thinking that you are better while you are not is detrimental to your growth process. For example, if you assess yourself as being able to tolerate anger and work through it by yourself while you are not, you will only succeed at repressing your emotions, which is quite destructive. A realistic, truthful assessment would require you to list truthfully where you excel and where you fail. Failure to determine the areas you ought to work on will lead you to become complacent while not acknowledging your strong points leads to defeat. Therefore, you need to take your time in quiet reflection to evaluate yourself.

WHILE GIVING YOURSELF THE LIBERTY TO MAKE mistakes, give others some allowance, too. The people around you are also prone to errors, both intentionally and unintentionally. You will not always have the right package delivered. You will not always have clothes that you purchased online to fit you. You will not always find that steaming cup of coffee on your desk every day. People are bound to make mistakes.

. . .

Even the best movies have bloopers, multiples of them even. Sometimes, the cast of a film has to repeat something several times until they get it. If you see many of them online, the entire cast keeps laughing even if they have to repeat the same scene countless times. If movies, which are scripted and directed, have bloopers, how much more the unpredictable life we lead. Give yourself some breathing space and give the same to others. Give room for mistakes, and you will be less angry when the people around you make mistakes. You might even laugh about it.

In the same breath, take time to enjoy the pleasures that life has to offer. It is easy to get caught up in the demands of your career, your job, your family, or your perfect schedule that you forget to see the beauty that life has to offer. You may still be engrossed in something that someone did wrong two weeks ago, or you could be worried about something that will come about until you forget to be present at the moment. When you do this, you miss the little pleasures of life which are the basis of having a fun life. Celebrate the blessings that are in your life now.

You do not have to arrive early at your workplace every day; be late one day. See the adrenaline rush you get before you get there. See how you dodge your boss to avoid him spotting you getting in late. Once you are late for one day, you become more thankful for the days that you arrived early.

Looking back to your early memories, you are likely to see that the most memorable ones, both bad and good, are those when something out of the norm happened. The day you had the most fun could be the day you defied the rules your parents set and went to the mall, not when you ate supper at 6 PM and was in bed by 8 PM. So, live a little. Go on and create those memories. Be accommodating of other people's bloopers, they will offer a great lesson for the future, and some laughs, too.

10

SEEK SOLUTIONS TO YOUR ISSUES

THE BENEFITS OF LEARNING HOW TO CONTROL YOUR anger are countless. For example, when you learn how to communicate appropriately and how to resolve conflict in a healthy way, your work life will benefit greatly. You will be able to create rapport and friendships with other people and managing your anger properly will cause you to feel healthier. It is also likely that you will sleep better in the night, your health will be on a better trend, and you could end up living longer. Here's how you leap the benefits discussed:

The first thing you need to learn how to do is to pay attention. Before you can begin to shift the reaction you give to anger, you need to spend some considerable time observing how you react when angry. Identify your anger triggers and these could range from traffic to financial issues. Next, pay attention to the signs of anger like frantic breathing or sweaty palms. Pay attention to the thoughts that come up, too. See where your thoughts go whenever you are angry or disappointed. Before you can begin to address issues related to your anger, you need to examine all there is to do with it and come up with ways to challenge every aspect of it.

Secondly, you need to seek resources available. The resources you would need to resolve anger issues could be in the form of classes, books, professional help, and others. A number of them most likely surround you. Go ahead and pay for counseling sessions or an anger management class. Many workplaces, however, offer the two services at no cost. There are also both physical and virtual support groups for which you would make an ideal candidate. If you are unsure about where to find these resources, talk to your doctor, your HR manager, or to colleagues who may have a clue about it.

Third, be focused on the solution. You will find that many strategies are focused on helping you overcome your anger and helping others around you to do the same. Majority of them we have discussed in the topics above such as mindfulness, exercise, pausing before you respond, and other relaxation techniques that are designed to help you be mindful of the responses you give to an anger trigger. Incorporate these techniques into your day, and you will find that utilizing them out in the middle of a crisis becomes quite natural.

If you feel that you cannot come up with a solution to the issues you are experiencing, it is advisable that you seek help. Many people find it difficult to coach themselves and would benefit from training by a professional or directly from a person who has dealt with similar issues in the past and overcome. Asking for help does not indicate weaknesses. It only shows your strong commitment and resolves to cause change and the ability to steer your life in the preferred direction.

Anger Management Class

The meaning of anger management is not as big as the word itself. Anger management is simply the process of learning how to recognize signs that you are angry, and then taking action to control the anger by calming down and dealing with the situation productively. Anger management is not designed to help you repress your anger; you only learn how to manage your anger alone and how to help others or deal with them when they are angry.

Some of the issues for which you may require help handling include:

- Constantly feeling irritated, hostile, and impatient
- Feeling like you need to hold on to your anger for longer every time
- Persistently focusing on negative experiences and persistently thinking negative thoughts
- Frequently arguing with others and having these fights escalate every time
- Becoming physically violent
- Giving threats of violence
- Keeping off different environments fearing that you will have anger outbursts
- Portraying out-of-control behavior like reckless driving, breaking items when angry, or doing things that put your children at risk

Anger management class will help you determine the presence of, or the absence, of the above frustrations and more so that you are better placed to express your needs, and you can stay in control of your faculties.

Anger management is done either in one-on-one sessions or in groups. A certified anger management counselor or an accredited therapist moderates the discussions, and the class can last anywhere between a few weeks and a few months.

When looking for an anger management class, make sure to verify the credentials of the therapist or the counselor. Also, ensure that the group is committed to maintaining the confidentiality of personal details expressed if you have that as a concern. Privacy and trust are also important because they create a sense of 'we' in the group, creating the impression that all members are united to fight for the same course, and that a problem to one person becomes a problem to many others.

Above all else, the anger management class needs to be one that allows you to view your anger issues from a positive angle. Some people take this class from a negative stance. They see it as a form of punishment, especially when the doctor or the boss recommends it. However, the attendee needs to reframe his thinking and understanding so that he begins to view the class as a grand opportunity to work on the self and to improve relationships.

Anger Management Support Group

An anger management support group is a therapy group made up of people who have dealt with or are in the process of dealing with anger issues. In these groups, members discuss all there is to anger, from triggers, to how they were able to deal with their problems. Members also teach other essential tools and hacks for dealing with violence. This group not only helps you overcome the issues you have now but also grows through your implementation of the solutions you have come up with. They teach you how to rebuild relationships also. A support group creates a sense of family because they celebrate with you for the progress you make and encourage you when you fail or encounter challenges.

The result of seeking solutions for your issues is that you will have a better grip of your anger. You will get the joy of having more control over your life, and more ready to overcome the challenges that life offers you. You will also begin to be more assertive in your self-expression because you do not have to be careful in your speech anymore, afraid that you may hurt someone.

In the end, learning how to manage your anger will offer you a bunch of benefits. It makes you better at communicating your needs. Anger management prevents social and psychological issues linked to anger. It keeps you from using your frustrations to get people to do what you want and turns you to a better communicator. It helps you avoid harmful and addictive coping behaviors, and enables you to maintain good health.

❧ 11 ❧

LIGHTEN UP WITH HUMOR

INSTEAD OF STRESSING AND MUSING, HOW ABOUT turning that anger into comedy? You see, many people fail to realize that anger is the force that drives comedy. Comedians realize this, and they will use the things that anger the society to come up with jokes. Anger does not only help to produce the things that many people can relate to but converting a problem into something people can laugh about turns the situation around. They begin to view themselves as winners, as though they are in charge of the situation, rather than as victims.

Humor heals and empowers. When you laugh about something, you assume power over it. Can you recall a time when you laughed at something that ought to have made you angry? You were probably complaining about something your spouse, parent, in-law, colleague, or friend did. When you think about it and suddenly it has you laughing, you begin to relax, and the issues start to release the hold they had on you. Some of the funniest stories we tell are those that petrified us when they happened, and now that time has passed, we have gained a better perspective and can see the humorous side of what happened.

The problem is that waiting for time to show you the humor is too long. You don't want to have suffered years of anger and become a bitter, angry person, just when the humor is beginning to reveal itself. The million-dollar question now is: how do you get to speed up this process? Here are some tips:

1. **Be distracted**

Researchers conducted a study where they initiated two traffic jams. In one of them, the drivers were left to their own devices, huffing, puffing, cursing, and fussing the entire time. In the other, the researchers created three distractions in the form of a puppy being walked down the road alongside the vehicles, an attractive man and a beautiful woman walking by, and a person doing stupid funny things nearby. The variables being tested in these scenarios were fuzzy and warm, sexy, and funny, respectively.

The researchers studied both groups to determine the frequency of them displaying their anger by yelling, honking, shooting their fingers, and stomping around outside their vehicles. The distracted group had fewer displays of anger, and the distraction that worked best was that of humor. From these findings, you can already see how having funny distractions, especially in situations and places that trigger your anger the most could work to keep off the anger.

- **Befriend Google**

The next time your anger has accumulated and you feel like your head is about to blow up with rage, especially driven by an issue you are sure should not get you mad, look on to the internet for help. Go ahead and Google funny videos and stories that have some familiarity with the issue you are handling. Find hilarious videos of people doing what you are doing or an even sillier response and laugh your heart out. The benefit of doing this is that it enables you to take your situation lightly. It also takes you out of the situation somewhat, making it easier for you to laugh at the other people's situations, and in the process, not fuss about your own.

- **Use the math**

If you spend an hour of your day laughing with friends, watching funny videos or a movie, it means that you have lessened the time you got to be angry by an hour. Therefore, if you are awake for 16 hours a day, you can only fuss for 15 of them. The more time you spend being happy, not necessarily watching movies and videos, the lesser time you have to be sad.

- **Be angry in a funny way**

Rather than expressing your anger in your usual disgruntled manner, try showing it in a way that gets you and others around you to laugh. For example, you could curse in a foreign language that others do not understand. As you circumvent your usual reactions and replies to anger, your brain will start to grasp the comic effect quicker and to let go of the negative emotions.

- **Make jokes about it**

We always assume that comedians do not get angry because they are continually making jokes and always seem happy. However, they go through the confusion, embarrassment, annoyance, and frustration that the rest of us have to endure. Without it, they would have nothing to write a comedy about. Therefore, the next time you are upset about something, especially about the not-so-heavy stuff, behave like a comedian and make fun out of it.

If by chance you are around an angry person who can't seem to crack a smile, assuming the issue he is angry about is light and the two of you are familiar with each other, go ahead and make him laugh. A story is told about a police officer who got a call to a home by neighbors who complained about the shouting match going on inside the house. As the police officer approached the front porch, the shouting escalates, and right in front of her, a TV gets thrown down from the second floor, and it instantly crashes at her feet. Instead of becoming angry and perceiving this to be a personal attack, the police officer proceeds to the front door and knocks on it. “Who’s there?” A man from inside yells.

“T.V. repair,” the officer yells back. The man inside laughed so hard and the laughter diffused the tension a bit, allowing the people inside to open the door and for the police officer to enter the house safely.

In tense situations, a joke is an ideal icebreaker. It lightens the mood and puts the feelings of those in the house back to perspective. In situations where you find yourself angry and cannot tell why, try to crack some jokes about it. Do not be sarcastic though, because this is not your typical environment that supports humor. Sarcasm may hurt other people’s feelings.

12

FORGIVE AND LET GO

We all have been hurt at a point in life. Your child refused to heed to your counsel and started abusing drugs. Your partner cheated on you and had an affair. A colleague sabotaged your work, so he could get the promotion. A parent constantly abused you verbally, physically, and even sexually in your childhood. People have had very traumatic experiences. Wounds caused by issues like these can last a long time; they could cause you so much bitterness, anger, and a desire to retaliate.

Nevertheless, the secret to overcoming the hurt is in forgiveness. Hard as it may sound, if you do not forgive, you may end up being the one who has to pay dearly. However, when you choose to forgive, you also choose hope, happiness, peace, joy, and gratitude.

Forgiveness may have different meanings to different people, but it primarily refers to the decision to let go of the thoughts of retaliation and all manner of resentment. You may always remember the words or the act that caused you considerable pain, but forgiving lessens the grip the hurt has on you, allowing you to be free from the control of what harmed you. It is also likely that just by choosing to forgive; you will become empathetic, understanding, and even develop compassion for the person that hurt you.

Forgiveness does not mean that you excuse what was done to you either or that you become friends with the perpetrator. It is only meant to bring you some pristine peace to help you maneuver through life more easily.

Some of the benefits of forgiving includes:

- It improves your mental health and wellness
- Boosts your self-esteem
- Enables you to have healthier relationships
- Makes you feel less depressed
- Lets you to release all the stress, anxiety, and hostility you may be holding
- Lowers your blood pressure

Holding a grudge is so much easier than forgiving. A grudge means that you are acknowledging and holding on to what a person that you loved or who should have loved you, did to you. It causes all the right emotions, those that go with what was done to you. You could feel confused, sad, and angry.

However, negativity does not produce any good outcome. Therefore, if you allow these negative feelings to crowd the positive ones, you will find yourself immersed and covered up in bitterness and a strong sense of injustice.

The effects of holding a grudge include:

- A grudge causes you to lose the enriching and valued connectedness you share with others.
- It causes you to carry with you all the bitterness and anger that you hold into every relationship in your life, putting you at odds with the people in your life and denying you the opportunity to enjoy new relationships.
- Grudges cause their holders to become so engrossed in what happened in the past so much that they forget what happened in the past.
- You develop anxiety and depression.
- You may sometimes feel like despairing because you think that your life has lost meaning or that you are at odds with your belief system.

REACHING THE STATE OF FORGIVENESS

Reaching the state of forgiving is quite a difficult but achievable task. When you forgive, it means that you are living. You must also have identified the areas of your life that require now entering into a new commitment with yourself to change by becoming accepting of the value that forgiveness has to offer you and the dynamics by which it can change your healing and have a list of the people you need to forgive. If you are open to it, consider seeing a counselor or getting into a support group to receive assistance going through the situation.

. . .

ACHIEVING FORGIVENESS ALSO MAKES IT NECESSARY for you to acknowledge the emotions that you feel in regard to the ill that was done to you and how these emotions have affected your behavior. You must then have the purpose to release them, along with the accompanying behavior, and agree with yourself that it is time to forgive the offender. Once you have made up your mind, you are likely to go through the process more comfortably, and you will not think of turning around. Lastly, choose to walk away from a victim's identity and to release the hold the offender has had over your life.

YOU WILL NO LONGER ALLOW GRUDGES TO DEFINE YOU, and you will no longer evaluate the quality of your life by the extent to which you have been hurt.

WHEN FORGIVING IS DIFFICULT

Forgiving can be quite difficult, especially when the person who offended you does not acknowledge his responsibility, or if he or she continues to hurt you in the same way occasionally. When this happens, you are likely to feel stuck. However, you should not let anything stand in the way of your personal growth. If you already decided to forgive, nothing should keep you from doing just that, not even the offender.

THEREFORE, WHEN THIS HAPPENS, YOU CAN CHOOSE TO take up some strategies to make coping with the situation easier. First, become empathetic so that you are able to see the situation from the other party's viewpoint. Ask yourself what could be causing the person to behave as he or she does. It is possible that you would have reacted in the same way had you been in the circumstances and situation that the person is in. Think, also, of the times when you hurt others, and they forgave you, too. Consider returning the favor by forgiving an undeserving person.

JOURNALING, PRAYER, AND GUIDED MEDITATION COULD also help to ease the intensity of the negative emotions. You could also talk to someone you look up to for advice on the steps you ought to take. This persOn could be an impartial loved one, a religious leader, a friend, or a mental health services provider. These people will provide you with an objective review of the situation and will help make the process of forgiving easier.

YOU NEED TO BE AWARE OF THE NATURE OF forgiveness as a process that needs to be done repeatedly. You do not just wake up, forgive, and move on. Even the small mistakes need to be forgiven repeatedly so that the hurt does not build up and cause large emotional wounds.

KINDLY NOTE THAT YOU DO NOT FORGIVE SO THAT THE individual can change his behavior. Forgiveness is somewhat selfish because you forgive for your benefit, not for the benefit of the other party.

YOU SHOULD ALSO KNOW THAT FORGIVING DOES NOT necessitate reconciliation. Only reconcile with people with whom you share an important relationship, and even then, it is not a requirement. It would be impossible to reconcile with someone who has died or one who is unwilling to speak to you. However, this does not mean that you shouldn't forgive them. You must forgive, even when reconciliation is absent.

LET GO

Once you have forgiven, you need to let the anger and the resentment go. You must also release from your remembrance the painful words or acts and the memories of the pain, the sleepless nights, the worry, and the tears you shed. By letting go, you are releasing the emotions that are tied to each of these events.

ONCE YOU DO THAT, REMEMBERING EITHER OF THESE acts should not drive you to tears and the memory of the offender should not drive you to anger either. You will have released all the emotion and your brain, too, will start to bury these events so that they are no longer in your conscious part, and you are able to move on from that.

CONCLUSION

Thank you for making it through to the end of *Anger Management: 12 Step Guide to Recognize and Control Anger, Develop Emotional Intelligence, and Self Discipline.* Let's hope it was informative and able to provide you with all of the tools you need to achieve your goals whatever it is that they may be.

Each of us struggles with some unresolved emotions of anger at various points of our lives, and it is important that we learn how to recognize and deal with the negative emotions in an easy sequential way that will guarantee you emotional growth, happiness, peace, and increased satisfaction.

The next step is to take up these 12 steps to get over anger in your own life by systematically going through the process of recognizing it, understanding it, learning how to express it calmly, redirecting your attention from it, and using the strong negative emotions to drive creativity.

You now see the value of empathy and understand how it drives you to understand your offender because you get to see from the offender's unique viewpoint. You are able to realize and acknowledge the possibly unique factors that could have led the person to do what he did. Understanding makes it easier to come to terms with reality. It is possible that you could be holding on to anger caused by a person who did not even realize that they were hurting you. Others will hurt you and not care about it, nevertheless.

You have also learned how to redirect and channel your negative energy and use it as a drive for activities that demand creativity. You could try out a new hobby like drawing or painting. Some people even turn it to humor. I bet you did not know that jokes are created from the negative experiences comedian has gone through. You can also behave like a comedian and try to come up with some light jokes to help diffuse the sadness and tension that an unfortunate event causes.

You have also learned about the role of forgiveness in the management of anger. It enables you to give up the ownership and right to all negative emotions so that you are disassociated from all negative emotions. This way, even if you remember the offenders and their actions, you will be okay, neither sad nor angry.

Finally, if you found this book useful in any way, a review on Amazon is always appreciated!

DESCRIPTION

Anger Management: 12 Step Guide to Recognize and Control Anger, Develop Emotional Intelligence, and Self Discipline gives you an outline of the 12 most critical steps that you should take to manage your anger.

To that end, this book is arranged into 12 brief chapters that detail the steps you ought to take in the process of managing anger by recognizing and controlling anger to develop self-discipline and emotional intelligence that you need to maneuver through life and to guide the relationships you form with others. This book begins by indicating to you the need for you to accept your anger rather than suppressing it. It would actually be impossible for you to deal with something that you have not taken ownership of.

Once you accept that you are angry, you need to understand where the nature of your anger by determining its origins, its triggers, and the signs your body produces to indicate that the anger is about to surface. Once you realize this, you can quickly take control of the situation. The techniques the book offers to deal with your anger once you have understood it includes pausing before you react, calmly expressing your anger, practicing empathy, redirecting your focus from the triggers of anger, and how to channel your anger in a creative way.

Lastly, inside this book, you will find a discussion on how different strategies you can take to incorporate all these steps into your daily routine. For example, you will see a guide to help you in the process of forgiving and for taking up humor to overcome anger in your life. Therefore, to get started on the process of overcoming anger, get started by purchasing this book today!

Inside you will find:

- A 12-step illustration of the most critical steps to take in your quest to overcome anger
- The most explicit definition and illustration of anger and its influence in your life
- Some interesting, relatable stories to help you identify with the steps discussed in this book
- A clear depiction of the exercises that are ideal for getting rid of anger and its influences
- The most engaging discussion indicating how you ought to redirect your focus from things that anger you
- A description of empathy and the right way to express it
- Advice on how to give yourself and others a break from responsibility

EMPATH

Step by Step Guide to Overcome Fears and Develop Your Gift for Highly Sensitive People

Jane Orloff

INTRODUCTION

This book is a study into the emotionally sensitive people and aims to provide guidance on how empaths can manage their gift. If an empath lacks awareness about the activities taking place in their minds and hasn't yet discovered their gift, they can almost consider themselves cursed. The vortex of emotions that they experience when they hang out in public places can leave them devastated.

Being an empath is not something to be ashamed of. On the contrary, it is a mark of strength, especially since empaths have an unmatched ability to empathize. Empaths have powerful introspective brains that keep churning new information, never resting. Nothing can escape their attention.

But on the dark side, empaths grapple with a cocktail of fears that hold them back from making progress. It doesn't matter whether these fears are real or untrue because they still have a domineering presence on the lives of empaths.

This book aims to help empaths overcome these fears and become proud of their gift. Being an empath is not a condemnation to a life of mediocrity. But you need to acquire some practical tips that will help you navigate through life with ease.

❧ I ❧
WHAT DOES IT MEAN TO BE AN EMPATH?

AN EMPATH IS A VERY UNIQUE BEING THAT THE AVERAGE person has a difficult time understanding. Although an empath's capabilities seem fascinating, they can potentially make their life agonizing. The following are some of the realities that an empath has to put up with:

CARRYING THE BURDENS OF OTHER PEOPLE AFTER INTERACTING WITH THEM

The average person doesn't see it as a big deal when they meet friends or acquaintances who have fallen on hard times and are having it rough. Words are exchanged and then it's over just as quickly as it began. But that's not the case with an empath. They tend to agonize over other people's pain as though it were their own pain. They could be carrying on with their day full of cheer, and then they run into a friend who informs them that they just lost a loved one, or are battling a terminal illness, and the empath will keep going back to the matter.

They don't have the capacity to just flick into a bin the thoughts attached to an unpleasant situation. They just keep going back to these thoughts, wondering what the answer to that other person's predicament might be. The empath will keep their mind buzzing with all the possible remedies. On one hand, it's a great thing. But on the other hand, it limits an empath's capacity to function in an adjusted manner. There are more people going through hardships than we could ever count. So, if an empath were to be distracted by all these people who are in a world of pain, then they'd hardly ever achieve anything with their lives.

MANY SOCIAL GATHERINGS ARE DRAINING AND UNCOMFORTABLE

An empath actively avoids social gatherings because they feel terrible for the most part. One of the unique capabilities of an empath is the ability to sense other people's thoughts and feelings. For this reason, when they are in the midst of a crowd, they tend to be bombarded by various energies emanating from other people. This weakens their confidence and makes them vulnerable, especially if the empath has no understanding of what's happening. This tendency to avoid social gatherings might make the empath seem anti-social, but it is merely an act done in good faith. They are only trying to preserve their sanity.

Empaths like socializing within small groups of familiar faces as opposed to large crowds. They are extremely good with one-on-one conversations too. Once they are comfortable with a person, the awkwardness fades away and their cheerful personality shines through.

Most people have a difficult time understanding why empaths shun crowds. The idea that someone could be affected by other people's thoughts and feelings sounds awkward to them.

One of the best ways for an empath to cope with this problem is to stick with their friends while out as opposed to being solo. This will avoid others from preying on the empath and making them feel pathetic.

NEVER-ENDING MOOD SWINGS

All empaths struggle with mood swings. The mood swings are brought about by the fact that empaths tap into other people's thoughts. As an empath, one moment you could be brimming with delightful thoughts, the next moment you could be depressed, and then back to being joyful again. There's no certainty to your moods. For the most part, your moods will be influenced by the people you stay close to or the information that you will feed your mind with. Empaths must be careful about the media that they spend time on. For instance, they should limit (or eliminate altogether) watching violent movies and disturbing news.

Watching violent movies can affect an empath's thoughts and cause them mood swings. Same with turbulent news; there is an ocean of sufferings going on in the world; people getting murdered, diseases claiming lives, and ruthless politicians taking advantage of their subjects. When an empath is constantly watching such kinds of things, it can go into their mind and affect them terribly.

Thus, an empath should stay away from destructive media and channel their energies into productive activities such as hobbies and positivity. They should form habits that encourage them to lead a life of meaning as opposed to seeking cheap and destructive thrills.

DEPRESSION

Considering that every human being is battling some form of challenge, depression cannot be wished away. It's always going to be there. But there's nothing ordinary with being in a depressed state 90% of your time.

This is one of the painful realities that some empaths find themselves struggling with. When an empath is exposed to so much pain, they tend to lose hope, and it weakens their resolve. Thus, they slide into depression.

For instance, an empath could be a gifted actor or musician, but most people in the industry tend to overlook them because they are not aggressive and in-your-face like the rest. And this can cause the empaths to be resentful, develop a bad attitude, and ultimately, suffer depression.

Sadly, not all empaths are aware of their condition and their capabilities. Their ignorance makes them suffer even more. At least the empowered empath knows what's going on with their lives and is ever ready to take measures to control the damage.

But when an empath doesn't understand how their gifts make them susceptible to pain, then they are thrown into a state of confusion, which breeds depression.

An empath should recognize their quirky capabilities and find a way of coexisting with other people without altering who they are; it will help get rid of the depression.

EASILY EXCITED ABOUT DREAMS, IDEAS, AND HOPES OF OTHER PEOPLE

An empath lives in their mind. Whether they are surrounded by a crowd or by themselves, they won't stop poring over small things inside their brain.

No one understands fantasy like an empath. It's one of their major outlets for the buildup of the frustrations. By escaping into a land of fantasy, they are finally free from the worries of the world.

They can create their own magnificent castles on the island of fantasy and put their own people there – people who get them. Fantasy offers them an escape and allows them to experience life on their own terms.

The average person might be somewhat dismissive of the things that take place in the mind, for instance, dreams. But it's different with an empath.

An empath has a huge interest in otherworldly matters and wants to understand what really their dreams mean. Thus, if they get a dream, they won't rest until they recognize the meaning behind it.

Empaths are also interested in poring over the ideas of other people. Once they meet someone they can get along with, most of the conversation is going to be centered upon ideas. They love exploring the different ways of thinking amongst people.

Empaths are also very receptive to the hopes of other people. They love to rally behind people so that their hopes might come true.

PEOPLE COME TO THEM WITH THEIR ISSUES

People are aware that empaths are kind. So, if they have a problem, guess to whom they will run to? It is both a good thing and a bad thing. On one hand, it does make the empath proud knowing that they can be of help. But on the other hand, it can lead to a lot of time wastage, especially if the cases are unwarranted.

One of the hard things an empath will have to practice is putting boundaries. They have to have boundaries so that they can protect both their time and dignity from abuse. Letting everyone have their way at your expense is simply being unfair to yourself. But an empath doesn't have the guts to just say "NO." They want to keep pleasing people even when it harms them.

Since people come to empaths with their problems, empaths can use this as a leverage to establish connections and advance their agendas as well.

Empaths have strong analytical skills and most people who present them with their worries and problems tend to get the best advice or solution ever. The analytical skills of empaths are developed through their intense thinking, and they help tremendously in boosting creativity.

ILL, SICK, AND NAUSEOUS FOR NO REASON

If you have been out on a rave without proper clothing, and then the following day you come down with a cold, that's understandable. But if you climb into bed healthy and wake up ill and tired, then that's not normal. Falling ill without any obvious trigger is something that empaths must cope with.

For the average empath who's not yet acclimatized to their condition, it gets even worse. Their illness can be as a result of their energy shield being tampered with and leading to loss of energy. For instance, if they watch something tragic, the resultant thoughts might harm their energy shield, and this could cause them to become susceptible to illnesses.

Empaths are terribly sensitive to many diets and foods. Their bodies tend to be aligned toward the foods that are organically grown. You will find some empaths repulsed by meats and processed foods and they will embrace vegetarian and vegan lifestyles. Because of their quirky eating habits, they are prone to becoming nauseous in the event that they consume foods that they are not acclimatized to.

Empaths should keep their health in top form by sticking to favorable diets, seeking regular medical checkup, and keeping active lifestyles.

CAN EASILY SPOT FAKE PEOPLE

Isn't the ability to glance at a person and tell whether they are genuine or fake amazing? Let's face it. The world is chock-full of insincere people who mean us harm. One of the strong capabilities of an empath is that they would immediately know whether a person is sincere or a fake.

When they meet someone, they start reading their energies, as well as their body language. They understand that genuine people will radiate certain energy and fake people will have questionable body language. It's not a learnable capability. It's more of a switch in their psyche that directs them in pinning down insincere and fake people.

If a person approaches an empath and straight out lies to them, the empath is in a position to detect that something is amiss. But sadly, they may as well second-guess themselves because of their low self-esteem, yet they are eventually vindicated when their fears come to pass.

An empath can prosper in careers where sincerity and honesty are demanded. This is because they can spot the people who are not genuine. They are so good at reading people's energies and making appropriate conclusions. Interestingly, they don't always use this capability to their advantage because of a tendency of downplaying their intuition.

FREQUENTLY ACCUSED OF BEING TOO SENSITIVE

An empath tends to approach life with a lot of caution. Nothing ever escapes their scrutiny. They could be engaged in a task that demands simple adjustments, but the empath is still going to be meticulous. This tendency of being too rigid and cautious has resulted in people calling them sensitive.

Empaths are very aware of how people talk to them and behave towards them. This makes them susceptible to things that don't hurt normal and well-adjusted people. For instance, if an empath is walking along the street, and they come across a person wearing a frown, they might mistakenly think that the frown is aimed at them. Then they start panicking and wondering why that other person hates them.

Empaths tend to raise concerns where there shouldn't be. This sensitive nature of theirs draws criticism from other people because they are difficult to get along with.

This sensitive nature limits the empath's capacity to form alliances or make connections with other people and drives them into seclusion. For people who haven't understood what drives an empath to behave the way they do, they can develop hatred towards them. But then empaths should put in the effort to see to it that they water down their sensitive side and get along with everybody.

VALUE THEIR EMOTIONS AND THOSE OF OTHERS A LOT

There's no other language that an empath understands more than emotions. Unlike empaths, most people are aware of or have only experienced a limited range of emotions. But then empaths have lived through many emotions – both the good and the worst.

For this reason, empaths tend to take their emotions very seriously. Whether they experience sadness or joy, they will turn it over and over inside their minds, all in an effort to seek the cause of their emotional state.

Empaths demand that other people respect their emotions as well. They don't want to open up to someone and then have that person dismiss their emotions. It crushes them. In the same breath, they tend to value other people's emotions. For instance, when someone tells an empath why they are sad, the empath will immediately offer sympathy and try to provide a solution.

2
WAYS YOUR GIFT CAN MANIFEST

There are various types of empaths and their gifts manifest in various ways. These are some of the ways that the gift of an empath can manifest.

EMOTIONAL EMPATHS

An emotional empath is receptive of the emotions that other people tend to emit. If they are riding a bus and they sit near someone who makes an outburst toward the driver, the emotional empath is likely to grow mad as well. They obviously have no reason to be mad, but somehow they are mad. This is simply because the anger emitted by the person seated next to the empath finds its way into the empath. And the empath perceives that anger as though it were their own. For the most part, their emotional state is defined by the people surrounding them.

In order for an emotional empath to survive these challenges, they have to develop a high sense of situational awareness. This means that they should stay away from situations that threaten their emotional balance. For instance, if they are in an environment where people are negatively charged, they should excuse themselves. This will see them avoid sifting other people's emotions and ruining their emotional stability. An emotional empath should also ensure that their time is packed with activity as opposed to just lying around. When the mind is engaged, there's a better chance of missing other people's emotions as opposed to when the mind is idle.

MEDICAL EMPATHS

Medical empaths are great at determining what ails a person. These people are so good at detecting someone who's battling an illness. By just a casual glance or a mere touch, they will not only know that someone is sick but can also tell what they are suffering from. Medical empaths have a natural aptitude for detecting ailments and they prosper in medical fields. A medical empath can establish rapport with sick people because they have an innate understanding of various sicknesses. They know how to make sick people drop their guards and open up about their condition without feeling judged.

But more interestingly, medical empaths have healing capabilities. Of course, this doesn't apply to all illnesses or all sick people, but medical empaths have the power to restore sick people into a state of health. The healing process could be triggered by something as simple as touching or speaking with the sick person. Their energies consist of restorative powers and this helps them transfer healing upon those that seek or need it.

In some instances, a medical empath can very well take on the symptoms of other people's illnesses. They could come across a person who's suffering a certain illness, and they are moved to the point that their body mirrors the symptoms of the ill person.

NATURE EMPATHS

The nature empath is most at peace when they are in the natural world. They have the capability to commune with elements of the natural world. Thus, a nature empath will always find a way of bringing nature into their lives. For instance, they might plant gardens around their residences, and hang canvas photos of their favorite things in nature at their homes. They cannot go for long without reconnecting with nature. And their way of treating depression or any other unfavorable emotion is by spending time with nature. This kind of empath is united with nature and they couldn't have it any other way.

The most hurtful thing for a nature empath is witnessing the destruction of nature. They tend to be passionate about matters touching upon the environment and are concerned with providing solutions for its wellbeing.

The nature empath can feel the vibrations of the natural world. They draw their power from spending time with nature. When they go for a long time without communing with nature, it can potentially bog them down.

For a nature empath, if they are up to facing a task that demands a ton of creativity, they can only reach their peak through spending time with nature, and this makes them extremely protective of all the elements of nature.

CLAIRCOGNIZANT EMPATHS

A claircognizant empath is one of the truly weird ones. They have the capability of knowing things by heart. Their intuition is on point. They seem to understand the true nature of circumstances without missing a mark. This inborn trait of telling right from wrong by heart surprises people. The more an empath develops this gift, the more powerful it becomes. And conversely, if they ignore their gift then it becomes watered down. An empath who has developed their claircognizant capabilities is definitely going to have a very accurate judgment on every situation that they get involved in.

The claircognizant empath is a master of detecting lies. They don't even have to gather the evidence first. The lie will pretty much stand out. But whether they will act on it or not is another matter entirely. For the bold ones, this is an incredibly helpful capability, knowing the number of liars roaming the world. This capability saves them needless pain.

This kind of empath is hardly frustrated for a long stretch of time. They just know what to do no matter their circumstances are. Their fine-tuned intuition helps them make the best decisions ever. Relying on their gut-instinct proves more rewarding than relying on their brain ever would.

SPIRITUAL EMPATHS

In a general sense, the world is made of both physical and ethereal matter. The physical world is apparent to every person, but that cannot be said of the spiritual world. The spiritual world is obviously beyond the understanding of the common man.

But not so for the spiritual empath; this person has a great understanding of the spiritual world. They cannot only perceive spiritual matters and events but can also detect spiritual entities.

For this kind of person, it is not uncommon for them to have a spiritual guide. They can commune with entities beyond the physical reality and are very perceptive of the matters taking place beyond the conventional reality.

Spiritual empaths have often been known to act as mediums. They can reach out to the souls of their departed loved ones and they can also establish close relationships with spiritual guides. Spiritual empaths have a heightened sensitivity to the internal makeup of most people. Thus, they can tell dangerous people from just a slight interaction.

The spiritual world is made of many different things and it takes a person with developed spiritual capabilities to discern the scope of that realm.

One of the advantages that spiritual empaths have over other people is the ability to be prepared against any sort of spiritual calamity. Most people are susceptible to spiritual attacks because they have limited understanding of how it works. But the spiritual empath is fully capable of detecting and warding off spiritual attacks.

TELEPATHIC EMPATHS

Having telepathic powers is nothing short of magic. This is the capability to tell what other people are thinking or are up to. A telepathic empath has a great situational awareness because they can tell what most people are planning. This allows them to create leverage and get out of harm's way.

It doesn't matter how closed-off one considers himself to be, a telepathic empath could still get past their barriers and access the contents of their minds. Telepathic empaths have the ability to tune into the general feeling inherent in a person or a crowd. This makes them great at reading people and gives them a head start in crafting an endearing self-image.

Telepathic empaths not only pick up information from other people but they can also transmit information to others. A telepathic empath could transmit their thoughts or energies into another person regardless of the time gap or physical gap separating them.

Although this gift is inherent, it still could use some sharpening. The empaths that put this gift into practice sharpen it, and those that fail to put it into practice end up stifling it.

Having telepathic powers is both a curse and a blessing. On the bright side, you can transmit your energies into other people, but then you can also read other people's minds, and considering that statistically most people are ill-intentioned, it can make you depressed.

PRECOGNITIVE EMPATHS

A precognitive empath has the capability of telling what the future will be like. He will catch a whiff of an occurrence long before it takes place. In other words, precognitive empaths have prophetic powers.

Whether this is good or bad varies from one person to another. Perhaps having the ability to tell what's in store for the future helps you prepare adequately, but then again having a glimpse into the horrors that wait is not particularly helpful, especially if nothing can be done about it.

A telepathic empath reeks of wisdom. They have the capability of looking into the future. This makes them not only aware of the course of their life or other people's lives but also puts them in a position of giving restorative advice.

A telepathic empath can prosper in vocations that utilize a person's ability to forecast the future. They can make great analysts in politics or financial matters and since their predictions are almost always accurate, success is sure.

Telepathic empaths are great at making decisions. Considering that they have a glimpse into the future, they put this ability to their favor, thus making decisions that align with projected outcomes.

Being a telepathic empath is a truly rare gift and those who have it are incredibly fortunate.

PSYCHOMETRIC EMPATHS

Do you develop an attachment to physical things such as photos and clothes? You might very well be a psychometric empath.

Psychometric empaths have a tendency of attaching meaning to various items and growing fond of them. These items elicit certain emotions that the empaths value greatly.

For instance, they might carry a photo of their favorite tree all the time, and the mere glance at that tree calls into their heart the feeling of joy and peace.

There are a wide variety of items or places that a psychometric empath could grow fond of and develop an attachment. But the items and places that often rank at the top are those that are related to their upbringing.

A psychometric empath is likely to develop an attachment to the period that they were small and had a lot of growing up to do. Thus, any throwback photo to that era carries a lot of emotions for them.

When they visit a place and become fond of it, they will be certain to take a souvenir that will remind them of that place some other day, and in effect call back the emotions buried in that souvenir. Psychometric empaths can also have an attachment to jewelry.

GEOMANTIC EMPATHS

Geomantic empaths have developed the capacity to detect the energies emitted by the earth. Thus, they are capable of identifying the status of the earth.

If a piece of land has suffered damage, the geomantic empath can perceive it, and they will put in the effort to restore that piece of land into perfect health.

This ability to communicate with mother earth puts a geomantic empath at an advantage since they can tell the state of the earth.

Geomantic empaths are in a position to tell when a natural disaster is about to take place. Generally, disasters are the major way that the earth communicates her displeasure at how humans treat her, and the disaster is her way of warning against any further abuse.

If human beings could take heed to the warnings of geomantic empaths, then there could be a peaceful coexistence between human beings and the earth. Sadly, most people who destroy mother earth only care about fulfilling their selfish needs without considering the harm that they inflict upon the earth and the subsequent punishment.

Geomantic empaths tend to prefer staying outdoors for most of their productive time so that they can be able to pick up the signals transmitted by mother earth.

FLORA EMPATHS

A flora empath can communicate with plants and become aware of the state of those plants. Most flora empaths tend to stick to a plant-based diet because they have grown accustomed to reading plants. They can feel the energies emanating from various plants and they are capable of communing with them.

Flora empaths like to spend a lot of time near plants so that they can be able to explore these plants and find out their statuses. They can tell whether a plant has borne damage from either humans or other destructive agents in nature. This capability of communicating with plants is rare.

Flora empaths who live in cities and don't have ready access to fields tend to plant their own gardens, and if there's a shortage of space, they will bring in plants into their living spaces. They have a deep-seated need to be close to plants. When they put a plant in their house, they will lavish it with attention.

If a flora empath went for a long period of time without any contact with plants, it could affect them and possibly trigger a depressive episode. And since they are commonly into plant-based diets, they have an innate capability of identifying healthy plants.

FAUNA EMPATHS

Fauna empaths have the capability of communicating and interacting with animals. They can give an animal just one glance and they would know whether that animal is in a happy or sad state. Fauna empaths share a deep connection with animals. They are not only capable of detecting what an animal is going through but they can also pass messages over to animals.

For this reason, animals enjoy cozying up to fauna empaths when the opportunity arises. Animals are very instinctive and can tell right away if a person means them good or harm. Thus, when they identify a well-intentioned person, feelings of delight surge through their bodies. It's not uncommon for fauna empaths to establish a deeper connection with an animal, for instance, their pet, than they ever could with their spouse.

Most fauna empaths understand that animals have the capability to process feelings. Thus, they are against all forms of animal torture. Fauna empaths will commit their resources into organizations that fight animal cruelty, and campaign against the cruel treatment of animals for commercial gain.

It's also not rare for a fauna empath to adopt a vegetarian or vegan lifestyle and stop eating meats as this aligns with their philosophy of shielding animals from harm.

3

BASICS OF MANAGING YOUR GIFTS

BEING AN EMPATH IS A BLESSING, BUT IF YOU FAIL TO manage your gift well, then it becomes a curse. The following are some tips to guide you in managing your gift.

IT'S OKAY TO PUT YOURSELF FIRST

You're the captain of the ship, why should others have their way at your expense? Learn to cater to your needs and take back the power that you so generously give away. Putting yourself first might sound like a selfish move but it is actually not the case. It is merely an acknowledgment to yourself that you matter every bit as the next person.

Some empaths have a tendency of not being sure of themselves. This habit pervades every aspect of their lives and puts them behind. When you second guess your every decision, you unintentionally invite people to question your competency. Never underestimate the power of people who are up to discrediting you; all it takes is creating lies and more lies.

When you put yourself first, you send the message that you have confidence in yourself and this naturally scares bullies away. However, if you let others have their way, never minding to satisfy your needs, other people will decide that you're a weakling and look for more ways to exploit you.

When you put yourself first you show the world that you respect yourself. People exercise caution when dealing with others who have demonstrated to have self-respect. But if people detect that you don't respect yourself, they will dismiss your input and find a way of ruining you.

LEARN TO SET BOUNDARIES

Another major challenge that empaths struggle with is establishing boundaries. The empaths who have no boundaries find themselves taken advantage of and they hardly ever make progress. If you set no boundaries people will definitely step in to take advantage of you.

Establishing boundaries is really a matter of imposing limits on how people can have access to your services or time. For instance, if your work demands a high level of concentration, you can ask people not to call you during work hours. This will boost productivity. If someone ignores your warning and keeps calling during work hours, it is a sign that they don't respect you, and this behavior warrants consequences. For instance, you could block their number so that they can never contact you again.

Setting boundaries is helpful, but for someone who is afraid of being on the receiving end of people's judgments. It can be particularly nerve-wracking, but all it takes is practice. The more you familiarize yourself with setting boundaries, the less it will affect you, and you will eventually get rid of the fear of judgment.

However, before you set a boundary, you have to think your situation through and be certain that you're taking the best decision. Setting a boundary on wrong terms is worse than not setting a boundary at all.

LET IT GO

Sometimes, the best plan is no plan at all. Learn to let things take their course without getting mad. This attitude will help improve your confidence. Letting things go gives you an opportunity to face your fears and understand that regardless of the outcome life is still going to move on.

This is not to mean that you should give up in the face of the slightest challenge! You should work diligently on your part and keep your focus on the goal. But if everything fails, you can now take the back seat and watch how things turn out.

An empath has a hard time being in a relaxed state and everything that they take part in is filled with too much tension and pressure. This not only hinders them from reaching their potential but also lowers the quality of their output. An empath must not shy away from acknowledging that they have tried all the tricks in the book and putting faith in their actions.

Empaths should also develop a thick skin so that in the event their actions generate a backlash, they won't crumble under criticism. If people are not criticizing you, then you definitely aren't making any major moves.

PROCESS YOUR OWN EMOTIONS

In a general sense, empaths are emotional minefields. They tend to harbor a variety of emotions. For instance, the emotional empath will take on the emotions of the people surrounding them, and considering that various people come with a wide range of emotions, such empaths experience many emotions.

If an empath hasn't yet recognized their nature, they can be under tremendous stress. So an empath should try to savor the emotions that go through their minds, for this will empower them to take helpful decisions along the way.

By processing your emotions, you should stop to see how your actions, other people's actions, and your environment, combine to shape up your emotional background. The more you process your emotions, the more you will grow accustomed to your quirky traits.

This process helps you gain access to the hidden parts of your personality that other people hardly ever get a glimpse of. Learning to process your emotions is a great step towards understanding your beliefs.

It also helps you develop your introspective qualities and boosts creativity. As an empath, it is critical to recognize the workings of your mind. This helps you cultivate habits that help you overcome your limitations and fears.

PRACTICE CELEBRATING

As an empath, the stresses of day-to-day living can take away all the fun and leave you drained, so much so that you hardly notice the progress that you have made. That's a terrible mode of living.

Always ensure that you stop to celebrate the great things going on with your life. If you achieve a goal, take a moment to celebrate the fact that you had the discipline and the diligence to make things happen.

When you celebrate your achievements, it improves your self-image. You stop seeing yourself as an average Jack or Jill and you become more skilled at tapping into your resources.

Empaths struggle with self-esteem issues. But celebrating your achievements goes a long way toward alleviating self-esteem issues because it makes you see your potential and that you are worthy of success.

It's critical to take a pause from time to time to take stock of your progress. This will help you come up with a plan of action that is both creative and effective.

Taking time off to celebrate your milestones is an opportunity to reward the people you have tagged along in your journey.

Obviously, there have been people who have helped you reach your goals, and the best gift you could ever give them is acknowledgment.

Learning to show appreciation for others improves your people skills and stretches your networking opportunities.

CREATE A PROTECTIVE SHIELD

An empath is susceptible to spiritual attacks that leave them drained of energy or in a depressed state.

Thus, empaths need to develop a way of shielding themselves from spiritual attacks and protecting their energy.

One of the best ways of putting up a protective shield is by donning crystals or garment embedded with certain stones.

Crystals are effective in warding off destructive spiritual entities. They help strengthen your aura and make it hard for destructive entities to penetrate.

When you don a protective shield, you put yourself in a position of power. This means that you can work without distractions, and for the most part, your thoughts will be stable.

However, when you leave yourself open to attacks, there's a wide range of destructive entities ready to pounce on you. They would then collectively put you in a depressive state.

Donning a protective shield is particularly helpful for emotional empaths who have the natural aptitude of "pulling" other people's energies and feelings and passing them off as their own.

This tendency of absorbing other people's energies can be incredibly limiting especially if the associated emotions are of a negative kind.

By donning the protective shield, an empath has time to engage in their activities without constant worry.

LEARN TO SAY "NO"

Most empaths are so scared of offending other people and this makes them have a hard time saying "No" to people.

The result of this habit is that people come to take advantage of an empath's naivety and this sets the empath back.

Saying "No" doesn't mean that you are a bad person. It merely means that you cannot accommodate the wishes of the other person without restraining your resources.

For instance, if someone comes up to an empath and asks to lend a significant amount of money, the empath might run to their bank and withdraw the entire sum without stopping to realize that giving away that money would probably leave them with little to cater to their means.

Their deep-seated desire to please other people causes them to make decisions that hurt might hurt them.

Obviously, it is hard saying "No" for the first time, but if you make it a habit, you will get into a position where you're not bothered at all to say "No".

Empaths think that by accommodating the wishes of every person they endear themselves to others, but they couldn't be more wrong. Taking a stand is what causes people to respect you.

USE SPIRITUAL GUIDES

Spiritual guides are there to show us the right way to go about our activities. The spiritual world is chock-full of events and entities, and when we go through it alone, it can be pretty hard to navigate through the noise.

Spiritual empaths are most adept at communicating with spiritual guides. Their guides help them to make the best decisions because they offer insight into the happenings of the spiritual world.

An empath could benefit a lot from having a spiritual guide who helps them chart through the difficulties of life. The spiritual guide can point to the exact things that stress them out and they can as well give them wisdom on handling their personal affairs.

Spiritual guides are also incredibly helpful in the sense that they offer protection. When you call on their help, they will come and fight away harmful spiritual entities that were trying to do you harm.

But before you can enjoy the assistance of a spiritual guide, you will first have to commit your mental and spiritual energy into establishing a strong bond with them.

The most important step is to clear the noise off of your mind and reach a state of serenity.

You can cultivate a close relationship with either one or a number of spiritual guides.

THE POWER OF VISUALIZATION

It can be tough being an empath. Think about it. One moment you could be happy, and the next moment you could be sad, not because you have reason to, but merely because you're in close proximity to a sad person. This irregular pattern of emotions can weaken your resolve, give you a bad attitude, and make you despair.

In such instances, one of the techniques of getting through the hardships of life is by utilizing the power of visualization.

Visualization empowers a person to live out their success in their mind. The understanding is that once you call on your mind to savor the end goal, then you're in a better position to actualize your plans.

Let's say that you intend to become a great business person in the tourism industry. Hanging out with people tends to drain you, and then doubts start to seep in about your competency to operate a successful business.

But through your mind's eye, you can see yourself owning a business that facilitates both regional and international tours. This is the power of visualization at work. It encourages you to take action that will make your desires come true. Many successful athletes, movie stars, and even writers have confessed to having used visualization to get to the peak of their careers.

4
EXERCISES

As an empath, you are susceptible to growing frustrated pretty much quickly. Unless you take charge, your gift can easily lower the quality of your life. It's not easy being ultra-sensitive and having to absorb the emotions of the people around you.

The following exercises are aimed at strengthening an empath so that they can develop a strong sense of self and be in a position to chart their lives by their own terms, and not as others wished.

1. IMAGINE BEING YOURSELF

The average empath struggles with forming a solid self-image. And even if they have an idea of what they want to be like, still they are limited because they never let themselves live out their ideas. Being yourself is one of the best things you could ever do to yourself. And a person who doesn't fake appears genuine and they are more likely to be appreciated by the world as opposed to a person who's trying to fake it.

The empath is obviously faking it in an attempt to win the approval of other people, but this doesn't always work in their favor. Where they expected familiarity and bonding, they might get hostility and distrust.

In order to become unashamedly yourself, you have to create that image first in your mind and then transfer it into reality.

Creating that image in your mind is not a terribly difficult thing to pull off. If you want to, you can borrow some aspects of your image from a person that you admire. But this person should act just as an inspiration otherwise you will become a copycat.

Once you have filled out all the gaps as to what you want your image to be like, you can now relish it in your mind, and then begin taking steps that will reflect your image.

2. INVOKE THE NAME OF A SPIRIT GUIDE

A spiritual empath keeps spirit guides who show them guidance whenever they feel lost or they run out of inspiration.

Depending on the sort of relationship that an empath cultivates with their spirit guide, they can seek assistance and or even become educated on the hidden secrets of the universe.

When an empath is going through a particularly rough time, they can call on their spirit guide, who may come down and offer assistance.

In order to be able to commune with spirit guides, an empath must have a very-well developed spiritual side to them. This makes it effortless to connect with their spirit guide and exchange information.

Empaths are vulnerable toward spiritual attacks, and if they don't put in the effort to shield themselves, they can be drained of their energy and sent into a depressive state.

In some cases, barely putting crystals on your body is enough, but there are more advanced cases that require something stronger than crystals.

For instance, when an empath suffers an attack from a horde of malignant spiritual entities, it will take more than crystals to repel those entities. In such a case, the empath can call on their spirit guide for protection.

3. THE POWER OF SHORT BREATHS

Another powerful exercise that an empath can embark on is taking short breaths. Considering that empaths can be exhausted from the powerful feelings and thoughts coursing through their minds, it is necessary to take short breaths in order to achieve a balanced state.

By taking quick breaths, empaths take enough oxygen into their lungs, and subsequently, into their brains, and get into a better position of fighting away unwanted emotions.

When an empath is in the middle of a crowd, it can be particularly exhausting for them, since they will absorb other people's energies and pass them off as their own. Getting rid of these emotions is not an easy task.

The first step that they must undertake is breathing in and out in short spurts in an attempt to ward off these emotions and feelings.

If an empath is dealing with emotional baggage of epic proportions, they might find themselves physically tired. And this too necessitates their short breaths in order to regain a state of balanced emotions.

Anxiety is a common problem for most empaths. They find themselves developing jitters a short moment before taking any action. There's nothing inherently wrong with being anxious, but if the anxiety stops you from taking any action, then there's cause for worry.

4. VISUALIZE AN ENERGY FIELD

If an empath leaves themselves open, they risk suffering a spiritual attack. This attack can come from energy vampires who prey on unsuspecting empaths.

One of the best ways for an empath to cover themselves against spiritual attacks is by forming an energy field around them.

The energy field goes around the top part of their auric field and is instrumental in warding off unwanted influences.

It takes some amount of mental resources to envelop an energy shield around a person, but then this shield is very critical in protecting that person against spiritual attacks.

An empath who is not aware of their capabilities will find themselves getting drained as soon as they start talking with someone who sucks the energy from other people.

An energy shield is made of exotic matter that repels unwanted spiritual entities and puts an empath in relative safety.

It is advisable for an empath to always envision an energy field around themselves before they go out into public places.

If an empath lacks the capacity to put an energy shield around themselves, they can always get assistance from masters who can call down the protective shields.

Empaths need to renew their protective shields on a constant basis lest the shields wear off and leave them exposed to spiritual attacks.

5. NOTICE YOUR BOUNDARIES (OR LACK THEREOF)

Boundaries are necessary for having a well-adjusted life. This is the measure that you use upon others. If you have weak boundaries or no boundaries at all, you are most likely going to struggle with the quality of your life. People can only respect you when you establish boundaries.

This is one of the greatest challenges that an empath faces. They find it so hard to set terms for people wishing to use their resources.

For instance, if an empath is great at offering life advice, which is common because of their introspective nature, you might find many people reaching out to these empaths for a dose of their wisdom, expecting the empaths to drop whatever they are doing and answer their question.

Obviously, this can be incredibly frustrating if an empath is engaged in some other resource-intensive activity. For instance, they could be at their day job or having some alone time, but since the empath is scared of upsetting people, they just put on hold whatever they were doing and fulfill the request of the other person, but when such requests compound, they drive the empath into a breaking point.

Thus, the empath must identify areas in their life that require boundaries, and establish whether or not they have put these boundaries into place.

6. IDENTIFY THE THINGS THAT OFFEND YOU

Different people are put off by different things. But the bottom line is that you require people to respect the fact that you don't want them to do certain things.

Depending on your background and experiences, there are certain things you wish that people stopped doing either to you or when they are around you.

You have to make a point of identifying these things and notifying the people that you socialize with.

For instance, if an empath loathes the idea of having to argue with others, arguments can easily become one of their turn-offs.

It is necessary for an empath to identify the various things that don't align with their personal philosophy. This can prepare them mentally when getting into various situations on what to expect.

For instance, if an empath is opposed to animal cruelty, it means that they will stay away from people or organizations at the forefront of animal cruelty, and they might even take the extra step of alienating themselves from friends who seem to be supportive of animal cruelty.

Identifying the various things that are not in agreement with your principles calls for deep introspection but the results are worth it.

It is the first step toward gaining respect from others and respect for yourself.

7. LEARN TO SPEAK UP

Another important exercise for an empath is learning to speak up for themselves, and especially being able to say "No."

The anxieties and fears that empaths harbor might hold them back from being assertive, and as a result it can cause them to be taken advantage of.

As an empath, you need to develop your assertive skills and be comfortable with asking for exactly what you want, telling it as it is, and saying "No" when the situation demands.

You're not Hitler simply because you couldn't come through for someone; you just did the right thing and enforced your limits, which shows that you have self-respect.

Empaths are particularly afraid of clashing with other people. In situations where tempers are likely to flair, an empath could find him or herself fleeing, but that's not how it's supposed to be. Empaths should be able to speak up for themselves and ask the person who's treating them unfairly to stop, lest they take more action.

Speaking up for yourself is not a call to be mean and hostile to other people; it is just a protective measure that an empath must take knowing too well that people are predatory.

At first, it is hard to speak up, and especially to say "No," but with practice, you can become a natural at it.

8. START TO TRUST IN YOURSELF

The reason most empaths have a hard time figuring out what they want and actually going for it is down to a lack of self-belief.

Sadly, you cannot achieve any recognition in this world if you don't believe in yourself, and even sadder, this responsibility cannot be shifted to some other person.

If you're incapable of trusting in yourself then you're probably a done case. But you don't have to be. Self-belief is not an inborn trait. It's learnable.

All the great people you can think of endured periods of self-doubt, but they had to learn and relearn how to develop self-belief, and this is what helped them scale the heights of stardom.

In order to understand the importance of believing in yourself you just have to look at the players of any kind of sport. There's always an action that results in a score. For instance, if we are talking about basketball, that action is putting the ball in the hoops.

It obviously takes self-belief for a basketball player to run across the court and put the ball in the hoops.

Trusting yourself is not as hard as it might seem. You only have to do one thing; take the first step.

The moment you cease being inactive and start taking action, you have made a tremendous leap in the right direction.

9. LOVE YOURSELF

At the end of the day, whether you perceive yourself as a capable person or not, you have to learn to live with yourself; to state it in a better way; you must love yourself.

If you love yourself, you won't be desperate for attention and you will enforce your boundaries and march towards your dreams.

It means that you should create a lifestyle that consists of a healthy diet and physical activity. If you love yourself, you won't have trouble stating your needs and wants, and people will be drawn to your positive energy.

10. SHOW COMMITMENT

Enough books to sink a ship have been written on how empaths can achieve a balanced state of emotions, but no advice would work if an empath didn't show commitment.

This is virtually the most significant factor in developing a perfectly balanced emotional state for an empath.

You have to be committed to the activities that will help you turn your life around, otherwise, nothing will ever work.

5
MEDITATIONS

EMPATHS CAN IMPROVE THEIR SITUATION BY TAKING UP meditation. Meditation is aimed at clearing the noise of the mind, which helps the person function at their optimum best. The following are some meditation techniques that improve the life of an empath:

1. LOVING-KINDNESS MEDITATION

This meditation is aimed at filling up an empath with love and kindness from both the external world as well as internally.

Empaths who are unaware of their condition are the most vulnerable because their volcanic emotions seem to be illogical.

This can lead to an empath developing self-hatred and a bad attitude that turns people away from them.

The loving-kindness meditation is aimed at restoring happiness into an empath's life. But in order to get results, an empath must practice it severally as opposed to just once and then forgetting about it.

First off, you have to ensure that the environment is right by settling in a quiet and serene area. You may put on some relaxing music for effect.

Recline on a sofa, prop your feet up on a table, and then shut your eyes. With your eyes closed, you can call to your mind the feelings of joy, happiness, love, and kindness.

If other thoughts arise in your mind, don't pay them attention. Keep focusing on the joy and happiness being generated within your mind.

The happy feelings should illuminate your mind so that it seems like a bright orb. At the end of it all, you will be elevated into a position of tremendous love and kindness.

2. FIRE MEDITATION

When you have been weak for so long, it comes to the breaking point where you just want to find the courage to face your reality.

Being an empath can easily lead you down the path of being a weakling. This is because empaths are so sensitive and much of people pleasers.

Thus, people tend to take advantage of the empath's timidity and get ahead at their expense. Of course, the empath is not okay with it.

This reality breeds resentment in an empath, but when they reach the breaking point, they are ready than ever to turn things around.

The fire meditation is a great technique to aid an empath that wants to turn their life around and develop the courage to stand for what they believe in.

The first order of business is to identify a quiet place in the outdoors where you will be undisturbed. Then you have to wait for the night and start a fire with wood to ensure orange flames.

Sit cross-legged before the fire and have with you all the reasons that hinder you from being the best version of yourself written on separate pieces of paper.

As the fire crackles in front of you, stare directly into it, and let that fire be transferred into your heart. Allow the fire to burn the cowardice that hides in you.

And then one by one, toss the papers into the fire, burning into ashes all the negative traits that have been holding you back.

3. PROGRESSIVE MUSCLE RELAXATION

Progressive muscle relaxation is aimed at restoring the full use of your body.

Scientists have found out that there's a huge correlation between the emotional state and the condition of a person's body.

For instance, if someone is always in a depressed state, their bodies, particularly the muscles, are going to deteriorate.

When you have a body that is not functioning at the optimum level, you deny yourself the chance to be as productive as you could be.

Putting your body into an optimum level ensures that you maximize your output, and this will make you more successful in your pursuits.

You can set your body into an optimum working level through progressive muscle relaxation or body scan.

This technique is basically a form of restoring your muscles into perfect alignment through stroking and light probes.

To get started, you will need to take a hot shower and apply oil all over your body. Then you can walk into a quiet room with white adornments and stand in the middle.

Starting from down going up, reach for your toes and give them a slight massage, rubbing and stroking them.

Next, move up to your calves and repeat the same, ever so tenderly, and then you can progress to every part of your body. At the end of it all, you will feel that your body is restored into a state of perfect health.

4. MINDFULNESS MEDITATION

Have you ever stopped for a moment to notice all the things taking place around you? I'm sure you haven't.

Most of us go through life almost as if we are held in a state of trance. We hardly ever pay attention to the minor things going on around us.

We could be eating a meal and not minding how we chew our food or noticing the environment, the color-blend, and the people around us. This tendency reduces us into mere robots.

Mindfulness is critical in having a rewarding life because it's the little things that surely matter.

Although most empaths have an innate ability to take notice of the small things, sometimes their emotional burdens can put heavy blinders on their mind's eye.

Thus, mindfulness meditation is critical in restoring their capacity to notice the small things about life.

There's no one way of practicing mindfulness meditation. It is merely a conscious decision that a person makes to notice more of the life happening around them.

For instance, when you stop to speak to someone, you shouldn't just drone on like a robot, but take the time to recognize other things happening around you. For instance, notice the buildings in the background, the birds lining the rooftops, and the sky.

If you're eating, don't swallow as though your throat is automated, but take time to savor the delicacy and appreciate the taste.

Always be present in everything that you are engaged in.

5. BREATH AWARENESS

The mind of an empath is always in a racing state, always on survival mode. It's not entirely a bad thing, but you have to acknowledge that this state could potentially ruin your chances of reaching your goals.

When your mind races, it tends to activate various emotions that tend to limit your capacity to be productive. For instance, it can activate anxiety, which is the root cause of procrastination.

When you're in a state of anxiety, you will look busy and yet not be productive at all. The anxiety will limit your capacity to concentrate and do something valuable.

One of the best ways of fighting away these unwanted emotions is through breath awareness meditation.

To start off, you have to make sure that you're in a quiet and serene environment. You can practice breath awareness meditation while sitting or standing. But for the best results, assume a cross-legged position on the floor of your house, and either close your eyes or put a blind on.

Stretch out your hands spread them apart, as though holding out an imaginary gift. Slowly, take in a lungful of air so that your diaphragm swells out.

Pause in that state and go through all your negative emotions, examining their validity. And as you exhale, let go of these emotions, and call on your imagination to watch these emotions go away in the form of little dark angels.

To achieve the best results, you have to practice the breath awareness meditation on the regular, as opposed to just once off.

6. KUNDALINI YOGA

An empath often undergoes periods of emotional torture that cause them untold pain both emotionally and physically.

But getting rid of these emotional pains is not as easy as visiting with a physician and getting a drug subscription.

It takes a remedy that will extend to the auric fields of a person to restore them into perfect physical and emotional health.

The ancient practice of yoga has been instrumental in delivering people from the shackles of emotional and mental bondage.

One of the popular philosophies of yoga is that every person has an inherent capacity to transcend the emotional limitations that we battle against. But in order to reach this level, we have to first activate what is known as the kundalini energy.

Practicing the kundalini yoga mainly involves making movements, deep breathing, and invoking mantras.

To get started, you have to first identify an outdoor environment devoid of disturbances. If there's none, you could always go back to your sweet home.

Take a position that you understand won't limit your movements. You can start moving your limbs or arms rapidly and then stop. Next, draw in lungful breaths and hold them before expelling them. And finally, invoke a mantra that is connected with the qualities that you want to cultivate in your life.

You can mix up the movement, breathing, and mantras for more impact.

7. ZEN MEDITATION

When we hear that someone has reached a state of zen, what comes to mind is that they have arisen to a state whereby they are no stranger to their thoughts.

Considering that an empath goes through a state of emotional turmoil, reaching a state of zen ought to be one of their life goals.

The emotional rainbow of an empath is extreme and varied, and it makes them susceptible to depression, especially for those people who haven't yet understood that they are empaths.

Reaching a state of zen will open them up to the wide spectrum of the emotional and mental universe. It will allow them to see how thoughts and emotions are connected both at the internal and external level.

The surest way of reaching this state of zen is through introspection. What does it mean to be introspective?

It simply means being capable of putting question marks to your actions, thoughts, attitudes, and habits.

It is not just a matter of observing these things but also developing a curiosity to explain why these habits take place.

For instance, if you have a tendency of being extremely angry when someone rejects you, you might question the root of this anger and find out that you hate rejection simply because one or both of your parents rejected you and you hate the taste of rejection. When you have this awareness, you won't be fazed by rejection anymore.

8. TRANSCENDENTAL MEDITATION

Most of us approach life at face value. We never stop to imagine what life is like from a different perspective. Thus, we are forever throwing familiar balls in the air and never getting out of our comfort zone.

Rising above our base needs is not as hard as it might seem. All we need to have is a dedicated mind.

As an empath, when you finally rise above your own state of being, you will acquire the knowledge about various qualities inherent in the auric field, and in that sense, you will acquire power.

To practice transcendental meditation, you have to find a calm room with preferably white decorations and a burning candle in the middle of the room.

You can assume either a sitting or standing position and shut your eyes. Then call on your mind to elevate you above your base needs and desires.

This exercise is resource intensive and it needs a great deal of mental energy to shut out the cravings of your mind and focus on transcending.

If you fail to transcend above your thoughts, don't despair. Just forgive yourself and carry out the meditation over and over again at the exact time. Before long, you will become great at transcending above your own state of being, and this exercise will bequeath you inner peace.

9. RAIN MEDITATION

Every person contends with some form of battle every now and again, regardless of age or background. But the difference is that well-adjusted people merely endure seasons of pain, albeit short ones, whereas empaths are in a continuous struggle for sanity.

These struggles trigger emotional turmoil in empaths and the compounding effect can crush them.

Before empaths can take steps in the right direction, they first need to shed off their emotional baggage.

Nothing does it so well than a rain meditation. This type of meditation achieves great results in cleaning out unwanted emotions.

To practice the rain meditation, you have to wait for a rainy day, preferably at night. But if you lack the patience, you can simulate the rain in your washroom and dim the lights.

Step out into the darkness on a rainy day wearing light clothes that will get glued to your body once the drops start hitting you.

With your head bowed down, start walking along the road, and call to mind all your fears, worries, weaknesses, anxieties, and pains.

As you call them into mind, make sure to combine them into one large basket of unwanted emotions. It should swell out inside your mind.

And then start getting rid of this giant basket of emotional pain. It won't occur in a flash as it is quite a burden.

As you walk through the rain, visualize the water washing away the unwanted emotions. Stay at it for long enough to witness the entire basket cleaned out and your mind restored to peace and perfect health.

10. SELF-INQUIRY

An empath spends most of their time turning things over in their minds. They develop a tendency of worrying. This habit of always worrying about how they appear in front of other people can be incredibly limiting.

It stops them from exercising their creativity to the maximum of reaching out to people for assistance when it's necessary. Living in your mind leads into challenges that well-adjusted people don't face.

A remedy against this state of affairs is practicing the self-inquiry meditation. This meditation is aimed at uncovering the true nature of a person, and in this case, yourself.

You have to be honest with yourself to make this work. When you get to understand yourself at the deepest level, your fears, worries, and the factors that drive you, you will be less likely to be swayed by what others think of you.

Practicing self-inquiry calls for a total makeover of your lifestyle. For instance, you have to stop consuming alcohol and sleep adequately.

In order to reach a point of thorough self-understanding, you will have to practice this meditation on a regular basis as opposed to making it a once-off affair.

When you learn the true nature of yourself, and by extension, of human beings, you will cease holding yourself back and letting others have their way at your expense.

6
MINDFULNESS

Mindfulness is the practice of exercising your awareness. Mindfulness encourages us to take notice of the things happening around us i.e. to recognize our reality.

By practicing mindfulness, our thoughts, feelings, and bodily sensations help us to have a thorough awareness of our present reality.

The following are some techniques of practicing mindfulness:

EAT MINDFULLY

Instead of wolfing your lunch down, you might want to go slow about it. Mindfulness eating incorporates the aspect of savoring food. You have to pay attention to how your food tastes. Also, you must chew your food slowly as this will aid in proper digestion. Most people tend to eat very fast whilst engaged in some other activities, and by the time they are done, they cannot even seem to comprehend the taste of that food. This tendency takes away the pleasure from meals. Eating very fast can possibly lead to digestive problems, too.

WALK MINDFULLY

A lot of your personality can be denoted from just your walking style. Outgoing people tend to walk in a totally different way than shy people. But that is beside the point. You can practice mindfulness by walking in an appropriate way. This involves carrying yourself in an upright posture and keeping your eyes on the lookout as opposed to looking down. You must not hurry your steps, but rather, you must walk in a fashion that makes it appear as though the soles of your feet were kissing the ground. Ensure that you take notice of the things that you come across on your way.

OBSERVE YOUR BREATHING

When we descend into the world of the dead, we are no longer breathing but now is the opportunity to get it right. Most of the breathing happens unconsciously. If we'd have to stop our activities just to focus on our breathing, we'd never get anything done. But then taking deep breaths is an integral part of washing away unwanted emotions and restoring a person's mind into a balanced state of emotions. Empaths tend to be constantly overwhelmed by negative emotions. One of the ways of fighting away these negative emotions is through practicing deep breathing techniques. Go to a serene area and slowly take deep breaths in and out.

CONNECT WITH YOUR SENSES

These are our basic senses:

- Touch
- Smell

- Taste
- Sound
- Sight

No matter where we are, we always have the opportunity of utilizing one or all of our senses. This is a great exercise of mindfulness.

If we are catching up with friends in a restaurant, we can catch the smell of the heavenly cuisines, watch the cars darting along the road outside, savor the taste of our order, touch our friends' pets, and enjoy the music seeping out of the speakers.

Empaths should not allow a single negative emotion such as fear to take center stage and cripple their capacity to enjoy various other things in life.

PAUSE BETWEEN ACTIONS

We live in a fast-paced world where a million things are vying for our attention. Slowing down might very well be an alien ideology.

For empaths, their anxiety makes them particularly quick whilst executing their duties.

For instance, if they have to make a move, it won't be a measured move, but rather a clumsy and quick attempt riddled with missteps.

It can make them look ridiculous and put them in a situation that they are always so much afraid of.

An empath should learn to take slow action. There's no harm to it. If they are delivering a speech, they should learn to pause between sentences, and have a sense of congruency.

ACTIVE LISTENING

Studies have shown that one of the habits that endear us to people is being an active listener.

Active listening is when you listen not merely to issue a response but to understand the perspective of the other person.

It's an incredibly rare ability. Empaths should develop this skill given that the alternative – speaking – tends to be somewhat challenging for them.

In active listening, you must face the person you're talking to, and keep direct eye contact.

If you want to show them your level of interest, make sure to repeat the last phrases that they utter.

Also, keep an open body language that sends the message that you're in agreement with whatever they are saying.

GET LOST IN THE FLOW

Your chances of achieving success significantly increase when you perform activities that you are passionate about.

For instance, if you have the gift of drawing excellent portraits but have average academic abilities, then following a career in the arts would be more rewarding.

You have to master the art of getting lost in the flow. Put on your desk all the materials you'll need and lose yourself in some serious artwork.

Considering that your work forms the majority of your life, you want to pick a line of work that won't exact too much pressure on you.

Empaths tend to do extremely well in creativity-driven careers.

MEDITATE

Meditation is another awesome way of practicing mindfulness.

It is basically the practice of calming down your mind and soul to reach a state of inner peace.

There are various ways of practicing meditation and each one has its pros and cons, but the ground rules remain.

You must meditate in a calm and serene area and you may or may not use mantras to reach a state of inner peace.

In order to enjoy the benefits of meditation, you want to make it a lifestyle choice as opposed to practicing it just once and then forgetting about it.

Meditation as a mindfulness technique will help you achieve the following:

- Joy
- Improved mental faculties
- Quality sleep

TRAVEL

Another great technique of practicing mindfulness is through traveling. There's a misconception that you have to be rich to travel.

As long as you have a job, there's surely a way of coming up with a budget that will let you hop on a plane and fly away. But then again, even traveling locally by train or bus still does the trick. When you get to experience new environments and meet new people, your mind broadens.

Here are some of the benefits of the above mindfulness techniques:

- Lowers stress: living in the moment will help you alleviate all the stresses that you might have accumulated. Most of the time, stress is aided by an idle mind. But when you pay attention to the small things in your environment, your mind will be occupied in deciphering these new experiences, and won't resort to raising internal alarms that trigger stress. Practicing mindfulness has also been known to boost the creative skills of a person. This means that you are in a better position to solve your problems and get rid of your stresses.
- Restores emotional balance: you can only reach a state of emotional balance when your mind is free of worries. Practicing mindfulness has been known to help in alleviating worries and putting the mind to a state of emotional balance. When you focus on the little things that are taking place around you, you deny your mind the chance to wander off into a state of worry. Consequently, you buy time to resolve your issues without necessarily suffering the pain of constant worry. Practicing mindfulness helps a person create a life that serves them as opposed to a life that is aimed at pleasing others and seeking attention.
- Increases resilience: enough research has been done to certify that the most important factor for success is being resilient. But being resilient is something that the average empath struggles with. First off, they have a poor attitude, which makes them give up at the slightest challenge. And then they have little or nonexistent self-esteem and this puts them in a state of perpetual anxiety. An empath can develop their resilience by starting to take more notice of the things going on around them. For instance, if you get

into a competition at school or at your place of work and come up short, look at all the factors that contributed to your failure, and then wait for the next round of the competition. Resilience is like a muscle; you get the most use from it by putting it into more practice.

- Reduce anxiety: an empath has a lot of things that make them anxious, but the biggest of all is the fear that they are not good enough. Empaths fear rejection. And the fact that they can absorb other people's fears and emotions doesn't help matters. You can only get rid of anxiety by convincing your mind that you are up to the task. When you take your time to pay attention to the things going on around you, you equip yourself with more knowledge and develop the necessary skills to overcome your challenges, thus banishing anxiety in all its forms.
- Slows aging: studies have shown that there's a correlation between emotional turmoil and getting old. In other words, the more mentally and emotionally disturbed you are, the more likely you are to get older. The process of getting old is irreversible; after all, nature must run its course. Just as this process can be fastened, it can be slowed down, too. Practicing mindfulness has been shown to be instrumental in slowing down the aging process. The reason behind it is that having an awareness of your present moment tends to ward off unwanted emotions and restores peace and calm in your mind. This promotes peace in your mind and slows down the aging process.
- Reduce physical pain: as an empath, being in a roller-coaster of emotions can also lead to physical pain. The body tends to constrict itself at certain parts in response to various emotional statuses. The pain is directly proportional to the severity of the depressive mood. But through practicing mindfulness, you can get rid of the

emotional baggage that has caused you pain in the first place. Mindfulness helps you to have clarity in thought and emotions. And it goes a long way in improving the quality of your life.

- Reduces depression: the truth of the matter is that everyone goes through a depressive episode from time to time. But when it comes to empaths, depression is their constant companion. There's nothing rosy about depression. It puts a person in a bad mood and harms their productivity. But through mindfulness, one can be able to achieve clarity into the problems dogging them and it sets them on a path to recovery from depression. Mindfulness also increases a person's knowledge and equips them with the ability to turn their life around. But in order to gain these benefits, you have to approach mindfulness as a lifestyle, as opposed to performing it just once.
- Improve sleep quality: to be productive, one of the areas that you have to be careful about is the quality of your sleep. If you get quality sleep, you are going to be more productive, and if you get mediocre sleep, you are going to be less productive. By practicing mindfulness, you eliminate the barriers that hinder you from having quality sleep. One of these barriers is anxiety. Mindfulness has been known to annihilate anxiety and restore balance to your emotional state. When you practice mindfulness on the regular, you will increase your capacity to have quality sleep.
- Improve concentration: one of the challenges of the modern-day world is that most people have a hard time concentrating. There's too much noise out there. And this makes it hard for a person to stay engaged in an activity. Thanks to practicing mindfulness, people can be able to get rid of the noise in their mind and escalate their focus.

7
CBT EXERCISES

COGNITIVE BEHAVIORAL THERAPY IS A SHORT-TERM treatment that takes on a practical approach towards solving problems. It seeks to identify the thought and behavior patterns that have contributed to the challenges that a person is facing.

The following are some of the exercises used in CBT:

JOURNALING

The purpose of journaling is merely to gather evidence about the challenges that the person is struggling with.

An empath tends to go through periods of intense emotional and mental activity. It really helps to put these experiences into writing.

By writing down your thoughts and experiences, you have a better idea of what's troubling you, thus you increase your chance of calling on your creativity.

You can document all the emotions, thoughts, and activities that take place in your life or those that take place on certain days only.

This will help you have a detailed report that can be analyzed and a pattern can be traced. For instance, it may become apparent to you that almost every Friday night you are in a bad mood.

The next logical step would be to ask yourself: why?

Maybe it's because you hang out at your favorite restaurant and other girls are always attracting guys while nobody bothers to approach you. But then it's not enough to make such diagnoses. A journal will help you answer various questions about why guys tend to not approach you. Is it your facial expression? Or is it that you're simply sending a bad vibe?

Besides helping you understand the root of your struggles, journaling will also improve your writing skills; which is a pretty marketable skill in this age of information.

UNRAVELING COGNITIVE DISTORTIONS

Our minds feed us beliefs basing on our experiences. Some of these beliefs are true but others are false. But then when a mind acquires a belief, it can be quite to shake it off, regardless of the fact that it is erroneous.

Empaths are at the most risk of developing false beliefs because they have intense emotional experiences, and when you put in their weak resolve and poor attitude, the storm is ripe for a blowing.

One of the ways for an empath to achieve emotional balance is through unraveling cognitive distortions, which is merely an act of identifying and challenging harmful thought patterns.

Some of the cognitive distortions that empaths have include:

- Polarized thinking: this is where a person thinks in absolute terms. If they are looking for a certain outcome, then they won't have it any other way. Such people fail to understand that there are gray areas that are just as rewarding.
- Overgeneralization: this is where a person takes one experience and assumes it to be true over the other cases. For instance, if you sit for an exam and fail, you might be tempted to think that you're dumb. Obviously, this is unfair to yourself because you cannot measure your intelligence basing on just one exam.
- Mental filter: this is where you ignore the positives and dwell on one negative experience. For instance, if your spouse has been generally supportive, and then one day he utters something terrible, you may have a hard time getting over that utterance, and forget about the years of the positive things that they actually did.
- Disqualifying the positive: this is a particularly difficult distortion to solve because it points to a flawed attitude and self-esteem. Such a person may receive a positive remark or compliment and still reject it. For instance, if they are told that their speaking skills are perfect, they will assign that compliment to political correctness or an insincere remark.
- Attempting to read minds: this is another cognitive distortion that hinders people from having a balanced emotional state. Such a person would jump into conclusions basing on light evidence. For instance, they might see someone with a frown and immediately assume that the person is mad at them.
- Fortune telling: this is not very different from jumping into

conclusions. It involves someone foretelling the future basing on very little evidence. For instance, if a woman at age 30 hasn't found a life partner yet, they might say that they will never find love basing on that assumption.

- Magnification and minimization: this is where a person exaggerates or minimizes the meaning or importance of certain things. For instance, a star soccer player who loses a penalty might exaggerate that experience and consider themselves to be a terrible player. And a player who wins an award might diminish the importance of that award and still believe that they are unworthy of recognition.
- Emotional reasoning: everyone is guilty of this. It runs on the premise: "I feel it; therefore, it must be true." Emotional reasoning can be extremely debilitating because it makes people believe their emotions even when they are erroneous.
- Personalization: this is where a person develops a tendency of taking everything personally. This habit limits them from connecting with other people and having rewarding relationships. The tendency to take things personally is indicative if a poor attitude.
- Control fallacies: this kind of person either believes that they are in absolute control of their lives or they have no control whatsoever. Both beliefs are wrong. No one ever has total control over their lives and no one has absolutely any control of their lives.

COGNITIVE RESTRUCTURING

Once you identify the various cognitive distortions and negative views that you have, you can start unraveling how they came about.

It's not enough to become aware of a certain cognitive distortion and leave it at that. You should also dig into the backstory of that cognitive distortion or inaccurate belief so that you can become empowered.

For instance, if you meet someone with a frown and automatically assume that they are mad at you when they are actually not even aware of your existence, it is obviously an inaccurate view.

Perhaps it might have originated from having to deal with a close member who used to frown whenever they were mad at you. So, the mere sight of a frown calls back that terrible experience, albeit subconsciously.

If you have a tendency of taking things personally, it means that you have a hard time being adjusted whenever people are around. They might do something innocuous but still, you will find a way of pointing out how personal their actions were.

This attitude might have stemmed from an abuse-laden childhood which saw you take all the blame and believe yourself to be flawed.

In effect, you have always viewed yourself through a negative scope.

EXPOSURE AND RESPONSE PREVENTION

This method is particularly helpful in treating cases of OCD. It involves exposing yourself into triggers for your OCD. The logic is that if you expose yourself enough times, you will eventually develop an aversion to the activity that you're attached to.

For instance, if you have a compulsion to masturbate, the trigger might be opening the computer and surfing the web. Instead of restraining yourself from accessing the computer or the internet, you might want to actually access the internet and learn to hold yourself back from watching porn.

If you start avoiding the computer or promise yourself not to open another webpage, the compulsion will incrementally add up, and at the breaking point, you will go back into watching porn with a vengeance.

By exposing yourself to your triggers you get to develop your resolve and the drive to overcome your challenges by proving yourself to have great character.

In the long run, this habit not only cures your obsessive compulsions but goes a long way towards establishing your character. It is critical in developing resiliency.

The world is more receptive to people who have a backbone. There's no other exercise that would strengthen your capacity to maintain your ground than the exposure and response prevention.

INTEROCEPTIVE EXPOSURE

The average young guy has incredible anxiety while mixing with members of the opposite gender; it's to be expected.

But then some guys have so much anxiety that they decide to shun all forms of female interaction.

They end up staying in their rooms for whole days and never coming out to socialize with other people because they will potentially run into females who will activate their anxiety again.

Being anxious is not much of a big deal, but when the anxiety cripples you so much so that you can hardly make any progress, then there's a problem.

The interoceptive exposure is aimed at putting people in contact with the things that trigger their anxiety so that they can finally be able to manage their anxiety.

For example, the young fella who cannot talk to women is put in direct contact with women, and this will force them to overcome their fear of speaking to women and stop viewing them as goddesses among mortals.

At the root of any terrible belief is an equally terrible experience. In order to change these beliefs, you have to supply your mind with evidence.

The young fella scared of talking to women thinks that he is horrible with women, and it's true because previous attempts have ended badly.

But then if he'd get himself to attend dates with hot women, their mind can develop a new belief: that they are great with women.

Nightmare Exposure and Rescripting

The fears that an empath carry can make them have a hard time getting a full night's sleep. They are scared of imaginary things coming up to their bed and trying to strangle them. They are scared of nightly entities that only their minds can conjure up.

The answer to these kinds of fears is not sleeping with the lights on but rather staying through the experience.

When it's night time, the empath should just walk into their room, and slide into bed as though it were the most normal thing.

Their heart will race and their fears will awaken, but if they still stay on the bed, they will finally realize that there's nothing to fear in that room.

The nightmares are merely creations of a fertile imagination and nothing more. The empath should be able to sleep without having to fight any monster or ghost.

In order to cement this newfound bravery, an empath should put into practice this habit of exposing themselves to their triggers.

When it's done enough times, they won't harbor fears about wrestling with formless nightly creatures anymore.

PLAY THE SCRIPT TO THE END

An empath can be held hostage by a type of fear that is manifest mostly at the mental level. Their fears will hold them back from making any progress.

For instance, an empath can mistakenly believe that when they deliver a speech, people will discover their lisp or terrible accent, and laugh at them.

Such an empath should attempt to live out the experience inside their mind and recognize that even in the worst-case scenario – that people should laugh – it won't affect them any bit.

Having this attitude helps an empath get rid of their fears and start living a life of meaning and purpose.

BODY SCAN

When you probe and apply slight pressure on various parts of the body, it is a great method of releasing the pain and tension that an empath's body has received.

The body scan is administered to the entire body and it can be done by an individual or someone can aid them.

Ideally, you should start by probing your toes and feet, lingering a while longer as you rub the toes, and then move slowly to other body parts.

The body scan promotes heart health and improves blood circulation.

RELAXED BREATHING

Breathing has proved to be a remedy for a number of problems. In order to get the best results, you might want to perform this exercise in a serene area with plants or trees in the background that ensure lots of oxygen-rich air.

While standing or sitting, you may slowly draw breaths in and out, eliminating all the unwanted emotions and breathing in peace and calmness.

CONCLUSION

One of the defining traits of an empath is an inability to forget about the struggles of other people. As soon as an empath meets someone that is in a world of pain, they start to feel for that person, and it doesn't stop even days after their interaction.

Empaths tend to absorb the energies of the people around them. This makes empaths afraid of hanging out in huge crowds. For the most part, people are not harboring positive emotions, and when an empath hangs out in a charged crowd, they would definitely pick up on these negative energies, thus ruining their moods.

The emotions of an empath are never stable. One moment they could be experiencing a high and the next moment they could be wallowing in a state of mental turmoil. This is down to their tendency of picking up people's emotions.

When the energies become too much, the empath can grow physically sick, and find themselves having to endure pain in certain areas of their bodies.

On the plus side, empaths are incredibly intuitive and have mind-reading capabilities. This means that they can tell what anyone is thinking. If you told them a lie, they could know it.

CPSIA information can be obtained
at www.ICGtesting.com
Printed in the USA
LVHW051917180520
655843LV00001B/14